THE
BATTLE OF
BRITAIN
A NATION ALONE

DEDICATION
To my good friends Bill Wood and Alick Grant, without whose kind and generous help this book would not have been possible.

ACKNOWLEDGEMENTS
Special thanks to Dr Michael Fopp, Director, Royal Air Force Museum, for his support and encouragement during the course of this project and thanks also to Dr John Tanner (formerly Director, Royal Air Force Museum) for his enthusiasm for the concept of an illustrated history to commemorate the Battle of Britain.

I would also like to thank, once again, the veterans of the air battles of 1940: Desmond Fopp, Pat Hancock, Brian Kingcome, Adolf Galland, Hans Schmoller–Haldy and Kurt Newald, for providing such frank and illuminating answers to, what must have seemed, an endless tirade of 'the same old questions'!

Finally, I would like to show my appreciation to the following for their active assistance during the preparation of *A Nation Alone*: Dorothy Sheridan at the University of Sussex; Brian Evelin and Sid Brown of the London Fire Brigade; Peter Murton and 'Bomber' Holdrick at the RAF Museum, Hendon; Flight Lieutenant Bill Fawcett, RAF Bentley Priory; Simon Potter and Nigel Gray for photographic assistance; Wing Commander Bob Rae RAFVR (T) and WO2 Andy Ingram RE, Christ's Hospital CCF; Mr 'Nobby' Kinnard; Mrs Mary Shulver; and not least, Jan and Richard Widdows for putting it all together and providing such kind hospitality.

THE BATTLE OF BRITAIN

A NATION ALONE

ARTHUR WARD

CHANCELLOR PRESS

First published in 1989 by Osprey Publishing

This edition published in 1997 by Chancellor Press,
an imprint of Reed International Books Limited
Michelin House, 81 Fulham Road, London SW3 6RB

Printed in Hong Kong

British Library Cataloguing in Publication Data
Ward, Arthur
        A Nation Alone: The Battle of Britain, 1940
        I. World War   2. Battle of Britain
        I. Title   II. Royal Air Force Museum
        940.54'21

ISBN 1 85152 653 6

CREDITS
Words, illustrations and all photographs by Arthur Ward, unless credited below:

Mass-Observation Archive: all excerpts copyright The Tom Harrison Mass-Observation Archive. Reproduced by permission of Curtis Brown Limited

The Hulton Picture Library pages 190 (top), 180, 27, 46 (top right)

Crown copyright (reproduced by permission of the controller of Her Majesty's Stationery Office) pages 40 (top left), 68, 69, 88/89, 121 (top), 126, 127, 136, 137, 156 (top right), 183

Royal Air Force Museum pages 9, 14, 15, 18, 19, 22, 23, 26, 31, 38, 39, 51, 55, 58, 59, 62, 63, 64, 70, 71, 74, 75, 86, 87, 94, 95, 103, 107, 123, 130, 138, 139, 143, 151, 154, 155, 159, 163, 167, 186, 195, 196, 197, 198, 199, 202, 203, 204 (bottom), 206

The Trustees of the Imperial War Museum, London pages 30, 35, 46 (top left), 47, 66, 78, 79, 82, 83, 125, 134, 142, 146, 147, 150, 171, 181, 190 (bottom), 191, 204 (top)

D Fopp 165, *N P W Hancock* 173, *K Newald* 200

CONTENTS

FOREWORD

by
Dr Michael Fopp
Director, Royal Air Force Museum

I am delighted to write the foreword to a book which takes a new look at one of the most important periods in the history of Britain and indeed the entire free world. It also gives me great pride to be able to do so because my own father is one of those featured.

The Battle of Britain, the first decisive battle to be fought entirely in the air, is now recognised as being the crucial initial step in the final destruction of the Nazi quest for world domination. In this excellent book Arthur Ward has combined the more familiar facts of that conflict with the less well known. He has not fallen into the trap that snares so many other writers by merely regurgitating myths and legends which, in some cases, fall a long way short of the truth.

Moreover, I am pleased to say, he has included the forgotten elements of the story: the ground-crews who battled against all odds to keep machines in the air, the civilians who kept going in spite of everything thrown at them by the Luftwaffe, the men and women of vital volunteer services; and the members of other Commands within the Royal Air Force who sustained the pressure over land and sea.

This book reminds us of things which are slowly disappearing into history, and it does so in such an interesting way: with visual images and graphic design, through the great effort that has been made to group together real objects associated with the times, and by the people involved remembering incidents both large and small.

I grew up in an RAF family, moving from place to place and country to country as my father pursued his postwar flying career in the Royal Air Force. As a child I was aware that he was an experienced pilot and I knew that he had flown Hurricanes and Spitfires "in the war"; but he very rarely mentioned his part in the conflict and I was a teenager before I realised that he was one of those heroic "Few" immortalised by Churchill's words. It happened when my sister was asked to write a history essay and he scribbled his reminiscences on a few scraps of paper for her. We were both very surprised.

As time went by I discovered more and when I made my career at the Royal Air Force Museum I obviously met many of the survivors of that long summer of 1940. With a few exceptions they were all the same, reticent to the point of being almost totally uncommunicative about their contribution. The cardinal sin then (and now) was to become a "line-shooter", a teller of tall stories. As a result here we are, 50 years on, and there is so much still to be told. *A Nation Alone* will not only help the children and grandchildren understand a little more about the great sacrifices that were made; it will also perhaps redress the balance, during their lifetime, for the small and shrinking number who survive.

Our people should feel proud of all those who participated in that great battle, from the courageous pilots to the long-suffering civilians who nightly braved the "blitz". Their story should be told not merely to the generations who were privileged to know them, but forever, so that never again may our country be "a nation alone".

Chapter One

*"Flying is still in its infancy; and in the
European war the aeroplane, though it has already
done so much, has given no more than a suggestion
of what its ultimate powers may be."*

*Claude Grahame-White,
Preface to "The Invisible War-Plane", 1915*

INTO THE DARKNESS

The spectre of predatory enemy bombers lumbering towards defenceless towns was a nightmare that haunted politician and ordinary citizen alike during the fragile peace of the interwar years. In September 1940 the vision would become stark reality for thousands of British people. These Vickers Virginias of 58 Squadron are over Worthy Down in 1934.

As the spring of 1940 merged into summer Nazi Germany stood poised to conclude her final act of conquest in Western Europe – the invasion of Britain. Few international observers voiced optimism about Britain's chances of survival, and indeed a successful conquest was widely thought to be no more than the final formality of a military campaign that had netted Germany vast territorial spoils with little apparent effort. A new warfare was abroad and Hitler had harnessed its power to full effect; nothing, it seemed, could stand in the way of "blitzkrieg".

After the Allied armies were so skilfully wrong-footed in France, resulting in the collapse of Franco-British opposition and the eventual humiliation of the Dunkirk evacuation, even the sceptical Führer began seriously to consider the possibility of continuing the war onto the British mainland.

After all, he held the good cards. At his command Britain, if she persisted to oppose his demands for a free hand in Europe, would be crushed and incorporated into the Third Reich. If on the other hand the British saw sense and withdrew from the contest, he would demonstrate his magnanimity and spare her further suffering.

Either way Britain was a spent force as far as Hitler was concerned, and could no longer prevent Germany from achieving her rightful position as the dominant force in Europe. His leadership, his vision and his military prowess had regained his nation's honour and erased the bitter memories of the 1918 armistice. Hitler's destiny would be fulfilled. Britain's resistance was little more than a minor irritation which, if it did not cease, would result in swift and terrible punishment.

Characteristically the British, perhaps due

A NATION ALONE

to ignorance of what was in store for them, saw things differently. With a resolve and tenacity born of desperation they clung to their islands and their independence and, facing a common threat, displayed a unity palpably lacking in peacetime.

Although national morale was largely intact, the same could not be said for Britain's armed forces. The Army had been defeated in France and was in a perilously weak state – short of guns, ammunition, vehicles and tanks and unable to provide much in the way of coastal defence. The Navy, still the largest in the world, was spread thin across the globe. The Home Fleet was busily engaged in defending the vital transatlantic sea-lanes, and in any case was unsuited for action in the narrow Channel waters across which the invading Germans would pour.

Only the "thin blue line" of British defence, the Royal Air Force, was able to offer real resistance to Germany's undoubted might. Clearly, before any invasion attempt, Hitler would have to be sure of total air superiority above the Channel waters and landing beaches of southern England – and to achieve this the RAF would have to be eliminated. Goering, head of Germany's Luftwaffe, promised his Führer an easy victory over the RAF. After their heavy losses in the Battle of France what was left of the British air force would be finished off over England. Intelligence reports showed the RAF to be weak, badly trained and

poorly led, and in direct combat over France their pilots appeared to cling to old-fashioned principles that owed more to the tactics of the First World War than to the high-speed techniques of 1940. The RAF, Hitler was informed, could be discounted along with the rest of Britain's defences. Nothing would stand in the way of invasion.

Far from being the final battle honour on a list of glorious German victories, the Battle of Britain was the fulcrum on which the eventual outcome of the Second World War turned. It was the first time in the war that Nazi fortunes took a turn for the worse. Although it was not then apparent, the RAF's victory in denying Germany the opportunity to mount a successful invasion of Britain led directly to the destruction of the Third Reich in 1945.

After the summer of 1940 Germany was forced to fight a war on two fronts – something that Hitler, in common with most military commanders, rightly feared – though only perversity drove the Führer to continue his grand ambitions against Russia. Britain's survival in 1940 also served as a beacon to the oppressed peoples of Europe and a signal to neutral America that, perhaps, German expansionism was not unstoppable.

The Battle of Britain was a complex affair. It was the first time that a major conflict was decided largely by the influence of air power. Both the RAF and the Luftwaffe made errors of judgment, but then there was no rule-book to follow and most prewar theories concerning air strategy were wrong or obsolete. Both sides suffered from poor intelligence, fielded aircraft of dubious technical performance and were bedevilled by inconsistencies in tactical deployment.

It was the Luftwaffe, however, that made the most mistakes. Goering was unaware that with radar the RAF possessed the most advanced early warning defence system in the world; he largely ignored it and discounted its relevance to his own tactics. Again, most senior airmen assumed that mass bombing would prove devastating and conclusive in its own right. The Luftwaffe's change of tactics halfway through the battle, when they were near to destroying the RAF's fighter force but instead decided on a policy of terror bombing, has long been criticised. Most observers at the time assumed, like Goering did, that the bombing of cities was a last resort that would be irresistible in its force.

Of the many factors that influenced the

outcome of the struggle the most significant was the aeroplane itself. Without the rapid developments in aviation technology there would have been no Battle of Britain, and probably no blitzkreig either. To understand fully all the fundamental aspects of the hectic summer of 1940 one must first know something about the development of the military aircraft as an effective weapon and the growth of air power as a significant piece of the strategic puzzle. And to do this we must look beyond the Second World War to the early days of aviation at the very dawn of the 20th century.

Before hostilities broke out in August 1914 the men entrusted with the defence of Britain had given little thought to the potential of the aeroplane as a weapon. With the benefit of hindsight, this lack of official enthusiasm for such a radical new invention seems hardly credible, but at the time only a very few saw the aeroplane as anything more than a scientific novelty. The Army, or more specifically the Royal Engineers then charged with the responsibility of developing British military aviation, had progressed from spotter balloons and kites to the earliest aircraft without seriously considering them capable of offensive potential. While field guns and howitzers could hurl powerful shells over great distances, aeroplanes could carry only a puny armament little greater than that borne by infantrymen.

In 1909 an event took place which, though not widely realised at the time, was to undermine the security Britain had long enjoyed and lift the lid off a Pandora's box of frightening possibilities. Louis Blériot's precarious descent onto Dover Castle's Northfield Meadow on July 25 after the first cross-Channel flight was an inspiration to other aviation enthusiasts and a commendably brave achievement which demonstrated the reality that the island fortress lacked a roof.

Official indifference to the potential of military aviation soon relegated Britain to the position of a mere onlooker in the frenetic developments taking place in Europe. Eventually the deterioration in international relations, the glaring inadequacies of Britain's domestic aircraft industry and the prevarication of the military forced the hand of an apathetic government. In 1911, at the request of Prime Minister Asquith, the Haldane Committee was convened to explore the possibility of a co-ordinated military aviation

Der Flieger-Leutnant Caspar warf als erster in diesem Kriege Bomben auf Dover hinab.

policy. In trying to gauge future requirements its members realised the need for an expanded air-arm within Britain's armed forces, and they even foresaw the forthcoming "fight for the supremacy of the air". The Haldane Committee certainly did not envisage a situation whereby air power itself could determine the outcome of battles, but it did recognise the reconnaissance potential of the new invention and urged that production of domestic designs was stepped up.

The new spirit of enterprise helped to establish companies like Avro, Sopwith (Hawker), Supermarine, Bristol, De Havilland, Blackburn, Handley-Page, Westland and Shorts and provided a bedrock of expertise which was to serve Britain well when two decades later the country sought to re-arm with aircraft capable of meeting any challenge. The most important outcome of the Haldane Committee, however, was the birth of the Royal Flying Corps (RFC), established by royal warrant on April 13, 1912.

As momentum towards conflict increased British military aviation was assigned merely reconnaissance duties and, on the outbreak of the war, the fledgling RFC was dispatched to France to spot for the guns and help the generals see beyond each shell-pocked horizon. With its naval air stations strung along the coast, the Royal Naval Air Service (RNAS) seemed best suited to offer some kind of air defence of the British mainland and, due to the Army's reluctance to release even a single aeroplane from front-line duties in France, it became the obvious and only choice as Britain's champion. Just how inadequate these defences were was plainly illustrated

Flieger-Leutnant Caspar, a hero of the fatherland after he became the first German aviator to bomb England in the Great War, portrayed in a contemporary postcard.

During most of the First World War Britain's anti-aircraft armament was woefully incapable of preventing a determined air attack. Antiquated weapons like this "pom-pom" were both inaccurate and in short supply. The gun illustrated is the actual weapon (a one-pounder) which fired the first anti-aircraft round in defence of London.

A NATION ALONE

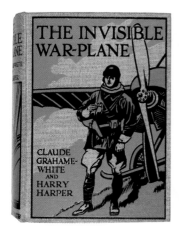

Claude Grahame-White's book *The Invisible War-Plane* reflected the popular image of military aviation in 1915, but until the advent of powerful engines and purpose-built weaponry reality remained rather less impressive than fantasy.

when a German seaplane casually dropped the first bombs on Britain at Dover in December 1914 without encountering any opposition.

Winston Churchill, then First Lord of the Admiralty, could hardly have been surprised. Only a day after assuming responsibility at the Admiralty in 1911 he had drawn up a charter for air defence which outlined four basic tasks: the destruction of enemy aircraft and airships at their bases; an interceptor force of aircraft based on the east coast; the concentration of anti-aircraft defences around military targets and the formation of a last line of defence centred on aircraft at Hendon, north-west of London; and the blackout of towns and cities to obscure them from the air. His prophesy in September 1914 that "aerial attack upon England must be a feature of the near future" had been fulfilled. Britain had fallen victim to a new warfare.

In Germany the early seaplane raids were intended as a gesture of defiance against a mighty rival and were only a hint of what was to come. The Kaiser's officers had been preparing an aircraft which would pose a far more serious threat – one against which, it was argued, no counter could be employed. The pages of contemporary science fiction were soon to become terrifying fact as London and the Home Counties became the arena for a spectacle unequalled in history. Germany had not been blind to the implicit opportunity which aviation offered for striking at the heart of its arch-enemy, and soon after the outbreak of hostilities her army and navy vied for a chance to deliver the first of a series of mortal

blows against the British mainland.

The weapon they hoped would achieve such decisive destruction and win the war was the Zeppelin, the huge cigar-shaped airship against which the unsuspecting British had prepared no defence. Perhaps taking comfort from the fact that she had not ratified the 1907 Hague Declaration prohibiting bombardment from the air, the Germans had excitedly developed Count Ferdinand von Zeppelin's invention into a formidable if unwieldy weapon of war.

Too big to remain a secret, the military Zeppelins were well known to the British public and even figured in the calculations of the Committee of Imperial Defence. However, they were seen as tactical rather than strategic weapons and no counter-measures were prepared. In 1908 an Invasion Inquiry had considered the possibility of German attack, but although contingency plans were not abandoned until 1917 they were concerned with repulsing a naval rather than aerial threat. The traditional custodian of national security was Britain's senior service, the Royal Navy, which strained at the leash like an impatient guard dog, eager to chase off any attempt by its rival to cross the North Sea.

The early raids revealed the inadequacy of the home defences. Although casualties were light, the British public suddenly realised that war could reach them as easily as it had their continental neighbours. The Zeppelins, relying on the properties of hydrogen for lift, were able to fly at altitudes contemporary aircraft could not reach, and on the rare occasions that

The distinction of the first victory in air-to-air combat is credited to one Corporal Louis Quenault, the gunner in a French Air Service Voisin III two-seat biplane. On October 5, 1914, while on a bombing mission behind the enemy lines, Quenault fired his machine-gun at a German Aviatik monoplane and shot it down in flames, killing both crew members.

ROYAL FLYING CORPS
Reconnoitring the Enemy's Lines.

one was tracked and held in the beam of a searchlight the motley collection of guns, many of pre-Boer War vintage, could merely spit defiance, their shells tumbling to earth well out of range of their giant targets.

As the aerial bombardment intensified even those who had been conspicuous by their contempt for air power had second thoughts. In 1916 responsibility for Home Defence reverted back to the War Office and Lord French was appointed Commander-in-Chief, Home Forces. It was now the turn of the RFC to provide a deterrent to the aerial threat and although fully committed to deployment on the bloody Western Front it was forced to form a Home Defence Wing. Barely equipped for the rigours of night fighting, the pilots of the flimsy BE 2 aircraft scoured the blackness for their elusive quarry. Always frozen, often blinded by the muzzle-flash of their guns if they did get an opportunity to fire, the young airmen hurled Hales bombs, Ranken darts and Lewis gun ammunition at their targets.

The breakthrough came on September 2, 1916 when Lieutenant William Leefe Robinson dispatched the Zeppelin SL11 in a conflagration over Cuffley in Hertfordshire, winning a VC for his skill and daring. As it would be a generation later, science allied with simple courage was the deciding factor in the nation's salvation. Armed with the new Brock-Pomery-Buckingham explosive bullets and equipped with more powerful aero-engines, the pilots of the Home Defence squadrons were able to inflict a terrible revenge on their unsuspecting quarry. The sight of Zeppelins, one after another, engulfed in flames and slowly collapsing earthwards soon became common, and for the first time aviators like Leefe Robinson were bestowed with accolades previously reserved for heroes from the army or navy. The Kaiser's dream of armadas of airships roaming at will over the cowering British died in the embers of the twisted carcasses of Zeppelins which littered the British landscape.

By 1917, however, Germany's lighter-than-air menace had been superseded by a more conventional heavier-than-air one. Flying in rigid diamond shaped formations, first Gotha and later Giant bombers from the crack "England Squadron" darkened the skies above Britain. Unlike the unwieldy Zeppelins these huge biplanes could maintain a steady course and, due to formidable combined fire-power, were able to see off even the most

ROYAL FLYING CORPS
Chasing a German Taube.

determined opposition. Mainly through reckless courage, pilots of the RFC were able to dispatch an occasional raider and improvements in anti-aircraft guns provided some success, but the havoc and destruction which resulted from the raids eclipsed even the worst the Zeppelins had managed.

A wave of consternation and anger at their apparent helplessness consumed the British population. To prevent an epidemic of panic the Government was forced to act, and to find a solution it sought the advice of a former enemy, the redoubtable former Boer leader Lieutenant-General Jan C. Smuts.

For the first few months of the Great War air combat was a leisurely affair more akin to jousting than a desperate struggle for supremacy above the battlefields of Flanders.

A NATION ALONE

At the Prime Minister's request Smuts proceeded to consider the radical restructuring of Britain's air forces. Initially he suggested the reorganisation of anti-aircraft guns into formidable and co-ordinated barrages and encouraged the organisation of fighter squadrons trained to attack in formation, not the penny-packets currently employed. As a result the defence of London was placed under the control of one man, Brigadier-General Ashmore. In control of the new "London Air Defence" operation, Ashmore formed the defences into distinct and separate gun and fighter-aircraft zones and encouraged the use of the new Sopwith Camels as rudimentary night-fighters. He also introduced more powerful searchlights and improved height-finding instruments and sound locators. Significantly his activities resulted in the first appearance of barrage balloons, benignly grazing the skies of London like so many bloated sheep. The integration of all aspects of air defence under one commander yielded enormous benefits which unfortunately were to be forgotten when, during the Second World War, responsibility for the management of aircraft and guns was divided between RAF and Army commands.

Before Ashmore had time to finalise all his preparations, however, the German air-raids

The problems associated with air-fighting during the First World War were many and varied. As this picture of the Lewis gun-mounting on an SE5A suggests, the pilot was exposed to the elements and no matter how securely the wing-mounted gun was braced, firing (via a "Bowden cable") caused such vibration that only close-range attacks were successful.

INTO THE DARKNESS

Night-fighters of the First World War were little more than hastily converted day-fighters such as this FE 2B biplane, which employed a "pusher" configuration to allow the front-gunner a clear field of fire.

increased in ferocity. As it would in 1940, lack of official information concerning the true state of Britain's defences encouraged a new bout of public cynicism. In search of whatever shelter could be found, people assumed squatter's rights in Underground stations and public parks, and confrontations with those in authority became frequent.

Encouraged to provide further solutions to the mounting crisis, Smuts' committee presented its final report to an anxious Government on August 17, 1917. It was an historic document for it recognised the importance of the aeroplane in its own right and argued that air-power should be independent from either army or navy control. The creation of a new Air Ministry was therefore recommended, with a suitable Air Staff as its executive. If Britain was to be protected from aerial bombardment it had to have the capability to strike deep within enemy territory and attempt to incapacitate the opposing war-machine before it, in turn, could inflict similar damage. Thus a truly independent air force had its genesis. At the same time the seeds were sown of a controversy concerning the offensive use of air power, one which would flower intermittently over the next two decades.

By January 3, 1918 the Air Council was in place and Major-General Sir Hugh Trenchard (who had been in command of the RFC in France since 1915) became Chief of the Air Staff. On April 1, 1918, in recognition of the aeroplane's impact on modern war and as a direct result of the German air offensive against Britain, the Royal Air Force (RAF) came into being.

As 1918 progressed, the introduction of new aircraft such as the excellent Bristol Fighter and the collapse of their spring offensive on the Western Front prevented Germany continuing the war over Britain.

Due to disagreements with the first Secretary of State for Air, Lord Rothermere, Trenchard almost immediately resigned from his post on the Air Staff. Instead of being removed altogether from high command he was offered control of the new Independent Bombing Force (IBF), which was being assembled in France in preparation for the strategic bombing of Germany. Although the IBF had few significant successes it did expose Trenchard to the full possibilities of bomber operations and further convinced him of the importance of an offensive air policy.

While the Zepelins and later the Gotha and Giant bomber raids did little to alter the course of the war, they had alerted the public to the potential horror of massed air assault. On the evening of September 3, 1917 a total of 132 people were killed and 96 injured by just 46 bombs from Gotha raiders. It was statistics like these which, when considered in the light of likely future developments in the size and capacity of aircraft, gave rise to frightening postwar calculations predicting unbearable casualties and destruction.

Though terrifying to those on the receiving end, the Zeppelin raids remained a curiosity to most of the population. However, Lieutenant William Leefe Robinson's timely victory over SL11 above the village of Cuffley in Hertfordshire in 1916 was greeted with national jubilation.

You did startle me ; I thought you were a Zeppelin.

The British public were fascinated by the whole concept of "war from the air", and the manufacturers of seaside souvenirs were among those who welcomed the opportunity to exploit such mass interest in a new area.

Curiously the Germans, who during the First World War had used their bombers as the first strategically deployed air force, were unable to repeat the achievement in the Second World War. While the Kaiser's air force had developed powerful multi-engined aircraft with great lifting power (for the time) and impressive defensive armaments its successor, the Luftwaffe of the 1930s, never possessed a heavy bomber with the equivalent potency of those employed by its predecessor.

At the end of the war in 1918, the RAF was the largest air force in the world. It possessed a staggering total of 27,333 officers, 263,410 other ranks, 22,647 aeroplanes and some 700 aerodromes. In order to preserve such a formidable force those who had been active

during its expansion sought to find good use for it, but the threat from the army and navy, keen to regain influence, was palpable.

After the General Election in December 1918 Lloyd George gave Churchill control of the Air Ministry to add to his responsibilities at the War Office. Early in 1919, at Churchill's request, Trenchard resumed his appointment as Chief of the Air Staff, a position he was to hold for an unprecedented ten years. His struggle to keep the RAF intact began almost as soon as he assumed office. In the closing months of the Great War Britain's new RAF had cost the tax-payer close on one million pounds a day. War-weary Britain had had enough of militarism and the dismantling of her war machine was inevitable. Being the youngest service the RAF suffered the deepest cuts and its 280 squadrons were reduced to barely ten per cent of their wartime levels.

To preserve the nucleus of the RAF Trenchard proposed new uses for his remaining squadrons, and it rapidly became the policemen of the Empire, with aircraft scattered right across the globe. The RAF's domination of recalcitrant tribesmen in Iraq, Afghanistan and parts of Africa seemed to vindicate all Trenchard's efforts, and helped promulgate a myth of invincible air power. It was a delusion the RAF was not alone in suffering, for the cult of the bomber caught the imagination of airmen the world over.

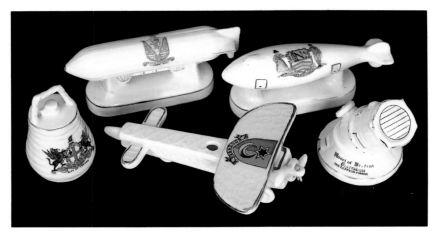

INTO THE DARKNESS

In the United States the ebullient *bête-noir* of America's military aviation theorists, Billy Mitchell, was busy demonstrating the vulnerability of battleships to attack by aircraft and Italy, in keeping with the international vogue for futurism, also produced its fair share of aviation prophets. By far the most famous and controversial of these visionaries was Guilio Douhet, whose seminal work *Command of the Air* was published in 1921.

Douhet had been much impressed by the achievements of the Italian air arm during the First World War, when many long-distance missions had been successfully completed. He then became head of the Central Aeronautical Bureau of the army and was closely involved with the development of military aviation, concluding early on that bomber aircraft were the key weapons of modern warfare. Because the bomber would always reach its target (in hours instead of days or weeks) it made traditional armament obsolete; flying high above the trenches and scarred landscape below, the bomber would press on to its destination and offer a formidable defence against the frail, underpowered fighters sent to engage it. Bomber aircraft would, he argued, end the stalemate that foiled land and sea power during the Great War.

Douhet went still further, maintaining that expenditure on interceptors would serve merely to dilute the resources available for bomber production: "The fundamental principle of aerial warfare is this: to resign oneself to endure enemy aerial offensives in order to inflict the greatest possible offensives on the enemy." Aerial bombardment, though terrible, would at least decide matters quickly and was a humane alternative to the stagnation of years of trench warfare with its heavy casualties and interminable misery.

However, most postwar experience was illusory, failing to provide a decent yardstick for long-term policy. Bewildered tribesmen and ageing, incapacitated battleships were no match for even the most outdated aircraft. The fact that aircraft could be prevented from reaching their targets was ignored, largely because recent events had presented no opposition. Trenchard even went as far as to state that "the aeroplane is not a defence against the aeroplane" – despite the fact that at the height of the German offensive over London in 1917 the "England Squadron" was suffering a rate of attrition of 20% because of improved fighter interception tactics.

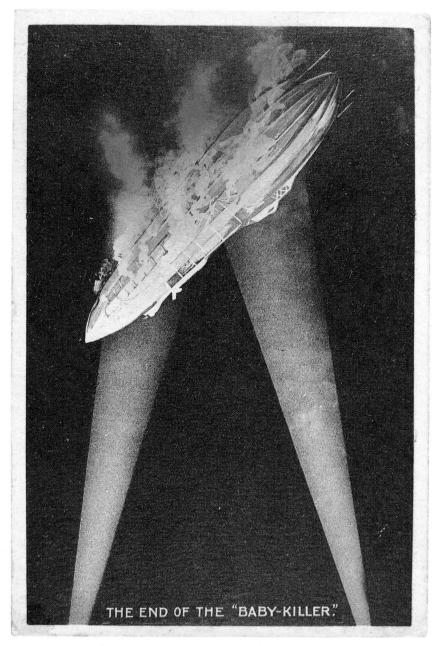

THE END OF THE "BABY-KILLER."

London had been an easy target to locate and attack. It was near to the coast and bombers were often overhead before interceptor fighters could reach combat altitudes. The serpentine thread of the Thames provided an ideal target indicator which was impossible to disguise. Would not similar missions to Paris or Berlin, if flown from British airfields, face greater difficulties? Not only were both cities well behind their frontiers, increasing the flight time of an attacking British force, but their geographic location also enabled interceptors to be scrambled well in advance of a raid. Unlike

Opinion in Britain was, understandably, uncompromising in its outrage against Germany's bombing campaign over England during the First World War.

A NATION ALONE

Marshal of the Royal Air Force Lord Trenchard inspects the first entry of recruits at Halton, the best known of the technical colleges set up for ground-crew training after 1922. Trenchard's vision and enthusiasm for Britain's air-arm was decisive in securing its expansion between the wars.

London, both cities could maintain a more effective blackout as there was no estuary to aid navigation. All these mitigating factors should have encouraged the policy-makers to reconsider their position and concentrate on an effective defence. If London's air defences could manage a 20% success rate, with all the capital's inherent disadvantages, then continental targets could expect to achieve better results against an opposing air fleet. At the very least the introduction of escort fighters was worth considering. Unfortunately the statistics were manipulated to suit the bomber protagonists and offence was still considered the best defence.

Germany, with no air force left to protect after the severe "diktats" of the Treaty of Versailles, did not need to create complicated doctrines to invent a use for air power. When the time was right the Luftwaffe would write a rule-book based on practical reality rather than speculation. Her immediate priority was to find a means of re-inventing an air force.

The ascension of Adolf Hitler to the lofty office of Chancellor in 1933 would provide

that means. In the interim, however, Germany's military aviators were not idle. True to the terms of the Versailles Treaty Germany did not possess an air force on the Fatherland's soil, but she did have one on Russian soil! With an irony revealed only by hindsight, Germany's Army Command had taken advantage of an agreement signed with Europe's other political exile, the Soviet Union, at Rapallo in 1922. Ostensibly concerning trade and diplomacy, the treaty concealed a military co-operation pact which provided facilities in Russia in exchange for German expertise.

As a result Germany was able to enjoy the use of a number of airbases for training purposes, the most notable being Lipetsk, between Moscow and Stalingrad. From 1924 German pilots in their Fokker DX111 biplanes were able to practise techniques which would later be used to such terrifying effect in Spain, Poland, Holland, Belgium and France and which would test the mettle of RAF pilots long shackled to the inflexible theories of formation flying and textbook manoeuvres. The roots of the "aerial artillery" techniques employed by the Luftwaffe within the framework of blitzkrieg can be traced back to their surreptitious training activities in Russia and the flight testing of prototypes in Sweden during the late 1930s. Moreover, the impressive and apparently passive developments in German civil aviation had created a cadre of skilled pilots and ground-crews easily able to adapt from mail-carrying Dorniers and Heinkels to bomb-carrying versions of the same machines. By the time Hitler came to power the success of Lufthansa and the cheerful showmanship of First World War veterans like stunt-flyer Ernst Udet had re-established German "air-mindedness" and instigated a programme of rearmament.

Some interested parties, like the *Daily Mail*'s Lord Rothermere, had not remained ignorant of the potential threat to peace posed by the ascendancy of the new Germany. As early as November 1933, in a *Mail* article headed *"We need 5,000 War-Planes!"* he claimed: "Not since the Dutch Fleet burnt British shipping in the Medway 250 years ago has this country been so inadequately protected against the possibility of foreign attack as it is today." Again, in 1935, Rothermere argued: "The safety of this country, and indeed its independence since the development of the air arm, rests above all on security against air attacks, to which Great Britain is more exposed than any other country in Europe."

Unfortunately, Rothermere tended to sensationalise the true threat of German airpower. Churchill, who was much more aware

of the practical limitations of offensive air operations, had to admit in 1933 that "Germany is already well on her way to become, and must become, incomparably the most heavily-armed nation in the world and the nation most completely ready for war."

The interwar period can be divided into two broad periods as far as Britain's investment in air defence is concerned. The first ten years saw a reluctance to increase the size and capability of the Royal Air Force due to financial restrictions and a not unnatural disinclination towards all things military; the second decade was characterised by the fear of initiating an arms race should expansion go ahead and the belief that protection from the predicted devastation of aerial bombardment could only be achieved through peaceful negotiation. As a result the RAF had to make do with aircraft of Great War vintage during the 1920s and wholly inadequate bomber and fighter designs to equip her depleted squadrons for most of the 1930s.

Britain's politicans hid under the sheets of appeasement in the hope that Hitler, like some bad dream, might vanish the next time they dared to peek into the gloom of international affairs. As the bad dream became a nightmare, it gradually dawned upon the nation's statesmen that they had neglected the defence of the realm. In 1936 the sum of £185 million was grudgingly allocated towards Home Defence and rearmament was stepped up, but by June 1940, only a month before the Battle of Britain proper, only 32 of the required minimum of 52 fighter squadrons were available for Home Defence. Prewar apathy

"Trenchard's Brats", the colloquial term for the growing cadre of recruits into the technical trades of the RAF, were taught all aspects of aerodynamics, engineering and aircraft construction. Here trainees to No. 1 School of Aeronautics at Reading get to grips with a strangely dismembered machine.

ABOVE Until the 20th century war games had involved only armies and navies, but with the advent of air power military strategists could explore the possibilities of deployment in three dimensions.

BELOW Public spectacles such as this one at Wembley were an important aspect of Trenchard's policy, designed to breed faith in and widespread support for the capabilities of the interwar RAF and its new role as "policeman of the Empire".

and a savage mauling in France before Dunkirk meant that of these squadrons only 25 were equipped with the modern Hurricane and Spitfire monoplanes.

If aviation in general had not achieved the aura of glamour which caught the imagination of a British public searching for an antidote to the interwar malaise, little development of any kind would have been likely. The flights of Alan Cobham, Bert Hinckler, Amy Johnson, Amelia Earhart, Jim Mollison, Charles Lindbergh and others established the aeroplane as the symbol of technological progress. Long-distance flights and world speed record attempts were to the 1930s what the clipper races and regattas were to the Victorians.

The bellicose Lord Rothermere had shown that even in the face of official indifference it was possible for Britain to produce world-beating aircraft. In 1935 he unveiled his private venture, the twin-engined "Britain First". A low-wing monoplane capable of matching the top speeds of contemporary front-line fighters, Britain First further vindicated the monoplane lobby and exposed the yawning gaps in Britain's aerial arsenal. In a gesture of public spiritedness (and in the name of the *Daily Mail*), Rothermere presented the aeroplane to a grateful Royal Air Force. Perhaps not unreasonably, he could not

resist this parting shot at his detractors: "Military historians will, surely, draw unpleasant lessons from the fact that it was left to a civilian enthusiast to inspire and provide what was to prove such a striking additon to our national defences." In RAF service, renamed "Blenheim", Rothermere's plane served in a variety of roles and was, for a time, Britain's pre-eminent medium bomber and only practical night-fighter.

As young boys carefully pieced together and painted "Skybirds" wood and brass model aeroplanes or rushed to the toyshop to choose one of the new "Penguin" aircraft construction kits made out of a curious material called acetate, they escaped to a fantasy world where air battles were fought in the Great War manner of Richthofen, Ball and Guynemer. The displays of Britain's aerial might during Empire Air Days and at the RAF Display at Hendon prompts both young and old to wonder just what a future air war would be like. It was unlikely to be the chivalrous affair depicted in *War in the Air, 1936* by "Major Helders". In this, a novel translated from the German, Britain and France go to war over territorial demands in Egypt; the British bomb Paris, reducing the graceful city to rubble in the style of Douhet and in response the French Army invades

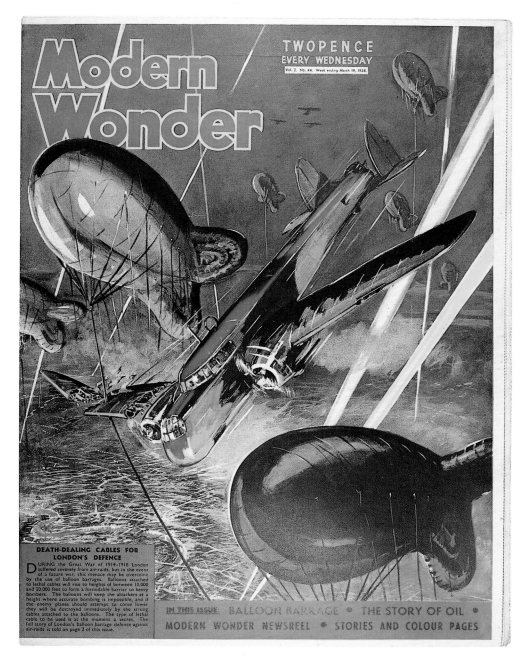

DEATH-DEALING CABLES FOR LONDON'S DEFENCE

DURING the Great War of 1914-1918 London suffered severely from air-raids, but in the event of a future war, this menace may be overcome by the use of balloon barrages. Balloons attached to lethal cables will rise to heights of between 10,000 and 20,000 feet to form a formidable barrier to heavy bombers. The balloons will keep the attackers at a height where accurate bombing is impossible, and if the enemy planes should attempt to come lower they will be destroyed immediately by the strong cables attached to the balloons. The type of lethal cable to be used is at the moment a secret. The full story of London's balloon barrage defence against air-raids is told on page 2 of this issue.

IN THIS ISSUE: BALLOON BARRAGE • THE STORY OF OIL • MODERN WONDER NEWSREEL • STORIES AND COLOUR PAGES

ABOVE & BELOW Regular air displays at Hendon, notably on "Empire Air Day", were hugely popular and of enormous importance in supporting the RAF's continual lobbying for funds to keep pace with aeronautical developments.

LEFT *Modern Wonder*, a popular science magazine in the 1930s, allocated a number of covers to the subject of air defence and the possible effects of huge air-raids.

Britain via captured airfields. The French "poilus" finally succumb to a withering assault by the remaining British squadrons and in a vindication of air power are forced to sue for peace.

War from the Air by L. E. O. Charlton listed further terrifying possibilities. Aeroplanes, he conjectured, might be "loaded with explosives, gas or thermite, or even the bacilli of disease . . ." but he admitted that they may fall prey to death-rays, demagnetisation or even chemically supercharged clouds which would burst into flames on the approach of an aircraft. In *Airfare* Edgar Middleton went as far as to suggest that houses and streets might need to be burrowed deep into the sides of hills or in underground cavities, but he warned: "The idea is of the farcical-humorous order judged from the standpoints of today. But then so was the aeroplane and the airship to the peoples of the early 19th-century period."

Today, much of what appeared in the popular press and on the cinema screen during the late 1930s seems little more than fantasy. The pronouncements of politicians on both sides of the disarmament lobby appear simplistic and extreme. Yet the anxieties of

A NATION ALONE

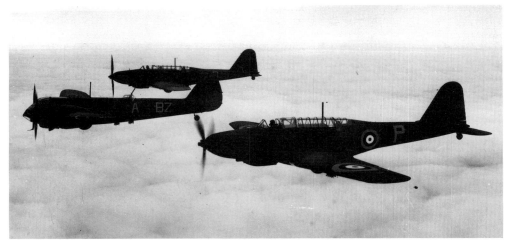

Fairey Battles of No. 226 Squadron accompany a Blenheim from 107. The Battle's chronic deficiencies were cruelly exposed during the war in France and it played a minor role in the subsequent fighting over England. The final ignominy came in early July: mistaken for an enemy raider a Battle was shot down by a fighter of 12 Group, adding tragically to the RAF's growing list of casualties.

A Hurricane of No. 501 Squadron pictured in France, 1940. The Hurricane was the mainstay of British air power in France, aided by Battles and Defiants, but the Spitfire was never put into service there.

men like Baldwin and Chamberlain and the success of prophetic films like Korda's *Things to Come* point to an underlying apprehension of the potential of air power.

If the bomber could "always get through" then the streets of Britain would be littered with the twisted bodies not only of soldiers but also of women and children. Gas, the nuclear weapon of the age, hung like the Sword of Damoclese above the heads of the population. Citizens needed no reminding of the terrifying effects of this unseen killer; its use in the trenches of Flanders had left a mark on nearly every family in the land.

As the various peace initiatives collapsed and crisis after crisis threatened to bring Europe to the brink of war it seemed that the prophets of doom would have their day. In Spain the destruction of Guernica by Hitler's Condor Legion confirmed all that the pacifists had most feared. In 1938 the Committee on Imperial Defence estimated Britain would suffer 1.8 million casualties in the first two

months of war. Twenty million square feet of timber would be needed for coffins and as this was an impossible figure mass graves would have to be dug. Activists on the Left warned that refugees would be machine-gunned and bombing would deafen survivors for life. Enemy bombers would glide across the coast with their engines switched off to avoid sound location (the public was unaware of Radar).

In response to Hitler's latest act of aggression – the invasion of Poland – Britain declared war on Nazi Germany. Hostilities officially commenced at 11 o'clock on the morning of September 3, 1939, and almost immediately the banshee wail of air-raid sirens could be heard across the capital. Churchill called London "the greatest target in the world", and it was estimated that 175,000 people would die during the first 24 hours of aerial bombardment. Although the first air-raid warning of the war was a false alarm, people had no illusions about the dangers that lay ahead.

INTO THE DARKNESS

By the end of September 1939 Poland, bludgeoned by Hitler's blitzkreig in the west and cruelly stabbed in the back by Stalin's Red Army in the east, finally succumbed to her sad fate. The Luftwaffe employed some 1,500 aircraft for the attack on Poland and its leader, Hermann Goering, in keeping with his Führer's wishes, was able to eliminate most of the obsolete Polish air force as it sat impotent on front-line aerodromes. Significantly the Luftwaffe also initiated its technique of close co-operation with the highly mobile ground troops and "Panzers" (tanks) of the army, ranging deep behind the front line to eliminate key targets and clear a path for the advancing troops. The principal of blitzkrieg had been proven to be sound.

"War Directive No. 1 for the Conduct of War" was the first of a series of famous orders prepared by Hitler laying down the methods and policies to be employed during successive campaigns. Although chiefly concerned with operations against Poland, it did not rule out the possibility of action against France and Britain. The directive stated: "In operations against England the task of the Air Force is to take measures to dislocate English imports, the armaments industry and the transport of troops to France." Hitler's caveat that "the decision regarding attacks on London is reserved for me" makes chilling reading – but supports the contention that he hoped to find a peaceful settlement with Britain and wanted to avoid direct confrontation.

The last paragraph ordered preparations for attacks on the "English homeland" but warned of the dangers of deploying insufficient forces. Bearing this in mind and aware of Hitler's anxiety about war on two fronts – perhaps also because as yet no target maps had been prepared, apart from hurriedly copied British Ordnance Survey maps and updated Lufthansa charts – the Luftwaffe erred on the side of caution and Britain was granted a sorely needed breathing space. There would be no Battle of Britain in 1939.

These were heady days indeed. On the afternoon of the declaration of war Churchill returned to his old job at the Admiralty. As the signal "Winston is back" was transmitted across the oceans sailors at anchorages all over the Empire cheered. Churchill spelt business and an end to indecision.

But it was the RAF that proved the most active service during the first days of war. In accordance with prior arrangements 160 Fairey Battle day-bombers of the Advanced Air Striking Force had left their bases in England and on September 2 landed at primitive grass airfields in France. More would soon follow, and precious fighters too. Though they did not know it at the time the Battle pilots had been equipped with death traps. It would not be long before the name of this aircraft became synonymous with posthumous awards for heroism.

Like their fathers before them the professional soldiers of Britain's regular army were mobilised and headed for the boat-trains to France. The ever-present threat of air attack meant that unlike "The Old Contemptibles" of 1914 the British Expeditionary Force of 1939 was not treated to the accolade of bunting, cheering crowds and regimental bands; the BEF troops moved quietly in small numbers and at night. The demands of a modern, mechanised army with 18,000 motor vehicles and some 100,000 different kinds of spare parts meant that shipping and port facilities were paramount. Civilians from the various port authorities around Britain were recruited and they hastily made all the necessary arrangements with their French counterparts. The advanced parties of anti-aircraft units and medical staff were soon followed by the main force of 160,000 men with 140,000 tons of supplies.

By the beginning of October, in a slow-motion replay of 1914, the BEF in position along a 55-mile front from Maulde to Armentières. The names of the towns, villages and crossroads traversed by this line were often found to match the Great War battle honours which emblazoned the regimental colours of the famous units involved.

The Hawker Hurricane was the first of the RAF's new generation of high-speed monoplane interceptors. Simpler to build than Mitchell's Spitfire – it used many of the jigs and machine-tools designed for Sydney Camm's famous Hawker biplanes – it was a robust and highly manoeuvrable aircraft. Unlike the Spitfire, which had a stressed skin construction, the Hurricane was often capable of flight even after substantial battle damage. These were based in France with 85 Squadron.

Scores of books were published in the 1930s warning of the dangers of impending attack from the air. This one, somewhat prophetically, shows a Luftwaffe Ju-87 "Stuka" dive-bomber homing in on Westminster, the vulnerable nerve centre of the nation.

From his headquarters in Arras, code-named "Brassard", Lord Gort, the BEF's Commander-in-Chief, went about making the best of his rather scant resources. The lack of recent investment was clearly illustrated by the paucity of modern weapons and the inadequacy of heavy armour available, and as Gort sent endless dispatches enquiring about the progress of promised reinforcemenets his troops settled into a familiar routine of drill, patrols, trench-digging and "blancoing". The songs their fathers had sung were replaced by "We're gonna hang out our washing on the Siegfried Line" and "When the lights go on again all over the world", and as boredom encouraged thoughts of loved ones and home, they looked forward to being back in "Blighty" for Christmas. As their French counterparts enjoyed the loud pleasures of bars and cafés the unfortunate tommies were forced to endure a strict black-out and security regime. Dispersed because of the threat from the air, they settled down to a damp existence under canvas or corrugated iron.

Facing each other across the tangled defences of no-man's-land the belligerents settled down to a long period of inactivity and tedium. On the Western Front, what American Senator William Borah dubbed "the phoney war" had begun. The troops of England, France and Germany added the nicknames "Bore-war", "La drôle de guerre" and "Sitzkrieg" respectively but it all amounted in the end to the same thing – an uneasy stalemate.

For some the phoney war would be very real indeed. None were to taste the bitter reality of combat more than the gallant Fairey Battle pilots bloodied so soon after their arrival in France. On September 20 three Battles of No. 88 Squadron were sent out on a border patrol. Their fate was quickly decided when, pounced on by Messerschmitt 109s, two of the underarmed and lumbering aeroplanes were sent spiralling to earth. Sergeant Letchford, the rear-gunner of the only Battle to survive, earned the distinction of destroying the first German aircraft to fall to the RAF over the Western Front. With a keen eye and good fortune he was able to dispatch an Me-109 in part-payment at least for the loss of his comrades. Ten days later a further four Battles, this time from No. 150 Squadron, failed to return from a reconnaissance over Saarbrücken and the type was removed from daylight operations.

Hoping for a collapse of the German home front through disillusionment rather than attrition, Premier Chamberlain was happy to see the offensive activities of the Army and Royal Air Force on the Western Front limited to reconnaissance and the odd skirmish. Even his Secretary of State for Air, Sir Kingsley Wood, was disinclined towards provocation. When urged to bomb Germany's timber resources in the Black Forest he exclaimed: "Are you aware it is private property? Why, you will be asking me to bomb Essen next!" Instead Bomber Command was used to drop propaganda leaflets on the German population in a further attempt to find a solution which avoided head-on confrontation. When leaflet dropping ceased on April 6, 1940, Armstrong-Whitworth Whitley bombers had unloaded a staggering 65 million fluttering missiles on the bemused citizens of the Reich!

The French were even less vigorous. Racked by doubt about their predicament they had not even produced an additional tank since the declaration of war, preferring instead to pour out touring cars by the hundred. The Maginot Line had set them back £58 million – surely it would provide all the protection needed? Unfortunately, it was extensively manned by an army of hastily mobilised conscripts who had no hunger for

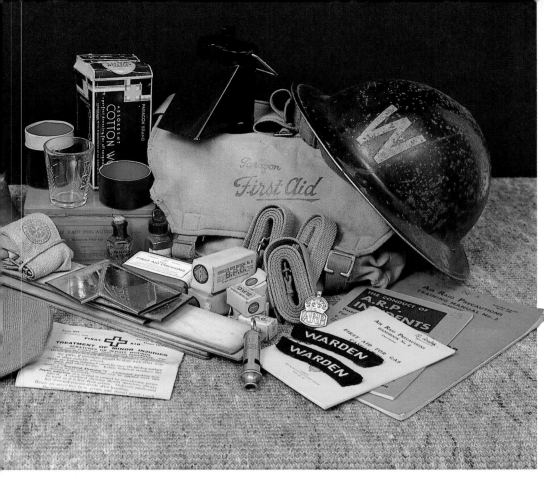

A fully equipped ARP warden was laden like a pack-mule. Apart from a robust Civil Defence gas-mask, a gas alarm rattle (left of picture) and an "all-clear" handbell, he also carried a shoulder-slung first-aid kit, information books, whistle, specially shielded lamp and, of course, the ubiquitous steel helmet. Though their role would be crucial during the Battle of Britain, hollow officiousness could easily engender both ridicule and dislike among the populace during "the phoney war".

glory but a high consumption of alcohol.

Though bulging with 1,800,000 soldiers the Maginot Line was an anachronism. It would have been more useful if it had been extended to the sea but the Belgians, fearful of insulting their German neighbours, refused any approach to extend it across their frontier. The Maginot Line may have been a wall of steel 400 miles long and bristling with guns and casemates but Belgium, the door in the wall, was left open and inviting.

Expecting an immediate air attack Britain had, since September 1, been plunged into darkness when a vigorous black-out was first imposed. On the assumption that each ton of explosives would claim 50 casualties hospitals were evacuated of all except the critically ill. In a little known but tragic side-effect of the crisis thousands of patients awaiting early treatment for cancer or other combatable ailments were left to their fate. The empty, sterile wards were made ready to receive the million-plus injured citizens it was predicted would occur.

Members of the Air-Raid Wardens' service which was formed in April 1937 were employed to enforce the Air-Raid Precautions (ARP) regulations. Donning black steel helmets stencilled with a bold white "W" and armed with hooded flashlights, wooden gas

rattles and solid brass handbells, these zealous public servants shouting "Put that light out" soon became almost as hated as Hitler. ARP was no joke: most people had read one of the many books available that outlined in graphic detail what was in store for Britain should the sirens go off. And the thing they feared most was gas.

Air-raid wardens were often based in rather spartan accommodation. Evacuated schools, sandbagged shelters and requisitioned offices were quickly converted into ARP posts and furnished with the array of equipment necessary for the official to carry out his irksome duties.

A NATION ALONE

In the late 1930s fear of gas attack gripped the public imagination in a manner similar to its modern equivalent – nuclear war. The authorities were quick to provide the essential protective equipment such as these ghastly gas-masks for babies, mass produced and ready for distribution as early as 1938.

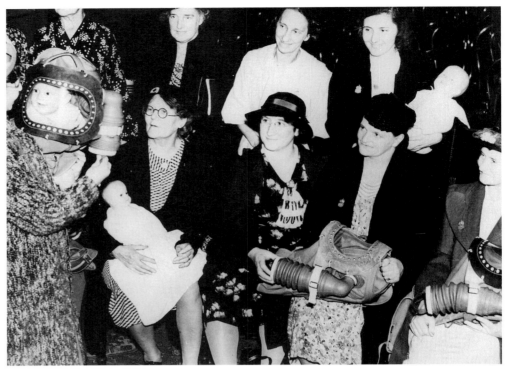

RAF establishments were far from immune to the threat of attack by gas. Here a decontamination crew pose in front of a Hawker Hector at No. 26 Squadron's base near Catterick, in North Yorkshire.

In *War on Great Cities*, published in 1937, Frank Morrison had warned: "The unrestricted use of lethal gas or bacteria upon the scale predicted by the experts implies a stampede of the threatened populations beyond all precedent." The Government shared Morrison's views and in March 1937 the first gas-mask factories were opened. These establishments managed a prodigious output and when war came everyone in the land was equipped with a mask. Slung in cardboard boxes tied with string or housed in bespoke cases for the more fashion-conscious, gas-masks were ubiquitous during the first months of war.

Gas-masks came in an amazing array of shapes and sizes. For children there was the "Mickey Mouse" version, so named because its goggle eyes and snout-like filter resembled the already famous cartoon character. Youngsters infuriated their parents by making "raspberry" noises, like breaking wind, every time they exhaled. A carefully timed blast was guaranteed to cause Victorian grandmothers to blanch! Adults' gas-masks were not nearly as much fun, being simple constructions of rubber and webbing with one-piece visors made of acetate that had the unfortunate habit of cracking.

New-born babies had one-piece masks that covered the whole body. Once the draw strings were tied only the baby's legs were exposed and the poor infant was cocooned in a grim container of pungent rubber. As babies' lungs were not sufficiently developed to draw air through the charcoal filter an accordian-like bellows was attached which the mother had to operate continuously while gas persisted. How she was supposed to keep this up for perhaps days on end was never explained, but at least some thought had been given to the matter and the mask on offer was better than none at all.

Respirators for wardens, police and ambulancemen were of altogether more sound construction, as was to be expected. Telephonists were able to don a version which

INTO THE DARKNESS

incorporated all the necessary paraphernalia of telecommunications into the mask itself. The services were issued with a mask containing a separate, interchangeable filter. Their haversack contained an anti-fog chemical to keep goggles clear from condensation and various ointments to deal with the multitude of blisters and burns that could be expected should gas be used.

Fighter and bomber pilots had patches of a special paint added to their aircraft, and it would change colour if gas was in the vicinity. Just what they were supposed to do (other than put their oxygen masks on) if gas was discovered was unclear.

A series of ARP handbooks covering the dangers of gas had been available since 1936 and among the advertisements for "Optrex", oilskins and Boots the Chemist's range of products which "could be useful in the preparation of a Gas Protected Room", the various gases and their properties were listed in chilling frankness. Gases like chlorine,

phosgene, mustard and Lewisite would have been familiar to veterans of the trenches, but modern nerve irritants bearing the initials CAP, KSK, BBC, DA, DM and DC were menacingly new.

An extract from the passage on phosgene makes it easier to understand the anxiety caused by chemical weapons and perhaps goes some way to explain the Government's reluctance to engage in offensive bombing: "Phosgene (Non-persistent) – This compound is a colourless gas at ordinary temperatures, though when liberated as a cloud it sometimes has a whitish appearance owing to condensation of water-vapour present in the air . . . It has a pungent odour rather like musty hay and is liable to cause coughing. In addition to being a very powerful lung irritant, Phosgene is also a tear-gas. It attacks the air cells of the lungs which, in severe cases, gradually become filled with inflammatory fluid resulting in interference with the passage of oxygen into the blood. In

The Alexander Korda production of H. G. Wells' story *Things To Come* played to packed cinemas in the late 1930s. In the film a city not dissimilar to London is attacked by an air fleet equipped with gas-bombs. The scenes of serried ranks of civilians collapsing under the influence of enveloping clouds of poisonous chemicals were powerfully dramatised. After the experiences of the Great War, when chemical weapons were used to such devastating effect, it is not surprising that strategicians assumed that aircraft would be used as the ultimate delivery system for modern chemical weapons. In an effort to prepare bewildered citizens for the effects of gas attack, ARP officers toured the country demonstrating the rather crude techniques then available to deal with gas contamination. Special decontamination squads were formed and ARPs regularly appealed for more recruits to join the rubber-clad army. Here Mr L. R. Allum of the Esher ARP broadcasts one such address to a curious crowd of civilians.

A NATION ALONE

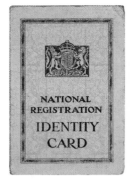

RIGHT As the need for efficient national security became even more urgent, "ID" cards for young and old were issued – with citizens required to carry them at all times.

ABOVE In the pre-television age it was the family radio that was the primary medium in announcing the unfolding developments of Britain's war effort. That meant the BBC, who then enjoyed a monopoly of broadcasting.

scarce and stocks of the "No. 8" batteries needed to power them ran out. Fear and frustration mounted – not least because ARP wardens, paid £3 per week (more than soldiers on active service abroad), seemed to have nothing to do except sit in their sector posts or boss people about.

In contrast to the severity of the black-out, the hours of daylight were extended by the introduction of "summertime" and, during the summer months, "double summertime". The last days of that Indian summer were exceptionally fine. In the eerie world of the phoney war pilots of Fighter Command could look down from their lofty galleries and see people swimming or sunbathing as they flew standard patrols. Weddings were running at twice the average rate and gossips muttered that the black-out was encouraging promiscuity. Entertainment of a more acceptable kind was made possible by the reopening of cinemas and theatres that had closed on the outbreak of war.

Yet beneath the mask of gaiety the more serious and tangible effects of total war were being felt. In anticipation of the much heralded air attack scores of families had their pets destroyed rather than see them tortured by gas or high explosives. A "Black-Out Budget" was introduced, raising the level of income tax by two shillings to seven shillings and sixpence in the pound.

this state exertion will cause the patient to collapse from want of oxygen, and death is then frequently the result."

However it was not gas but the black-out, a joke turned sour, that was to prove the immediate killer. Trees and telegraph poles sported bands of white paint, kerbs, steps and car running-boards were painted white and even bowler hats could be converted by the addition of a circlet of white material. Newsreels showed novelties such as pets parading around with tail-mounted lamps or sporting huge luminous bows, though they failed to disguise the havoc caused by the need for such measures. Road casualties more than doubled and by the New Year more than a fifth of the population had come to grief in one way or another trying to find their way through the gloom. People fell into ditches, tripped over kerbs or stumbled into the paths of cars whose headlamps had been masked save for a narrow slit that was all but invisible on foggy nights. Supplies of torches grew

INTO THE DARKNESS

The new Emergency Powers (Defence) Act introduced by parliament on August 24, 1939 began to take effect. This enabled the government to suspend Habeas Corpus, the right to free assembly and the right to demonstrate, and forbade public dissent. Newspapers were prevented from publishing weather forecasts, and inventions filed at the Patent Office could be commandeered for government use. For the first time policemen were armed and patrol cars with two Lee Enfield rifles stowed between the front seats became a familiar sight. Aliens were detained and sent off to dismal internment camps. The defence of the realm was to be pursued without the unnecessary complication of parliamentary debate.

As in the Great War, a Ministry of Information was established when hostilities commenced, at first under Lord MacMillan. Under him and his famous successors – Sir John Reith, Duff Cooper and Brendan Bracken – the Ministry and its sister department the Political Warfare Executive (concerned with overseas propaganda) were responsible for disseminating an enormous amount of messages intended to show people how to behave in wartime. Soon the towns and villages became cloaked in a mantle of posters and notices, many of which are now recognised as masterpieces of design.

The initial posters were not a great success,

merely urging the citizen to "Keep Calm and Carry On" or "Defend Freedom with all your Might". One in particular was a spectacular disaster: "Your Courage, Your Cheerfulness, will bring us Victory". The public, being encouraged to fight for democracy, were unhappy with a message that seemed to urge sacrifice in order to protect "us"—namely the Establishment.

A further set of instructional posters followed. One headed simply "Gas Attack" appeared to assume the reader was an imbecile who would not know how to don a gas-mask when the need arose. A survey carried by the Mass-Observation organisation reinforced the widespread feeling that the government was in danger of patronising its electors. It argued that people were becoming irritated by too many rules and regulations and were broad-minded enough to accept the hard facts of the current situation. Mass-Observation, an army of "pollsters" which grew out of an anthropological study programme in the mid-1930s, became a useful means by which the Ministry of Information could gauge public reaction to Home Front propaganda. Members of Mass-Observation collected a huge amount of information on public anxieties, morale and attitudes, and by discreetly employing "overheards" or provoking discussion in pubs and shops its "observers" formed a rich patchwork of wartime social history. This

As the German Navy and Luftwaffe stepped up the pressure on Britain's over-extended supply lines, thrift and economy became priorities for a beleagured nation. Posters encouraged the householder to save waste bones and grow more vegetables – "dig for victory".

During the first year of war road accidents caused by the black-out took a heavier toll of life than enemy action. Car headlamps were fitted with special shields, flashlights were baffled – and quiz books and party games assumed a new importance.

A NATION ALONE

Evacuated children about to board a train to take them to the safety of designated reception areas. For many it would prove a traumatic experience, and by April 1940 nearly 700,000 had returned to the cities from billets in England and Wales.

provides a refreshing and often hilarious alternative to the official versions.

As the propagandists became more skilled at their craft more effective means of presenting government directives were found. Probably the most memorable posters at this stage were the "Careless Talk Costs Lives" examples designed by "Fougasse", showing Hitler and his cronies eavesdropping on gossips in the most unlikely settings.

One poster dealt with a problem which for many is the most significant memory of the phoney war years. Headed "Don't do it, Mother – Leave Your Children in the Safer Areas", and portraying a concerned mother of two boys being urged by a phantom Führer pointing to a distant city to "Take them Back! Take them Back! Take them Back!", its message was clear: in order to save the lives of innocents, evacuation would be essential.

Britain had long been divided into "Evacuation", "Neutral" and "Reception" Areas should the need for a mass evacuation arise. Local authorities in the Reception Areas had provided the government with an estimate of the number of billets available to house the

exodus of city dwellers. Provision was made to relocate almost 5,000,000 people. In the event, some 3,500,000 had moved to the safer areas by the end of September. In fact more than half this number moved in accordance with private arrangements either to friends and relatives in the countryside or, for a lucky few, to enjoy a relatively luxurious war in small hotels or guest houses. Between September 1 and 3 over 1,500,000 citizens moved to billets organised under the auspices of the local authorities. Of these, 827,000 were children about to set off on a journey that would turn into an adventure or a nightmare – depending on individual fortune.

The pleas of unhappy evacuated children and the absence of massed bombing raids were the dual causes of a return home that plagued the plans of the government. By the beginning of April 1940 nearly 700,000 evacuees had returned home from billets in England and Wales; Scotland, more remote from the immediate danger area, witnessed an even greater reverse evacuation.

In overall terms the scheme had failed. The objective of moving civilians and especially children away from danger was not met. Even at its height the operation resulted in the evacuation of only half of London's school-children, and the capital was the Luftwaffe's major target. An attempt to reintroduce evacuation in February 1940 was even less successful: only a fifth of the children eligible for evacuation had registered to leave by the end of April.

Evacuation nevertheless had important social consequences. For the first time privileged families came face to face with the result of inner-city squalor and neglect. Many could not believe that children endured lifestyles that encouraged them to urinate in the corner of living rooms, sleep underneath beds (poor parents would have had pride of place on the mattress) and shun the use of soap and water.

Not only evacuees were subjected to official labelling and numbering. From October 1939 until 1952 every civilian had to carry a National Registration Identity Card. As the phoney war progressed civilians became increasingly annoyed by repeated requests to show identification, especially if the uniformed enquirer had been well known to the carrier in peacetime.

Unlike the euphoric rush that met Lord Kitchener's call to arms in 1914, there was no immediate stampede to recruiting offices in 1939. In 1938 the Government published a "Schedule of Reserved Occupations" as a means of preventing the rush to arms that had deprived British industry of skilled men during the Great War. When war was declared on September 3 the government immediately passed the National Service Act (Armed Forces), which provided for orderly conscription via the "call-up" method. By December 1939 nearly 1,500,000 men were in military service, with the vast majority in the Army and the balance divided between Navy and Air Force.

In January 1939 the government had distributed a booklet about opportunities for National Service subtitled, "A guide to the ways in which the people of this country may give service." It detailed occupations available across the range of services, armed and otherwise. Part-time jobs could be had in ARP, rescue and demolition, first-aid, decontamination squads, the Police War Reserve, Observer Corps, Auxiliary Fire Service, Women's Land Army, Coastguard, Royal Naval Reserve, Territorial Army, Auxiliary

Territorial Service (for women), Royal Air Force Volunteer Reserve and Civil Air Guard. As a result there was hardly a household that failed to offer National Service personnel. Home from work, civilians donned tin-hats (nicknamed "battle bowlers") and went off for a night's fire-watching or triangulation practice at an Observer Corps post.

By the beginning of 1940 more than 40,000 women had exchanged the fashion of the day for the fashion of the duration. Newly outfitted in rough military serge, they bolstered the home defences in either the Women's Royal Naval Service (WRENS), Auxiliary Territorial Service (ATS) or the Women's Auxiliary Air Force (WAAFS).

No stone had been left unturned to ensure that the nation was best equipped to meet the foe. A register of scientists had even been compiled, enabling the services to benefit from the latest in technology and science. The wisdom of this far-sighted move was to be acknowledged in just a few short months.

Apart from the more dramatic measures which were putting Britain onto a war footing, other more detailed precautions were taking place. In an effort to frustrate attempts by the Luftwaffe to home in on regional transmitters the BBC closed them down and provided only

By the outbreak of war Lord Rothermere's "Britain First", now in RAF guise and renamed with a more militant patriotism the "Blenheim", was equipping several squadrons. This row of Blenheim IVs are pictured with No. 535 Squadron at Odiham, Hampshire, in 1939.

The needs of war soon turned Britain into a vast armed camp. Civilians donned all manner of uniforms, manning the ramparts of Civil Defence to release regular servicemen for more pressing duties. The photograph shows cheaply produced fire-guard's helmets, a 1940 service issue respirator which had a separate filter unit more powerful and less restricting than mast-mounted versions, and an assortment of Civil Defence armbands. The telephonist's gas-mask came complete with headset and integral microphone. The steel helmet (top right) bears the Morris Motors Fire Brigade insignia, while those on the far right were worn by rest centre personnel, rescue workers and firemen (chief fire officer) respectively.

a single "Home Service" to keep its avid listeners amused and informed; dangerous animals at London Zoo were destroyed in case they escaped during an air-raid; the National Gallery carefully packed up its collection of fine paintings and secretly transported them to a disused mine in Wales alongside the treasures of the British Museum; the Bank of England, BBC variety department and even Billingsgate fish market shifted operations outside the immediate danger zone of London; a special evacuation of government codenamed "The Black Move" was prepared should Westminster and Whitehall be reduced to rubble by the Luftwaffe; and it was rumoured that the government and royal family might have to flee to Canada if things became too dangerous on the Home Front.

Civilians with nowhere to go, or no inclination to leave their homes, were catered for by the provision of corrugated iron bomb-shelters named "Anderson Shelters" after the Minister for Home Security, Sir John Anderson. By the outbreak of war almost 1,500,000 of these flimsy-looking but surprisingly robust contraptions – once they had been buried in back gardens – had been supplied by the government. To supplement them covered trenches, dug during August, were completed to offer protection for over half a million people. And so with windows taped, doors gas-proofed with carpeting and stirrup-pumps oiled, the citizens of Britain waited anxiously for the first notes of air-raid sirens to herald the start of the inevitable bombardment.

Whilst General Ironside (Chief of the Imperial General Staff, 1939–40) courted the press and challenged: "Come on Hitler, do your worst!" and added to an enthused *Daily Mirror* journalist, "We [the Army] would welcome a go at him," it was in fact the Royal

The air of light-hearted unreality that characterised the phoney war is captured by this example of popular sheet music. Similar sentiments were expressed in songs such as "We're going to hang out the washing on the Siegfried Line." Once Hitler had demonstrated the terrible power of blitzkrieg, however, the mood quickly became less flippant.

detonate on the mud-flats of the Thames estuary were Royal Navy counter-measures prepared to neutralise the mysterious weapons, but not before they had severely damaged the cruiser *Belfast* and the battleship *Nelson*.

With the approach of the harshest winter in 45 years, and suffering rationing, coal shortages and burst pipes, the British desperately needed something to cheer them up. The Royal Navy provided a tonic in December when it cornered the pocket-battleship *Graf Spee* at Montevideo in Uruguay. Her captain, Langsdorff, scuttled her rather than see his ship destroyed at the hands of the British force blockading the port, but though it was an "own goal" news of the destruction of the *Graf Spee* was celebrated as a significant victory and brightened the gloom of blacked-out Britain.

During the following months crowds flocked to cheer the prisoners released from captivity aboard the *Graf Spee*'s supply ship *Altmark* and rushed to see a downed Heinkel bomber in Scotland. Newsreels sensationalised the sporadic raids the RAF made against German ports and shipping. Understandably, each early event received media attention out of all proportion to its overall effect on the course of the war.

Signs that the phoney war was indeed temporary were first noticed in April 1940, but they were not the result of activity in Britain, France or Germany. It had long been appreciated that Germany's supply route for its badly needed iron-ore presented a tempting target, and the Norwegian port of Narvik was the avenue by which Swedish iron-ore reached the Reich. Churchill, characteristically, had long waited to mine Norwegian waters; Chamberlain, the appeaser, was able to acquiesce as Norway, distant to the real flashpoint of France, offered the chance of a successful diversion.

Norwegian waters were mined on April 8, and Chamberlain announced that Hitler had "missed the bus". The next day the Germans began their operation Weserübung (Weser-exercise) and ruined everything that Britain had planned by invading Norway and Denmark. Britain and France had been assembling an invasion force with the intention of securing key Norwegian ports, and they had not expected the Germans to beat them to it. As the Luftwaffe secured airfields all over Norway and landed fresh troops and supplies, the Allied invasion force

Navy that was bearing the early brunt of the conflict. Within hours of the declaration of the war the liner *SS Athenia* was sunk by a German torpedo, heralding the start of the U-boat campaign against the British economy. On September 7 the first of the hundreds of Atlantic convoys set sail, and the desperate struggle to maintain the ocean lifeline was on. On October 14 Captain Gunther Prien of U-47 manoeuvred his nimble submarine into an attack position inside the fleet anchorage at Scapa Flow and sank the battleship *Royal Oak*. Of all the weapons Hitler employed it was the U-boat and not the bomber which nearly brought Britain to its knees.

During November 1939 nearly 100,000 tons of shipping fell victim to a different kind of seaborne weapon – the mine – and of the various types encountered by far the most worrying was the parachute-dropped magnetic mine. Only after one had failed to headed for the coastal towns of Namsos and Andalsnes and the port of Narvik.

In a salutory lesson, both sides learned that the key to the successful invasion of a defended coast was air superiority. With control of all the airfields the Luftwaffe was able to range at will, remorselessly pounding the enclaves of cold and ill-equipped Allied troops, and by May 2 the garrisons at both Andalsnes and Namsos were forced to retreat. At Narvik, despite repeated attacks by both naval and infantry forces, the Germans (now on the defensive) were able to hold out. Although the Royal Navy was able to inflict severe damage on the Kriegsmarine ships present it was clear that without air-cover maritime force could no longer win battles.

The disaster in Norway resulted in swift recriminations back home. Chamberlain's already shaky tenure was shaken still further. In the House of Commons the ensuing debate was conducted in an electric atmosphere, but the Prime Minister's defence lacked conviction. Reminding the house that the failure in Norway was "not comparable to the withdrawal at Gallipoli", he skilfully took a swipe at Churchill, the man responsible for both adventures; but Churchill, his moment yet to come, would not be drawn. It was Leo Amery, ex-minister and respected arch-imperialist who, shifting attention back to the overall handling of the war, enshrined the occasion and sealed Chamberlain's fate. After a lengthy critique of Britain's war effort he turned to Neville Chamberlain and quoted Cromwell's famous words: "You have sat too long here for any good you have been doing. Depart, I say, and let us have done with you. In the name of God, go!"

The following days witnessed desperate activity as Chamberlain sought the support of political friend and foe alike, but his efforts were to no avail. At last, realising he had lost the battle, he chose a successor. Of the two contenders, Lord Halifax and Churchill, the former seemed most suitable, but Halifax, a peer of the realm, felt there would be a constitutional conflict should he take a seat in both houses. To the surprise of both king and country Churchill, the adventurer, emerged as Prime Minister. His moment had arrived. Writing later he summed up his feelings on that momentous day, May 10, 1940: "I felt as if I were walking with destiny, and that all my past life had been but a preparation for this hour and for this trial."

At 5.45 am precisely on the morning of that same day Adolf Hitler had continued his own walk with destiny and brought the phoney war to an abrupt end. Along Germany's frontier with the Low Countries the drone of aero-engines could be heard, piercing the still air of dawn. Junkers Ju-52 transport planes – the Luftwaffe's much loved "Auntie Ju" – headed for targets on the broad Meuse River and among the fortifications of the Belgian border they prepared to dispatch their paratroop cargo. As sunlight flickered down through the leafy canopy of the impenetrable Ardennes, blue-black smoke from exhausts spiralled up through the tree-tops: the Panzer divisions were on the move. "Fall Gelb" (Plan Yellow), the German offensive against the Allies, had begun.

Chapter Two

"We seem to bring down aeroplanes
at the rate of a hundred a day.
That's very good . . . if it's true."

*Woman to Mass-Observation Unit, commenting on the BEF's
performance during the Battle of France, May 1940*

BRITAIN AT BAY

The German top brass survey their next target – one which must have appeared temptingly close after their easy successes in Poland, the Low Countries and France. But the British, protected by the grey waters of the Channel and the North Sea, were always likely to prove a different kind of enemy . . .

The Battle of France should have been an evenly matched contest: 136 German divisions and 149 Allied divisions faced each other across the wilderness of no-man's-land. Though the Wehrmächt fielded nearly 2,500,000 combat troops the Allies had over 2,000,000 men supported by 3,600 tanks, many of them superior in design to German models. In the air the Luftwaffe was much stronger than the Allied forces – it had 3,000 serviceable aircraft as opposed to an Allied total of 2,000—but although many French machines were obsolete it was recognised that Allied air power could be reinforced by squadrons in Britain should the need arise.

The imbalance that weighed the odds in favour of Germany was the deficiency in Allied leadership and planning. General Gamelin, the Allied Supreme Commander, was more used to fighting in the manner of 1914 than 1940; his abilities, notable though they once were, did not extend to an understanding of the strategems of blitzkrieg.

Thus led, the Allied armies were wrong-footed from the start. Leaving his flank dangerously exposed, Gamelin rushed to counter the German offensive that was punching through the Low Countries. Distracted by such astounding exploits as the German capture of Eban Emael, then the most powerful fortress in the world, Gamelin ordered the mobile forces of the French First Army, with the BEF in tow, to cross the Belgian frontier in a repeat performance of August 1914.

The real threat was elsewhere. Confounding the experts, Hitler's tank commanders had found that the Ardennes was not only penetrable but also defended by edgy, second-rate troops. Sweeping through the thinning

A NATION ALONE

ABOVE & RIGHT The awesome power of the Luftwaffe was conveyed all too convincingly by the blitz on Rotterdam on May 10, 1940. These unpublished snapshots clearly demonstrate the effectiveness of incendiaries on concentrated built-up areas, and the bombing of the Dutch port seemed to bear out the widely held theory that there was little defence available against a large concerted air-raid.

woods and onwards to the River Meuse, the Panzers of General Heinz Guderians's XIXth Armoured Corps bypassed the silent and immobile defences of the Maginot Line. Its designers had invested the wonder of the age with air-conditioning, electric lifts, railways and even solariums – but they had not thought it necessary to allow its turret-mounted guns to fire to the rear. Napoleon had said, "The side that stays within its fortifications is beaten." Erwin Rommel, then the young commander of the crack 7th Panzer Division, would have agreed.

Too late, Gamelin realised that the main thrust of the German offensive was aimed further south towards the mighty fortress at Sedan, fulcrum of the Allied line. On May 14 Sedan, isolated and overwhelmed, surrendered to the Wehrmacht (Holland capitulated the same day). Thirteen days later Boulogne was captured and the Allied garrison at Calais surrounded. Germany's use of mobile ground forces, supported by the aerial artillery of the Luftwaffe, had cut a swathe through France and isolated 60 Allied divisions still bogged down in Flanders. On May 19 Gamelin was replaced by the older but more popular General Weygand.

By May 25 the Belgian Army had surrendered. Further fighting in Flanders was pointless. The previous day Hitler had ordered his Panzer commanders to halt, fearful that their already over-extended supply lines might be broken. As the Germans rearmed and refuelled a precious breathing space was created that gave the Allied troops trapped in the north time to prepare a defensive perimeter centred around Dunkirk. On the evening of May 26, from his headquarters in Dover Castle, Admiral Ramsey (Vice-Admiral, Dover) initiated "Operation Dynamo" – the plan for the evacuation of Allied troops via Dunkirk.

Meanwhile further south the French (now under Weygand, who had replaced Gamelin on May 19) fought on with renewed vigour. Regrouping 40 battered divisions north-east of Paris, Weygand prepared a last stand along the Somme and Aisne rivers. But it was already too late. On June 5 the second phase of the German offensive commenced and forced the French to fall back to the Seine. On the 9th the Panzers broke through and the rout of the French armies began. Paris, declared an open city on June 13, fell the following day.

Italy had entered the war on the side of Germany on June 10. Attempting to snatch some glory in France as she writhed in her death throes, Mussolini ordered his army to cross the Alpine frontier. An advantage of six to one did not save the Italian troops from a severe drubbing at the hands of France's élite Alpine division, but sadly such victories were droplets in a sea of misery. By mid-June it was clear that France's fate had been sealed.

There had been hectic activity in the air as well as on the ground. Unfortunately air operations were undertaken amid the same atmosphere of confusion that had prevented the armies from achieving any notable success.

When Germany invaded France, the RAF had six fighter squadrons in that country. Four of these were equipped with Hawker Hurricanes, the two remaining squadrons (part of the BEF Air Component) with obsolete Gloster Gladiators. After some hectic

BRITAIN AT BAY

fighting on May 15, the Gladiator squadrons 607 and 615 were partly re-equipped with Hurricanes and ordered to cover the retreat to Dunkirk, but the biplanes never made it back to Britain, being set alight by their ground-crews to prevent them falling into the hands of the rapidly advancing German forces. This set the pattern for events that followed: unless aircraft could remain serviceable they were destroyed by their reluctant fitters and riggers – or, with increasing frequency, by free-roaming Messerschmitt fighters.

Shortly after Germany began her offensive in the west the Hurricane squadrons were increased to a total of eight: Nos 1, 73 and 501 were with the Advanced Air Striking Force, Nos 3, 79, 85, 87 and 501 with the Air Component. On May 13 a further 32 precious Hurricanes were sent to France in response to pleas from the French Premier, Reynaud. Churchill wanted to send more but Dowding, Commander-in-Chief of Fighter Command, was unrelenting in his refusal to commit any more to the catastrophe across the Channel.

On May 16, Dowding sat down and drafted a letter to the Under-Secretary of State for Air – a communication which has since become one of the most famous documents relating to the conduct of the air war during 1940. In it he pointed out that his fighter strength in Britain stood at a mere 36 squadrons, and he reminded the Air Council that they had set a minimum requirement for the defence of Britain at 52. This minimum had been calculated on the basis of offensive operations from Luftwaffe squadrons located in Germany. Now, with the possibility of attack from France, Britain's defences were in danger of being outflanked and the reduction in Fighter Command squadrons became even more worrying. The line had to be drawn somewhere; if it were not, there would be insufficient fighters left to protect the nation.

On May 21 the Hurricanes of the Air Component, under the command of Air Vice-Marshal Blount, were recalled to Britain. In future they would fly their remaining sorties in support of the BEF from airfields in the south of England.

The Hurricanes of the Advanced Air Striking Force meanwhile fought a valiant rearguard action in France. By June 15, temporarily reinforced by 17 and 242 squadrons, the five existing fighter squadrons in France were assigned to the protection of the remaining evacuation ports. Nos 1, 73 and 242 squadrons patrolled Nantes, Brest and St Nazaire, while Nos 17 and 50 provided air cover above St Malo and Cherbourg. By the 18th all Fighter Squadrons were ordered back

Detached from the sophisticated early warning systems available to fighter squadrons in Britain, the Air Component of the BEF in France operated in a rudimentary style not that different from the RFC over 20 years before. Navigation was basic in the extreme, and without the benefit of electronic aids aircrews had to rely on cumbersome manual calculators like those shown on the left in the picture. On the seat to the right is a well-worn all-in-one Sidcot suit which was worn over aircrew uniforms and was fitted with capacious pockets for storing maps and emergency rations. The flying helmet is a 1940 pattern "B" type fitted with earphones and to which a combined microphone and oxygen-mask was attached. The flying goggles (Mk IVs) are fitted with a flip-up sun-visor to aid the pilot when searching for the proverbial "Hun in the sun".

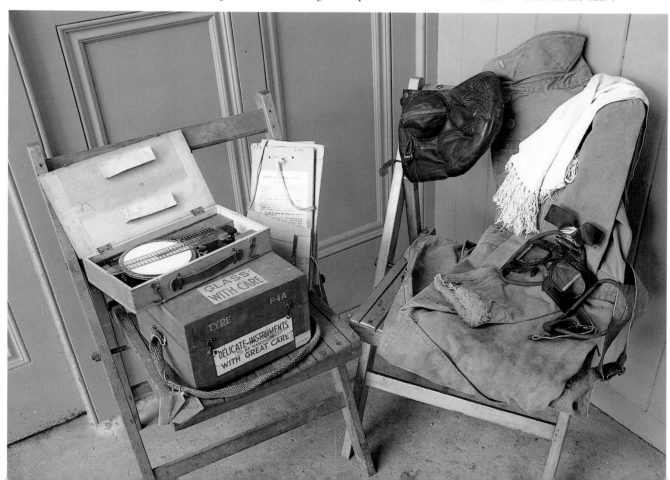

The Defence Committee of the War Cabinet, pictured in 1941. Back row, left to right: Air Chief Marshal Sir Charles Portal, Chief of the Air Staff; Admiral of the Fleet Sir Dudley Pound, First Sea Lord and Chief of the Naval Staff; Sir Archibald Sinclair, Secretary of State for Air; David Margesson, Secretary of State for War; General Sir John Dill, Chief of the Imperial General Staff; Major-General Sir Hastings Ismay, Chief of Staff to the Ministry of Defence and Deputy Secretary (Military) to the War Cabinet; Colonel Leslie Hollis, Senior Assistant (Military) to the War Cabinet and Secretary to the Chiefs of Staff Committee.
(continued on next page)

to Britain. As German forces played leap-frog over the airfields and supply depots the RAF's retreat from France was anything but orderly. Lack of fuel and spare parts meant that many aircraft, so sorely needed back in Britain, were left behind. If there was time they were destroyed – if not, the job was left to the Luftwaffe. The adventures of two Hurricane pilots illustrate the chaos that reigned during the RAF's last days in France . . .

Pilot Officer Pat Hancock was a trained Spitfire pilot. In keeping with the muddled bureaucracy prevalent at the time he was posted to No. 1 Squadron in France, then equipped exclusively with Hurricanes. Arriving at the squadron HQ north of Arras on May 12, he found himself particularly unwelcome; fresh pilots without aircraft to fly were just simply a nuisance, adding to a squadron commander's burdens.

Within three days of his arrival and still without an aircraft, Pilot Officer Hancock was sent on temporary secondment to No. 501 Squadron – and en route he realised the scale of the disaster which engulfed France. Confusion and panic reigned, and on one occasion he found himself defending a shot-down German rear-gunner from an inevitable lynching at the hands of French peasants. On arrival at No. 501 he was billeted in the basement of a local pub, but at dawn he discovered that in response to intelligence reports of an imminent parachute attack the squadron had fled, leaving him once again stranded and without a mount. Joining the retreat, this time in the back of a Crossley lorry, he was finally repatriated with No. 1 Squadron and, delight of delights, given a plane to fly.

After only one and a half hours' local flying in the Hurricane to familiarise himself with its handling characteristics, Pilot Officer Hancock was ordered to join the rest of the squadron on patrol. And his first contact with the enemy was brief and spectacular. Ordered to cover the retreat of the BEF south of Dunkirk, the squadron of 12 Hurricanes intercepted a formation of Heinkels intent on

sealing the fate of the troops. A dozen Hurricanes against around 150 Heinkels was not exactly fair odds, especially as the RAF at this time refused to drop its traditional formation attacks, presenting an easy target for keen German air-gunners.

Selecting a Heinkel 111 as a target Hancock was disappointed to discover that even the expenditure of a large amount of well-aimed Browning ammunition did not guarantee a "kill". On the contrary the Heinkel's rear-gunner benefitted most from the encounter, managing to pepper Hancock's new Hurricane with 7.9 mm machine-gun bullets.

Without the use of elevators, unable to make sense of the damaged air-speed indicator and with the throttle jammed in emergency boost, the unfortunate Pilot Officer attempted a landing. "I had the choice, after going through several phases of panic, of either smashing into a hangar or hitting a Blenheim. After three passes of the airfield, going much too fast, I hit the Blenheim, cutting it in half. I discovered later that–fortunately–it was unoccupied. I tore it apart and burst my petrol tank in the process. Fuel was everywhere, but there was no fire–otherwise I wouldn't have survived."

The reception he received from his Flight Commander, then hurrying to the scene in a lorry, is best left to the imagination. The lucky German air-gunner had unwittingly destroyed two RAF machines with a single burst–a record which may stand to this day!

Pat Hancock retired from the RAF as a Wing Commander having seen service all over the world. His experience of the Battle of France, though brief, has remained sharp. His overriding recollection is of the turmoil caused by the threat of air-power rather than the effect of it. In a shocking period, one of the major shocks was to see the devastating effect that the air war was having on the French population, without any bombs going off. The mere sight of a parachute, even though it was attached to a solitary airman who had baled out was enough for villagers to flee in anticipation of an imminent invasion by "les parachutists".

Another example was that of Desmond Fopp. As a boy in Australia, he had been captivated by the exploits of aviation's pioneering spirits, especially those who flew single-handed from Britain to the Antipodes. When his family moved to England he was determined that he would learn to fly, and

joining the RAF Volunteer Reserve gave him his opportunity. Volunteering in the wake of the Munich Crisis in November 1938, he had amassed over 200 hours' flying time by the outbreak of war. Classic aircraft like Hawker's famous interwar biplanes the Hart, Hind and Audax and the De Havilland Tiger-Moth had been his mounts as a student. His flying training was completed under full-time service conditions at the controls of the Harvard, an American state-of-the-art monoplane, while stationed at the Flying Training School at RAF Brize Norton.

After six or seven hours of conversion training, without the aid of pilot's notes, he qualified as a Hurricane pilot. The fighter was "an unruly beast compared to the Harvard, and five times more powerful!" Sergeant Fopp, fighter-pilot, was ready for war.

He joined No. 17 Squadron, then exchanging their outdated Gauntlet biplanes for Hurricanes and, without any combat training, took off with his new colleagues from Kenley and headed for Le Mans in north-west France. With no clear instructions the squadron assumed standing patrol duty. The activities of a vigorous French "Fifth Column" prevented any opportunity of intercepting the enemy, since each time a flight of Hurricanes took off its course would be relayed to the Germans by observant collaborators. On the station, life was chaotic and many of the senior officers were rarely to be seen, preferring instead to sample the pleasures of local hostelries.

There were some highlights amid the general depression of inactivity. Once the

For Britain the Battle of France was pervaded by muddle and continuous relocation, with RAF units moved progressively nearer the coast as the German advance bit deeper into French territory. These pilots of No. 17 Squadron are seen trekking out of Le Mans in June 1940.

(continued from previous page)
Front row: Lord Beaverbrook, Minister of Aircraft Production; Clement Attlee, Lord Privy Seal [Deputy Prime Minister]; Winston Churchill, Prime Minister and Minister of Defence; Anthony Eden, Foreign Secretary; A. V. Alexander, First Lord of the Admiralty.

A NATION ALONE

As chaos reigned in France it was important that RAF aircrews did not fall victim to the guns of the BEF as well as those of the Luftwaffe. This Air Diagram, distributed in May 1940, warns of the dangers of poor air-to-ground co-operation.

DO YOU KNOW THE RECOGNITION SIGNAL?

DO NOT TRUST TO MEMORY ALONE. ALWAYS CARRY WITH YOU A NOTE OF THE RECOGNITION SIGNALS FOR THE DAY IN A FORM, OF COURSE, THAT DISCLOSES NOTHING TO THE ENEMY.

Squadron, their Hurricanes weighed down by "essential provisions", made their way from Le Mans to Dinard. There the disgruntled RAF pilots found the local Armée De L'Air units had decided that further resistance was useless, leaving the business of air cover to their British colleagues.

Suddenly, it was time to move again. Without warning, save the sight of the CO climbing into his aeroplane, the squadron hurriedly prepared to evacuate its brief home at Dinard. Those with aircraft escaped, those without made their own way home. Sergeant Fopp had a tense moment when a young Pilot Officer tried to relieve him of the Hurricane he had been flying in France. Not in the mood for pleasantries, particularly since the officer in question had been conspicuous by his absence on recent patrols, Fopp's "reasoned argument" won the day. The squadron, now a

A souvenir postcard sent home by Private H. A. Ward, 5th Battalion, the Buffs (BEF). He escaped from France via St Nazaire aboard the *Lancastrian*, but the steamer was attacked by Stukas and over a thousand troops perished. Ward, having rescued several comrades, was a survivor; but a few days later, ordered to collect firewood from a West Country beach, he was killed by a recently laid mine intended to blow up invading Germans.

BEF had started to withdraw to the coast rich pickings could be found among the increasingly large amount of stores abandoned en route. At Le Mans the Army had "dumped" an enormous stockpile of excess stores, and to Sergeant Fopp's delight it included 200 brand-new motorbikes. No. 17 squadron holds the unique if dubious honour of being the only RAF formation to ride the famous Le Mans racing circuit, and Fopp's own charger was a 500 cc Norton. The racetrack revealed further rich pickings: the NAAFI had based itself in one of the stands and to the relief of the inquisitive pilots this too was found to be vacant yet well-stocked.

"Liberating" all the drink and cigarettes they could carry and stuffing the surplus into every empty space in their aircraft No. 17

pattern of dots above the distant horizon, was eventually joined, and to his surprise Sergeant Fopp discovered that landfall was to be the island of Jersey.

It was June 17, and though Jersey was not officially demilitarised until the 28th it was considered unwise for the squadron to stay in order to prevent a possible German attack on the unarmed island. Indeed on the 11th 18 Whitley bombers had approached Jersey airport to refuel en route to a raid on newly belligerent Italy. The CO of the bomber force heatedly ordered the airport controller Charles Roche to turn on the airport lights. Professing that black-out regulations were in force, the hapless Mr Roche eventually threw the switch. Minutes later the Lieutenant-Governor of Jersey was on the phone ordering the lights to be extinguished as they were "inviting the whole island to be bombed by the Germans". From Jersey, No. 17 squadron fled to neighbouring Guernsey, where the tiny airport's narrow runway threshold resulted in damage to the tail-wheel of Sergeant Fopp's Hurricane as it clipped a hedge along the airfield perimeter.

On June 19 No. 17 Squadron, exhausted and with only two serviceable aircraft, landed at Tangmere in Sussex. Today a retired squadron-leader with 37 years' RAF service behind him, Desmond Fopp sums up the Royal Air Force activities in France as "almost useless".

For many pilots the RAF's presence in France had tragic consequences. As usual the blow fell heaviest on the unfortunate pilots of the Fairey Battle squadrons, whom it will be remembered had barely survived their baptism of fire at the beginning of the French campaign.

This reconstruction of a typical RAF office around 1940 includes many intriguing "period pieces". From left to right: brass mess drinks tray, gun-metal paperweight, replica of a Schneider Trophy-winning Supermarine S6, aircraft recognition chart and booklets, pages showing foreign air force insignia from the 1937 edition of *The RAF Pocket Book*, Rotol emergency repairs booklet, aircraft instrument information books and officer's forage cap.

A NATION ALONE

Once the German offensive had begun the scale of the assault was soon recognised. An enormous column of tightly packed Panzers, armoured cars and transport lorries, stretching for over a hundred miles, began to snake its way to the eastern banks of the River Meuse. The French Command prevaricated and, amazingly, ordered the Allied air forces on further reconnaissance missions to see if the "prize target" was a feint. Eventually, after increasing pressure from the Air Defence Commander-in-Chief, British Air Forces in France, Air-Marshal Barrett, the squadrons of the AASF were released with orders to attack the German assault troops.

Some 32 Fairey Battles were scrambled in search of rich pickings. However, within minutes 13 aircraft had been shot down and all the remaining aircraft had been damaged. On the afternoon of May 10 a further ten Battles fell to the guns of Luftwaffe fighter-planes. Powered by the same Merlin II "V"-type engine as the Hurricane but carrying a crew of three and up to 1,000 lbs of bombs, the Battle was no match for the nimble German fighters. The aircraft was to the RAF what the Stuka would become to the Luftwaffe – a liability if unprotected by a close fighter escort.

The next day a further eight Battles were sent against targets along the Meuse bridgehead, but they never even reached their objectives. Cut down en route, only one aircraft returned to its airfield. On the same day a complete squadron of Blenheim bombers (No. 114) was destroyed before it had time to take off from its airfield; engines running, the aircraft were decimated by a low-flying squadron of Dornier 17 bombers which suddenly appeared out of the eastern horizon. On May 12 nine Blenheims of No. 139 Squadron were "bounced" by 50 or so German fighters, and two badly shaken aircrews returned.

With only a handful of Fairey Battles left Barrett, under increasing pressure from a hysterical French Command, was ordered to press forward further attacks against the German river crossings, and the bridges at Maastricht were selected. Knowing that he was sending his remaining crews to almost certain death Barrett asked only for volunteers. No-one declined.

In one of the most moving and tragic operations ever undertaken by the RAF the remaining aircraft of the AASF set out for virtual suicide. Despite the gallantry of men like Flying Officer Garland and his observer Sergeant Gray – with their aircraft severely damaged they dived headlong into the bridge at Veldwezelt and earnt the RAF its first Victoria Crosses of the war – the raid was futile; without destroying a single bridge the Battles were hacked from the sky. The incredulous German flak gunners, in position for two days, could not believe their luck. With losses of over 60% the RAF suffered its worst defeat of the whole war, and within hours the AASF ceased to exist. The Fairey Battle was consigned to the pages of aviation history and was never used in anger again.

The disaster in France was total and irrevocable. As the advancing German troops scrambled down the sand-dunes along the coast at Dunkirk the scale of their victory was revealed. Scattered along the beaches was the debris of a routed army. In their struggle to get home the British troops had left a staggering amount of vital equipment to the mercy of the tide; amid the bomb craters and barbed wire entanglements lay all the stores and heavy weapons of the BEF. An impressive total of 338,226 troops (225,000 of them British) had been plucked from the beaches by the "little ships" and relays of Royal Navy destroyers and corvettes – but they had left everything, save their rifles, to the Germans. For weeks to come the British Army, though essentially intact and safely back in Britain, had barely enough weapons left to equip each soldier.

On June 17, in response to a request by the Prime Minister, the Chiefs of Staff Committee produced a report outlining Britain's chances of surviving a German invasion. The 13th paragraph summed up the Committee's feelings: "Our conclusion is that, prima facie, Germany has most of the cards; but the real test is whether the morale of our fighting personnel and civil population will counterbalance the numerical and material advantages which Germany enjoys. We believe it will." Sir Hastings Ismay, Churchill's representative on the Chief of Staff Committee, recalled that "the report contented Churchill, and the conclusion undoubtedly represented the views of the nation as a whole."

The day after, largely on the basis of such optimistic evaluation, Churchill made one of his most famous speeches: "What General Weygand called the Battle of France is over. I expect that the Battle of Britain is about to begin . . . Let us therefore brace ourselves to

BRITAIN AT BAY

Reichsmarschall Goering had good reason to be satisfied with the performance of his mighty Luftwaffe: in Poland, France and the Low Countries it had demonstrated what many Germans believed to be an invincible power. Tours of wrecked and mangled enemy aircraft had by 1940 become a commonplace military relations exercise for the "Iron Man".

our duties, and so bear ourselves that, if the British Empire and its Commonwealth last for a thousand years, men will say, 'This was their finest hour'."

The "finest hour" was yet to begin. In the meantime Britain, isolated and alone, prepared to throw all its resources into the coming fight. On May 14 the newly-appointed Secretary of State for War, Anthony Eden,

made an appeal to the nation. Tuning in to the 9 o'clock news on the BBC Home Service the people of Britain heard the Secretary of State warn of the dangers of the new warfare being encountered on the continent and in particular the threat from parachute troops which the Germans had dropped far behind the front lines. "In order to leave nothing to chance, and to supplement from sources as yet

A NATION ALONE

RIGHT Tank-traps called "dragon's teeth", like these at Horsham in Sussex, were scattered across open parkland, on either side of major roads and along the various redoubts or "halt-lines" that traversed southern England.

FAR RIGHT This curious white tower is a 1940 addition to Dartmouth's medieval castle. Designed to appear as part of the old fortress, it was built to house a 4.7-inch quick-firing gun that covered the entrance to the harbour.

RIGHT Pill-boxes were situated at any location considered vulnerable to either a parachute or gliding landing or along routes likely to be taken by German infantry divisions. This is one of a pair that provided enfilading fire-cover across a large arable field near Epsom in Surrey.

ABOVE In the summer of 1940 all that stood between Britain and the all-conquering Wehrmacht was a narrow strip of sea, and the breathing space between the fall of France and the start of hostilities against mainland Britain enabled the completion of hastily improvised defence works along the south coast. This pill-box covered the sea approach and expanse of beach at Slapton Sands in Devon.

untapped the means of defence already arranged, we are going to ask you to help us in a manner which I know will be welcome to thousands of you." The result of Eden's broadcast was the birth of one of the largest unpaid armies the world has ever seen—The Home Guard. The rush to the recruiting offices was immediate and overwhelming. Eden had expected the scheme to be well received but never in his wildest dreams had he assumed that within 24 hours the Local Defence Volunteers (as it was then called) would number over 250,000 men.

At first it was impossible to arm the LDV with anything like effective weapons, for what remained in the nation's armoury was needed by the regular troops, so the enthusiastic but untried platoons of militia found themselves equipped with all manner of unlikely instruments of war. Some, it is true, were armed with pitchforks and broomsticks, though the true symbol of the LDV – the "pike" – was not issued until later. A length of drainpipe capped by a lethal 17-inch bayonet, the weapon was immediately unpopular and was rarely seen on parade.

Most recruits were armed with hastily improvised hand weapons, usually entrenching tool handles sporting adapted infantry bayonets. Others came readily equipped with personal sporting weapons and even flintlocks of unknown design or vintage. Later a large consignment of 1917 pattern American "Springfield" rifles arrived but these were never really popular and their .300 calibre made them incompatible with the much-admired British service rifle, the .303 Lee Enfield Mk 4.

Churchill took a keen interest in the activities of the LDV. He considered the prefix "Local" uninspiring and urged Eden to choose a more "compulsive" name, preferring the suggestion of "Home Guard". Not content to let his involvement rest there and concerned that anti-tank defences were still inadequate, he advanced further ideas. With contacts made while dealing with the German mine threat when he was at the Admiralty, Churchill proposed the development of a "sticky bomb" which could be thrown at armour. This and other volatile weapons were soon in production and a range of projectors, to supplement basic manpower, were quickly manufactured.

Saloon cars could be transformed into armoured vehicles with the addition of a few strategically placed sheets of boilerplate and chicken wire to repel German stick grenades. The lethal Fougasse appeared, buried under sandbags at the roadside. This was an oil drum which when ignited by pulling a string spewed out a flaming mixture of oil and petrol – thus, it was hoped, ambushing any unsuspecting enemy patrol.

As invasion fever gripped the country the LDV dutifully manned roadblocks, river crossings and country footpaths. Obstacles boasting descriptive names like "Dragon's Teeth" and "Hairpins" were established in an effort to deny the German armour access to main roads. In the fields steel girders and wooden poles were erected to reduce the space available for glider landings.

Inevitably there were some fatal accidents. With so many men armed with unfamiliar and deadly weapons perhaps more accidents than those that occurred could have been expected. On the night of June 2, for example, four people were shot dead in separate incidents for failing to notice or stop at LDV roadblocks. Fortunately the early days of the Home Guard were characterised by comic rather than tragic events, as the records of the Northamptonshire Home Guard testify.

Having been tipped off that a parachutist had been seen descending on local fenland, "A" Company of the Peterborough District LDV turned out rapidly "in civilian clothes with arms and ammunition, eager to defend the city at all costs". Rifles loaded, the men were deployed to ambush the invader. Suddenly a fast-moving car appeared and, bracing themselves, the nervous reception committee advanced towards it, bayonets fixed. With a cry of "Blimey, it's the old man!" the volunteers soon discovered that its occupant – complete with straw hat, breeches, leggings and revolver – was their own commanding officer. Nevertheless, an interception had been made and in the absence of a steel-helmeted and jackbooted parachutist the company decided to retire to the local pub.

The comedy did not end there, however. In the words of the official history: "Having got their rifles loaded, only a very few volunteers knew how to eject the rounds without firing, and to save the face of the Battalion the officer in charge took the men into a side street and personally unloaded all the rifles in the dark and in the rain."

All over the country similar events were happening, but despite their shortcomings the willing volunteers of the LDV helped to shore up the defences of the country during its darkest hour. As the rumours of German parachutists dressed as nuns or disguised as Allied soldiers (there were thousands of French and Polish troops now stationed in Britain) swept the country an altogether more sinister reception was being planned in total secrecy – and often under the very noses of local militiamen.

Once it became clear that France would be occupied by enemy forces the planners in Britain were forced to consider the possibility of a continued German advance across the English Channel. It was obvious that one of the key reasons that defence in France had crumbled was the ease with which the Germans were able to race on to each objective. There was perhaps as much active collaboration behind the German front as resistance and the German infantry, unimpressed by ambush or sabotage, were able to press on with confidence.

To prevent the same calamity from overcoming British resistance it was decided to form "stay behind units" which could attack the invasion force from the rear should they form a bridgehead. The covert operations of these very special forces are one of the most intriguing aspects of the home front.

ABOVE The Home Secretary's broadcast to the nation on May 14 called for men between the ages of 16 and 65 to come forward for duty in a new national militia – the Local Defence Volunteers. The keenness with which men were prepared to don khaki drill and put their lives on the line astounded everyone and recruiting posts, like this one at Wimbledon, were inundated with eager volunteers.

ABOVE RIGHT LDV recruits took on their new responsibilities with gusto and one battalion known as "Tickler's Army" designed its own armoured car.

OPPOSITE PAGE Despite their flimsy appearance Anderson shelters were a practical solution to the problem of providing refuge for thousands in anticipated target areas. After receiving a self-assembly kit of parts families set to work bolting the corrugated iron structures together and buried them in back gardens.

Without attracting any attention the various military intelligence organisations set about creating a network of Auxiliary Units, as they were called, designed to create as much havoc as possible behind the enemy lines.

In great secrecy and with little fuss "recruiters" using the Home Guard as a cover approached potential candidates considered best equipped for the risky and thankless task ahead. Those best suited for the job included gamekeepers, miners, woodsmen, fishermen and especially poachers. Once enrolled the "auxiliaries" were schooled in the art of sabotage and survival. A handbook was produced, labelled *The Countryman's Diary 1939*, which contained a catalogue of ideas for killing, maiming, blowing up or incapacitating whatever or whoever came the way of its well-versed owner.

If invasion took place the Auxiliary Units, scattered in forests and woodlands all over Britain, would retire to prepared positions in hides, underground bolt-holes or remote cave systems. With only ten days' supply of food and water issued they were expected to live off the land until the moment when, in response to enemy presence, they leapt into action and ambushed troop concentrations or penetrated enemy headquarters. Many hideouts were constructed in the grounds of some of Britain's grander homes, as experience in

France had shown that German generals selected lavish accommodation for their command centres. In a variety of ingenious ways an underground network was extended until some 20 Auxiliary Unit centres were established, each commanding an unspecified number of irregulars. Tunnel entrances were built under cover of faked bombing raids, and to avoid suspicion the excess soil was scattered among the freshly made bomb craters.

If Germany had invaded, there is no little doubt that once captured the brave Auxiliaries would have faced the firing squad, for posters already prepared by German printers spelt out the penalty British saboteurs would receive. Three special Home Guard battalions were created to provide a cover for the Auxiliary Unit's activities; the 203rd in the South of England, 202nd in the north and 201st in Scotland. However the Auxiliaries' names were never officially recorded and it is likely that if questioned the official Home Guard would have denied their existence. To this day most of what occurred concerning the development and implementation of the Auxiliary Units is still classified. The men who spent the invasion summer in damp underground hideouts were probably mostly middle-aged in 1940 and therefore the secret of their activities is unlikely to ever be fully revealed or understood.

BRITAIN AT BAY

The British Army was home from France, but though it had the will it lacked the resources to offer serious resistance to Germany. Hitler, by contrast, had 200 battle-hardened divisions to employ. Sir John Dill, General Ironside's replacement as Chief of the Imperial General Staff (CIGS), could count but a tenth of this number and his best divisions had left their equipment in France. Britain had only 500 field-guns and almost no anti-tank weapons with which to oppose a German assault. With over 800 miles of assailable coastline to defend – stretches of which could boast only one machine-gun to every mile of beach – desperate measures were used to shore up the gaping breaches along the sea perimeter.

Trees were felled, beach-huts filled with pebbles to provide rudimentary anti-tank obstacles, and the sea ignited to test the principle of a "flame barrage". Some of the most bloodthirsty and dramatic experiments were conducted without much secrecy and often for the benefit of newsreels – the theory being that if German troops got wind of what was in store for them should they land, they might have second thoughts about trying!

General Alan Brooke had been newly appointed as the Commander-in-Chief of Britain's Home Forces within the area designated "Southern Command", and it was this command that would bear the brunt of a German invasion. By mid-July he had completed the voluntary evacuation of many of the inhabitants within a narrow coastal strip extending from Sheringham in Norfolk to Portland in Dorset. Unimpeded by onlookers and local residents, he was able to continue to fortify the invasion coast. Improvisation was

ABOVE In an effort to confuse the Wehrmacht should it manage to secure a bridgehead on British soil, all directional and information signs were removed and locations became anonymous.

With most of its heavy equipment lost in France, the British Army had to rely on its reserves of small-calibre weapons. The No. 4 Mk 1 Lee Enfield rifle was a popular and very accurate weapon, but it was no match for modern armour. The Bren machine-gun [on the work-bench] provided more powerful fire-support; its high rate of fire (500 rounds per minute) and great accuracy over long range (600 yards and more) made it the ideal choice for installation in pill-boxes, whence saturation fire could be delivered to prepared killing grounds.

essential as the available resources were pitiful. St Margaret's Bay at Dover – a high risk area – was protected initially by only three anti-tank guns, each with six rounds. Aware of such deficiencies, Churchill had expressly forbidden any practice firing!

Of all the defences which sprang up along the coast at this time, the most memorable and representative of the period was the "pill-box". First encountered by the British Army in 1917, the concrete pill-box was a German idea, and seeing the excellent protection it provided from direct hits from even the largest field pieces the British decided to imitate the new structures. Under the command of Major General Taylor of the Directorate of Fortifications and Works a variety of easily constructed pill-boxes were designed. To

house rifle-armed infantry small hexagonal versions were built with walls 15 inches thick. The Bren gun, able to command a greater field of fire and thus a more valuable target, was protected by a heavier pill-box with walls 42 inches thick.

The largest pill-boxes were designed to mount either two-pounder or six-pounder anti-tank guns, and as these would be prime targets for the dreaded German 88 mm gun every effort was made to keep their frontal area to a minimum and extend the depth of concrete and brick to protect the crew inside. If the extended crust of the invasion beaches was penetrated the squads of regulars, reservists and volunteers who manned the isolated pill-boxes would be expected to rake the occupied beaches with fire until either lack of ammunition or a German contact charge removed them from the inventory of war.

Beyond the coastal defences the south of England was traversed by a series of "stop lines" – barriers along which, it was hoped, the enemy advance could be checked. Essentially these were coordinates on maps in the War Office for in reality most stop-lines were hastily improvised anti-tank ditches reinforced with the odd pill-box. Two more substantial barriers, the so-called "GHQ" lines, were constructed. One bisected England south of London along a line from the Thames Estuary to the Bristol Channel; the other ran north from the Thames Estuary as far as the Firth of Forth. It was here the bloodiest battles would be fought on British soil should the coastal defences be breached.

If a landing either from the sea or the air was imminent it would be signified by the use of a codeword: "Cromwell". The ringing of church bells in the invasion area was a signal to the local Home Guards to take up their positions. In theory the bells were to be rung only by order of a Home Guard who had himself seen at least 25 parachutists land, but in practice – as witnessed by the invasion scare of September 7 – Home Guard commanders all over the south of England unleashed them directly they got receipt of "Cromwell" and regardless of the intelligence situation.

Civilians had to be prepared for a possible invasion, too, and with this in mind the government distributed its famous invasion leaflet in mid-June. Entitled "If the Invader Comes", it was an earnest attempt to provide the population with a clearer idea of what to do should they be confronted by the spectacle of a platoon of German infantrymen advancing up the local high street.

The threat of invasion was very real and the government, unsure of exactly how the German offensive would first manifest itself, was leaving nothing to chance. Stories from France had confirmed ministerial doubts about the ability of civilians to withstand the pressures of modern warfare; morale had collapsed in France because the population had been confused and had no clear instructions from central government.

To prevent a collapse of public morale in Britain, with streams of refugees clogging the roads, contagious defeatism and the harmful activities of "Fifth Columnists", the War Cabinet decided to pre-empt public anxieties and try to put the emergency into perspective.

The first few sentences set the tone: "The Germans threaten to invade Great Britain. If they do so they will be driven out by our Navy, our Army and our Air Force. Yet the ordinary men and women of the civilian population will also have their part to play."

The leaflet contained six points, which it was hoped would cover all eventualities and provide a set of rules to follow if the reader found himself embroiled in the war zone. The central theme was the instruction to "Stay Put" – the authorities did not want a continental-style rout. It also included advice on who to trust: "If you keep your heads, you can also tell whether a military officer is really British or only pretending to be so." One wonders how many unfortunate encounters with Polish, Dutch and Belgian soldiers in British battledress resulted from this rather simplistic piece of advice.

On June 20 Mass-Observation presented a report to the MOI of its findings concerning the public reaction to the "Invasion Leaflet". As always, its discoveries were illuminating: after spending a disproportionate amount of space criticising the layout and paper used for the leaflet (apparently many households had disposed of their copy because it was taken to be a cheap circular), M-O observers gathered public reaction to its contents.

One "working class" woman commented thus: "Looks pretty black doesn't it, really? We've got that list of things to do if we're invaded. I don't know! You can't say we're not prepared. They keep telling us these things every day – if only people will listen." One housewife was rather more direct in her appraisal of the situation: "It all depends on common sense, really – and British people haven't got any."

Fortunately not everyone held such a low opinion of British characteristics and an elderly woman probably captured the spirit of the time best with the following statement: "I'm not worrying. I haven't even read it. I don't think they'll come because our boys are too good for them – and if they do come we'll get some sticks and beat them back."

The last sentence is not so ludicrous when one considers the fact that at the time more than one RAF airfield was defended by airmen armed with lengths of four-by-two surmounted by a tangled crown of barbed wire or iron spears fashioned from the bars protecting the windows of airfield buildings.

Mass-Observation's report was concluded

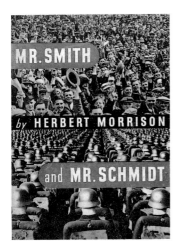

ABOVE In order to increase wartime production it was important that workers appreciated the value of their labour – and the need for long hours of overtime.

BELOW Every day householders received a deluge of different emergency instructions covering every possible wartime contingency.

RIGHT As Britain prepared to fight fascism from abroad she also had to contend with a noisy fascist minority at home. Oswald Mosley was in prison, but the British Union of Fascists mounted a vociferous if unpopular campaign for his release.

with a request for a more "lively, visual and perhaps concise" approach to future information. With "parachute fever" gripping Britain, the teams from Mass-Observation gained much information in the pubs, shops and bus-queues of the nation. The sample of their overheard conversations that follow are included to create a clearer impression of the Britain of 1940 – and the character of its phlegmatic and irrepressible people. Traffic warden, about 50, to bus-driver: "Let me know if you see any of them parachute fellows about, Harry. I don't want them disturbing my pullets now they've just come on to lay." Pub landlord to visitors: "Hello, you lot. Haven't seen you for ages. What have you done – dropped by parachute?" Middle-aged man in pub: "If one landed near me, I'd follow 'im and slit 'is throat."

During a survey in July 1940 Mass-Observation discovered that only 17% of the people questioned thought that Germany would effect a landing. However, 80% were still convinced there would be major air-raid damage. Many people thought, as did Churchill, that the Irish Republic might be invaded or prove sympathetic and helpful to the Nazi cause.

Day by day, as the nation enjoyed an unexpected respite from further encounters with Germany, the public mood grew more confident. Indeed the carrying of gas-masks

had declined to such an extent that should chemical weapons have been used the effects of a sudden terror raid would have been devastating. Churchill, too, was becoming increasingly confident that Britain could fend off an invasion attempt. In a letter to the Dominions' Prime Ministers on June 16 he wrote: "Of course their numbers are much greater than ours, but not so much greater as to deprive us of a good and reasonable prospect of wearing them out after some weeks or even months of air struggle." Survival nevertheless depended not only on the stamina of the weapon users but also the weapon makers. The enormous vigour displayed by a population thought by many international commentators to be facing imminent defeat is a component of victory every bit as significant in its way as the achievements of the fighter pilots of the RAF.

Under the direction of Churchill's coalition government – Beaverbrook, Morrison and Bevin – factories began to work 24 hours a day, seven days a week. Bank holidays were cancelled and normal working hours were increased to shifts lasting from 8 am to 7 pm. Vast amounts of overtime were worked and it was not uncommon for employees to fall asleep at their lathes or work-benches.

Since it was obvious that the Germans would need to gain air superiority in order to effect a landing, production resources and effort were concentrated on the manufacture of aircraft, and especially fighter-planes. The "Shadow Factory" scheme had been introduced in 1936 and motor-car manufacturers were encouraged to switch over their facilities to aircraft production. In 1938 "Scheme L" was initiated by the Air Ministry, providing for the production of 12,000 new aircraft within three years.

Of all the contingencies for war which were planned during the 1930s it was the expansion, coordination and dispersal of manufacturing which proved the most far-sighted. The Battle of Britain was, as we shall see, a numbers game. The Germans had never expected to be in a position to attack the British mainland so early and especially with the forces required to prepare the way for invasion. Thus their production plans did not forsee the need to step up the manufacture of aircraft outside the numbers required for continental activity. Indeed once France had been conquered Hitler was keen to see a partial demobilisation to prevent disquiet on his home front.

BRITAIN AT BAY

Hurricanes of No. 56 Squadron flying in rigid formation patrol in the skies above southern England. Such textbook procedures would be shattered when the pilots encountered the loose, hunting groups of Luftwaffe fighters.

Meanwhile, however, British fighter production figures steadily increased throughout the summer of 1940. In May the total stood at 325, in subsequent months the figures were 446, 496, 476, 467 and in October, when the immediate crisis had passed, 469. In June 1940, with available production facilities at full stretch, Germany could manage only 220 fighters per month. Throughout the summer her production was lagging far behind Britain's and was never even as much as half of the British totals.

The dispersal system encouraged a much broader manufacturing base than had previously been available. Soon furniture-makers, coach-builders and panel-beating firms were busily engaged in the manufacture of aircraft parts. Dispersal also ensured that no single factory – and, consequently, target – produced all the components for a particular machine. The wisdom of this policy was demonstrated when the birthplace of the Spitfire, Supermarine's Woolston factory at Southampton, was badly damaged during the Battle of Britain. Production of the immortal fighter, though impaired, continued apace at other locations.

One such location was the giant 1,414-acre Castle Bromwich plant at Birmingham. This had been set up by Lord Nuffield, better known as William Morris, doyen of the British car industry. In 1938 Nuffield had offered his services free of charge to the nation, and in particular to the Air Minister Kingsley Wood. Soon the mighty Nuffield organisation had rolled up its sleeves and was heavily involved in the accelerating rearmament programme.

Nuffield subsequently became Director-General of Maintenance and head of the somewhat clandestine Civilian Repair Organisation. Under his control the CRO charged Morris Motors with the recovery, repair and redistribution of damaged or unserviceable military aircraft. Battle-damaged or simply worn-out aircraft did not long lay idle on airfields and even during the heat of battle were withdrawn to CRO factories for repair to ensure they were back in action in as short a time as possible.

It was not unusual, for example, for a Hurricane which left Hawker's factory on a Saturday and was damaged on the following Tuesday to be back in action with its squadron before the weekend. Often recovery and repair was managed within a 24-hour period. From its headquarters at Merton College, Oxford the absentees from Cowley's production lines organised a veritable army of contractors who,

As the threat of invasion intensified during 1940 publishers had a field day turning out handbooks on self-defence, clandestine warfare and sabotage. The authorities, however, continued to urge caution, prevailing on people to stay at home should fighting break out.

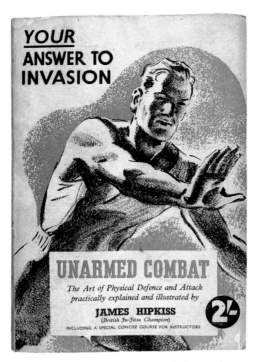

YOUR ANSWER TO INVASION

UNARMED COMBAT

The Art of Physical Defence and Attack practically explained and illustrated by

JAMES HIPKISS
(British Ju-Jitsu Champion)

INCLUDING A SPECIAL CONCISE COURSE FOR INSTRUCTORS

2/-

seven days a week, raced out to jobs on site or brought badly damaged machines back to the appropriate workshops.

By mid-July the CRO (now under the direct control of Beaverbrook at the Ministry of Aircraft Production) was repairing an average of 160 fighters a week and returning them good as new to the RAF, and by the end of 1940 a staggering total of 4,196 aeroplanes had passed through the hands of the ex-car builders. Aircraft which had crashed or were beyond repair were "cannibalised" and parts used for less badly damaged planes. Reparable Equipment Depots witnessed scenes of "mass grave-robbing" as CRO progress-chasers descended on them in search of spares.

Another valuable operation run under the auspices of the new Ministry of Aircraft Production was the Emergency Services Organisation, a first-aid facility for battle-damaged factories. It was said that ESO's main stock-in-trade was "telephones, tarpaulins and enthusiasm", but it is thanks to the voluntary work of its members that factories like Supermarine were able to regain some form of production within a short space of time. ESO could provide emergency repairs or back-up supplies if gas, electricity or water services were damaged and offered spare tools, labour, transport and even bomb disposal services to ensure Britain's manufacturing network was intact.

"The Aircraft Builders", the MAP account of its wartime activities, gives us some idea of the spirit of camaraderie that lasted during the Battle of Britain period. "Although the practice of mutual aid has rarely been the subject of an official report, it is well known that this feature is the backbone of the ESO. Craftsmen, tackle, transport, know-how and every class and type of equipment have been provided at short notice when the need has been urgent. Things are produced like magic from the air."

Everywhere the production of armaments took priority. Disused underground tunnels were converted into aircraft parts factories, and they even set up an aircraft construction group known as "London Aircraft Production" that concentrated on the production of Halifax bombers. Nor must the railway industry be forgotten. The London, Midland & Scottish Railway Board had turned its engine workshops over to aircraft production as early as 1938, and by the time the Battle of Britain reached its height more than 100 pairs of Hurricane wings alone had been produced. In April 1940 the Doncaster works of the London & North-Eastern Railway began production of Botha, Barracuda and Sea Otter components as well as thousands of parts for Spitfires and Hurricanes.

Although many of them toiled under difficult conditions the civilian population, encouraged by Churchill's tenacious example, withstood the demands of war production with a strength and determination which has often been overlooked. But as they worked and as an immediate German invasion failed to materialise, "fifth column fever" spread. Hysterical reports of parachute landings increased. Matters were not helped by the activites of the traitor William Joyce, who transmitted sedition on Radio Bremen. "Lord Haw Haw", as he was dubbed by a largely unimpressed British public, did manage to stir up some rumours and seemed to have a gift of knowing precise details about suburban streets or small-town factories.

A "Silent Column" was launched, a clumsy and patronising attempt by the government to silence the gossip which riddled everyday life. In July 1940 anti-social citizens like "Miss Leaky Mouth", "Miss Teacup Whisper", "Mr Secrecy Hush-Hush" and "Mr Pride in Prophesy" appeared in the press and on posters to dissuade rumour-mongers. On the 17th the BBC broadcast the programme "Chatterbugs" which featured the ludicrous

BRITAIN AT BAY

"Snodergrass", a gossip who soon alienated himself from his colleague during a 30-minute comedy sketch. Incidentally in an effort to prevent deception by German broadcasts the BBC, in a break with tradition, allowed its announcers to name themselves before each report so that people became familiar with each announcer as a personality.

Shops put up signs saying "No Fifth Column Within Please". An old man of 74 was given a seven-day prison sentence for gossiping and even an abusive vicar was not exempt from the wrath of a local authority over zealously interpreting the government's wishes concerning meetings and assemblies in wartime. Research showed that people were becoming confused about exactly what they could and could not talk about.

When questioning a sample of Londoners about their opinion of the government's "Silent Column" campaign, Mass-Observation found that only 26% of people thought it was a good idea. The attempt to padlock the mouths of Britain failed and was soon replaced by a more moderate request to "Talk, grumble but give nothing away". The Ministry of Information had still to find its best approach.

As the military inactivity continued people began to relax a bit more. A survey in an anonymous Suffolk village revealed the following gem from a middle-aged mother unhappy about a battalion of Scottish troops being billeted near the village: 'They go up the pole them young fellers when they've had a drink or two. They don't do no harm, though." A more elderly woman, however, was not so sure: "Did you hear them last night? They aren't half a rough lot, them Scotsmen. Nearly had a fight down at the Shepherd and Dog last night. I reckon there'll be trouble soon if they don't behave more. The lieutenant is having a gay old time with the girls too."

Meanwhile details were finalised to make things as awkward for the invader as possible. It became an offence to show any sign which could indicate "the name of, or the situation of, or the direction of, or the distance to any place". As a result road signs, signposts, street names and even the platform signs at railway stations were removed. Woe betide any hapless dispatch rider who got himself lost. With no signs anywhere to guide him and a public alert to the threat of fifth columnists and saboteurs, his was an unhappy lot.

Buses were fitted with wheel locks to

prevent them from being moved. Private cars, on the other hand, were either immobilised by lack of petrol, drained of oil and mounted on blocks for the duration or, if mobile, had to have their rotor-arms removed from the distributor whenever they were left unattended. If this was not done, policemen were empowered to deflate tyres and tear out ignition leads.

The number of petrol pumps in the south and east was greatly reduced and the remainder prepared for demolition; in France, the petrol-fuelled Panzers had simply queued up at garages and helped themselves to what was available. Derelict vehicles were pushed into fields to provide makeshift glider barriers around which farmers continued to work. The Motor Trade War Executive, alarmed at the fall in demand for the products of its members, issued a series of posters urging drivers to "Keep Your Car on the Road . . . and Men in Employment!" and "The Nation Needs Road Transport."

Some new vehicles did nevertheless appear on the roads. Perhaps the most curious of all was the Beaverette, a light armoured car sporting twin Vickers "K" guns and mounted on the Standard 14 hp motor-car chassis. Originally ordered by the Ministry of Aircraft Production for the protection of airfields and aircraft factories, nearly 2,800 of these ungainly but effective vehicles were produced, the majority ending up in Army service.

A NATION ALONE

Unsure of exactly what was going to happen next, Britons watched for any sign that might herald the invasion. It was hard to believe that Hitler had limited the activity of the Luftwaffe to nuisance raids and reconnaissance missions during the weeks since Dunkirk. Perhaps he had no further territorial demands? Or perhaps his scientists were perfecting some new means of transporting Panzers across the Channel floor, in the manner expounded by some prewar fiction. No-one knew.

What they did know was that any future battle would start in the air, and that it would be up to the RAF to protect Britain initially. When France fell, Hugh Dowding at Fighter Command breathed a sigh of relief and said, "Thank God we're alone." One anonymous interviewee of Mass-Observation was probably nearer the attitude of most ordinary people when he stated: "We usually pull through in the end." Time and the young pilots of the Hurricane and Spitfire squadrons would provide the answer.

Chapter Three

"If Chicago gangsters can have bullet-proof
glass in their cars I can't see any reason
why my pilots should not have the same."

Air Chief Marshal Hugh Dowding,
speaking to the Air Staff, Air Ministry Conference, 1938

DESIGNS FOR WAR

Contrary to popular myth it was the Hurricane, a direct descendant of Hawker's biplane fighters of the mid-1930s, which bore the brunt of Luftwaffe aggression during the Battle of Britain, and not the more technically advanced Spitfire.

The Royal Air Force of 1940 was a formidable weapon. Since Hitler came to power in 1933 it had undergone immense change, and in 1940 it was a more sophisticated, well-armed and better trained organisation than it had ever been. The old doctrines claiming the invincibility of the bomber had been challenged and replaced by a new belief that if it came to a contest defence against bomber fleets would now be possible. This new concept for air defence was encouraged by two inventions, both developed during the 1930s: the high-performance monoplane and, perhaps more radically, "radio-location".

If heavily armed fighters could out-perform bombers they could shoot them down. If they knew where to find the bomber formations then force could be brought to bear and the destruction of bombers would be both possible and practical. The Hurricane and Spitfire fighters and the new science of radar met both criteria and proved that an air attack against Britain, especially during daylight, could be repulsed, or at the least seriously disrupted. However, these new weapons were only just ready for the Battle of Britain and were as much the result of individual conviction as official foresight.

For metal monoplanes and radar to be viable many new sciences and disciplines had to be integrated in a way that had previously been unnecessary. Were it not for the efforts of an expanding scientific and engineering technocracy during the 1930s Britain would have fielded an air force in 1940 that any Great War aviator would have felt at home with. Instead the RAF had exchanged its slow, poorly armed biplanes and primitive communications systems for fast eight-gun monoplanes with enclosed cockpits protecting a pilot linked to his airborne colleagues – and a radar-guided control network by modern high-frequency radio equipment.

The sharp edge of the new RAF, the monoplane, was not an invention peculiar to the 1930s. During the First World War most

The North American Harvard was the RAF's first modern monoplane trainer. It had an enclosed cockpit, retractable undercarriage, powerful engine and wing-flaps, enabling fledgling fighter-pilots to enjoy the security of close instruction prior to the daunting prospect of a solo flight in a Hurricane or Spitfire.

air forces had experimented with monoplane fighters and throughout the spring of 1915 the German Fokker E1 reigned supreme in aerial combat. So effective was the "Eindecker" that the period of its ascendancy was dubbed the "Fokker scourge".

It was Dr Hugo Junkers who developed the first truly modern monoplanes towards the end of the Great War. The "tin-donkeys" as they were known were cantilever monoplanes which required no external bracing. What is more, they were constructed entirely of metal and clad in the corrugated 2 mm Duralumin skin which became Junkers' trademark. The war was over before full-scale production could proceed and all Junkers prototypes, in accordance with the rulings of the Versailles Treaty, were scrapped alongside the remainder of the German Air Force.

During the 1920s there was little stimulus for development of aircraft design. The RAF made do with modifications of First World War designs and equipped its squadrons with aircraft like the Avro 504, Vickers Vimy, Bristol Fighter, DH9A, Gloster Gamecock and Armstrong-Whitworth Siskin. Biplanes could out-turn monoplane designs and the multitude of struts and bracing wires effectively resulted in a box girder wing structure, the flimsy appearance of which belies a strength and rigidity capable of absorbing enormous stress. The biplane was assumed to offer the most suitable fighter configuration, though it was accepted that bombers might be more suited to the monoplane format as they would not be subjected to the rigours of aerobatics. All the fighters and bomber designs in service with the RAF during the 1920s and early 1930s were built to a common and recognised formula; improvements in performance were the result not of developments in aerodynamics but the sum of steady advances in engine technology.

In 1925 the Fairey Fox light bomber appeared. At a time when air-cooled radial engines proliferated Richard Fairey had opted for the American Curtiss D12 liquid-cooled in-line engine. The aircraft's sleek lines and high-performance engine caused a sensation when it was discovered that, although intended as a light bomber, its streamlined airframe made it faster than the current front-line RAF fighters.

Rolls-Royce in turn produced their own uprated engine – the Model "F" or Kestrel as it was later named. The Kestrel will always be associated with the series of Hawker biplanes designed by Sydney Camm that began with the Hart day bomber and went on to include the Fury interceptor, Demon two-seater fighter, Audax army co-operation variant, Hart trainer and Hind day bomber. So successful were these aircraft that nearly 3,000 variants were built during the early 1930s.

The clean lines and polished cowlings of Hawker's biplanes are the epitome of the interwar fighter and represent the high-point of wire and fabric construction. Hawkers had been struggling since their takeover of Sopwith in 1920, but the success of the Hart derivatives guaranteed their future and enabled the company to concentrate on a monoplane design that benefitted from the valuable experience gained from the biplane programme.

Meanwhile, other factors were at work which hastened the arrival of even more powerful engines than Rolls-Royce's Kestrel. In December 1912 Jacques Schneider announced his intention to offer a trophy to the winner of a new speed and performance competition for seaplanes. Believing that the future of aviation would centre on a network of hydroplane flying services, and convinced that the earth's abundance of ocean provided ideal and ready-made "airfields", Schneider was determined to encourage the active development of the seaplane.

The first competition was held in 1913 at Monaco. Many contestants were eliminated at the early stages, which tested seaworthiness and basic handling capabilities, but the essence of the contest was the speed course consisting of a triangular closed circuit of 150 nautical miles. The fastest team won the trophy for either its parent nation or national aero club, depending on what basis the challenge was made. Three wins within a five-year span would secure the trophy for all time for the successful entrant and its sponsor.

The 1913 Schneider Trophy race was won by a Frenchman, Maurice Prévost, piloting a Deperdussin float plane. One of the few aircraft which survived the inevitable soaking of seaborne operation, the Deperdussin averaged the hardly stunning speed of 45.75 mph, though its 160 hp Gnome rotary engine had enabled the frail monoplane to achieve bursts of up to 100 mph along certain sections of the offshore course.

In 1914 the contest was won for Britain by Thomas Sopwith and Harry Hawker, whose

DESIGNS FOR WAR

The Spitfire – legendary symbol of the RAF's performance in the Battle of Britain. Its harmonious shape appears to be as much the result of nature's ideal requirement for flight as it is the product of technical development by the plane-maker R. J. Mitchell.

Sopwith Tabloid seaplane was piloted by Howard Pixton at an average speed of 86.8 mph. The First World War then interrupted the contest and competition did not resume until 1919.

The crowds that flocked to the first postwar Schneider contest were treated to the first view of a new seaplane from a stable which would soon become synonymous with the Schneider event – Supermarine. During the war the Supermarine Aviation works had been concerned chiefly with producing marine aircraft. This is not surprising since it was the Admiralty Air Department and not the War Office that was the company's principal customer. Supermarine's most successful Air Department design was the N1 "Baby", a single-seat pusher biplane flying-boat notable for its advanced lines and graceful wooden hull. Working on the design team was a young and talented technical draughtsman, Reginald Joseph Mitchell.

Poor weather conditions and an unfortunate accident prevented Supermarine's entry for the 1919 competition, the Sea Lion I (based on the N1B Baby design) achieving success, but its design did set a precedent for subsequent Supermarine machines. Mitchell was soon promoted to chief designer and quickly determined to provide a more worthy

ABOVE Formation flying was considered the pinnacle of achievement for RAF fighter-pilots. Here a stack of Hawker Fury Mk Is position themselves for the camera.

RIGHT Although nearly 20 years had elapsed since the end of the First World War, the RAF of the mid-1930s was still equipped largely with obsolete biplanes which would not have looked out of place above the shell-cratered terrain of the Somme. Typical of the interwar inventory was this Hawker Audax.

DESIGNS FOR WAR

challenger for the next competition.

Supermarine's success came in 1922 at Naples when Captain Henri Biard, piloting a Sea Lion II, averaged a speed of 145.7 mph to snatch the trophy from the holders, Italy. Although other competitors enjoyed the full backing and sponsorship of their own governments, Britain's win had been financed solely by Supermarine. Support in kind was provided by the engine manufacturer Napier, who supplied a new 450 hp Napier Lion engine on loan for the competition. On its return to Britain the victorious Sea Lion was purchased by the Air Ministry and used in high-speed seaplane evaluation research.

Supermarine's success in 1922 was, unfortunately, short-lived. Lack of government support and strong competition, notably from America, had denied the company a follow-up victory in 1923. It was also becoming increasingly obvious that Mitchell's Sea Lion design offered little further scope for development. In order to regain the coveted Schneider Trophy a thoroughbred racer was now needed.

Mitchell was able to rethink his plans for high-performance seaplanes in time for the 1925 competition – and the aircraft that emerged from the construction sheds of Southampton's Woolston Works in August 1925 could not have been more different from the familiar Sea Lion. Mitchell was convinced that the future lay with monoplanes and not

biplanes which, for all their merits, presented unfavourable drag coefficients.

His solution, the Supermarine S4, was perhaps the most attractive of all the Schneider Trophy aircraft, and the resemblance of this cantilever monoplane to its famous military descendant – the Spitfire – is

Frog ("Flies Right Off the Ground") scale-model flying aircraft were extremely popular with "air-minded" boys of all ages during the years before the Second World War. Designed to echo the shape of the new monoplane fighters then coming into service, the robust tin and paper models were powered by strong rubber-bands and capable of a surprisingly wide range of aerobatics.

unmistakable. The graceful curves, gently rounded wings and predatory bearing of the new design hinted at greatness. Yet before it was able to demonstrate its true potential the S4 was destroyed during trials only a day before the competition was due to begin in Baltimore.

After the 1925 competition the government at long last realised that Treasury support was essential if Britain were to regain the trophy. National prestige was at stake and it was becoming increasingly obvious that the competition was an important stimulus for research and development – a fact that would have important ramifications for future military aircraft. As a result an RAF High-Speed Flight was formed and the Air Ministry commissioned an assortment of racing seaplane designs. Supermarine provided three machines to help equip the national team for its enthusiastic practices at Felixstowe on the Suffolk coast.

Though smaller and stronger than its predecessor, Mitchell's S5 closely resembled the S4. It was constructed of both wood and metal, and if its Napier Lion VIIB engine was unsupercharged it still managed to deliver 870 hp. While the aircraft was wire-braced it had a lower frontal area than the S4 and drag was much reduced. At Venice in 1927 Flight-Lieutenant Webster and the S5 flashed across the finishing line at over 280 mph to regain the trophy for Britain. The legend of Mitchell and his monoplanes was reborn.

Before the next race, in 1929, events took place which created the framework within which Mitchell's Spitfire fighter would be

created. First Supermarine (and its designer) was bought by the industrial giant Vickers, then Mitchell decided to approach Henry Royce to see if the great man and his company could provide a more powerful engine than the Napier power unit which, it was now realised, had reached the limit of its development.

Rolls-Royce had foreseen the need for more powerful engines than its Kestrel, which was still employed in RAF biplane fighters, and the result was the "Buzzard". It was not one of Rolls-Royce's great successes, managing a power output of only 825 hp, but it paved the way for a promise to Mitchell of an engine twice as powerful; the company's chief engineers – Ernest Hives, Cyril Lovesey and A. J. Rowledge – were instructed to start their quest.

Within a year the Rolls-Royce "R" engine was producing a startling 1900 hp in test-bed running at Derby. This enormous increase in power was the result of a whole host of innovations: a new Rolls-Royce alloy Hydaminium was employed to keep the weight of the engine to a minimum and while still containing the power which resulted in an internal crankshaft loading of nine tons; to prevent distortion and burning the engine's exhaust valves were filled with sodium, which dissipated the great heat of combustion; a new fuel was developed to prevent premature detonation, the resulting cocktail of 78% benzol, 22% aviation spirit and a touch of tetraethyl lead being fed to the engine by a supercharger at over three and a half gallons per minute.

The sophistication of the new engine was apparent as soon as it was fitted to Mitchell's new S6. Almost incredibly, the 36-litre engine weighed only 1,500 lbs. Its frontal area was so low that the S6 narrow fuselage matched the width of the supercharger housing. Once in place the "R" engine was linked up to a subtle cooling system which Mitchell had employed in favour of traditional drag-inducing radiators. The wings of the S6 were used to disperse the great engine heat so fuel had to be contained in the aircraft's metal floats. A large oil tank was built into the tail-fin, which helped with further cooling. The engine oil circulated to and from the oil tank through rows of pipe-shaped radiators along the fuselage.

Unlike most other aircraft of the day the S6 (like the later Spitfire) was of stressed skin construction – that is, the aircraft's rigidity

DESIGNS FOR WAR

was due to the structure of its external panelling and not internally braced formers clad in thin, unstressed fabric coverings. Stressed skin construction (or monocoque as it became known) allows internal spaces to be used for machinery, passengers or freight and results in a much more efficient solution to the power/weight equation. In every aspect the S6 was subjected to minute scrutiny in order to improve the aircraft's aerodynamics.

The 1929 Schneider competition took place at Calshot. Britain entered not only the Vickers Supermarine S6 but also the Napier Lion-powered Gloster VI Golden Arrow. The efforts of Mitchell and Rolls-Royce were not in vain: on September 7 the S6, with Flying Officer Waghorn at the controls, took the contest with an average speed of 328 mph.

Britain needed only one more victory to win the Schneider Trophy outright. Mitchell was confident that this could be achieved and set about uprating the S6 with a modified "R"-type engine capable of some 2,350 hp. With the country in the midst of an economic depression Ramsay MacDonald's Labour government felt that investment in further competition was an unnecessary extravagance, but at the last minute a guarantee of £100,000 from Lady Houston averted cancellation and the British challenge went ahead.

On Sunday September 13, 1931 Flight-Lieutenant Boothman, flying the S6B, crossed the finishing line at Ryde Pier off the Isle of Wight to the loud applause of spectators and learnt that he had averaged a speed of 340 mph. Later Flight-Lieutenant Stainforth took

the plane to a world speed record of 407.6 mph. Britain had captured the Schneider Trophy outright – and the monoplane was at last elevated to a position of pre-eminence in aviation.

As a result of the rapid developments in aviation technology, and more especially the achievements of the RAF High-Speed Flight, the Air Ministry decided to issue a specification for a new single-seater fighter to replace the Bristol Bulldog biplanes which then equipped most of the "Fighting Area" squadrons within the Air Defence of Great Britain (ADGB), Fighter Command's predecessor. The new specification (F7/30) called for the highest possible speed at 15,000 feet, highest possible rate of climb, good manoeuvrability, good fighting view, four .303 machine-guns and all-metal construction. A later specification (F5/34) raised the requirement to eight guns.

Fresh from his Schneider Trophy victories Mitchell submitted his design for appraisal by the Air Ministry. Designated Supermarine Type 224, the new fighter bore a greater resemblance to the later Junkers Stuka than it did to a high-performance fighter. The plane, its design featuring an open cockpit, cranked wings and massive spatted undercarriage, was powered by the new Rolls-Royce Goshawk engine of 660 hp. The Type 224 employed an extremely complicated cooling system to prevent the evaporatively-cooled Goshawk

Popular toys reflected the increasing public interest in all things aeronautic. The Sky Birds kits of wood and brass (this one is a First World War Fokker DVII) were the first built to the later universal scale of 1:72 and, once painted, made very convincing items. Toy searchlights were available in abundance as, later, were cheap metal replicas of the Hurricane and Spitfire. The two motor vehicles are toy models of the "De Dion Auto Cannons" used in London and Paris during the First World War to fend off Zeppelin raids. The appeal of interwar aviation is demonstrated by the Imperial Flying Boat jigsaw puzzle and by Aviation, "a game of aerial tactics" popular from the early 1930s. The Frog "Penguin" construction kits were the forerunners of today's plastic models, but were made of an early form of acetate more akin to Bakelite than modern polystyrene. The one shown (right foreground) is a scale replica of a Hawker Fury.

A NATION ALONE

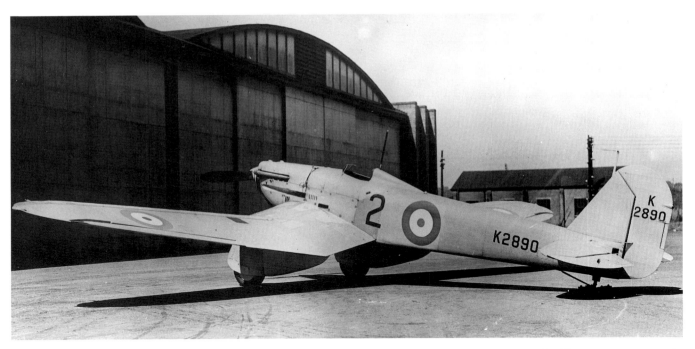

Designed to meet the requirements of Air Ministry Specification F7/30, Mitchell's Type 224 prototype for Supermarine was not a success. Though it led directly to the development of the graceful Spitfire, it resembled the Junkers 87 Stuka dive-bomber more than a high-speed interceptor fighter.

from overheating, and virtually the whole of the wings' leading edge consisted of condensers which turned the steam from the engine into water. The coolant water was fed to collectors in the undercarriage fairings and was in turn recirculated around the engine's cylinders.

The Type 224 was not a success, achieving a top speed of only 238 mph when it first flew in February 1934. The advanced cooling system developed faults, especially during aerobatics when the water and steam was apt to become dangerously mixed. The F7/30 competition was in fact won by the Gloster SS37, which entered service as the RAF's last biplane fighter, the Gladiator. Interestingly this aircraft was not of all-metal construction.

Perhaps Mitchell, having achieved over 400 mph with the S6B, had been somewhat contemptuous of the Air Ministry specification. Certainly he had underestimated the difficulty of incorporating a high rate of climb, manoeuvrability and good pilot visibility into his new monoplane – disciplines unnecessary in his racing seaplanes. Two other monoplanes, the Bristol Type 133 and the Vickers Jockey, did not meet the specification and nor did any of the biplane submissions – Hawker's PV3, Westland's PV4, Bristol's 123 and Blackburn's aptly-named F7/30. The losers went back to the drawing-board and Mitchell in particular was determined to see his reputation upheld.

Germany, meantime, was beginning to

rattle the sabres of militarism once more: in 1932 she walked out of the Disarmament Conference and subsequently withdrew from the League of Nations. Although her still "illegal" air force was equipped with biplane designs like the Heinkel 51 and Arado 68, Air Ministry intelligence was aware that monoplane fighter variants were being considered by the German Air Ministry. Based on the not unrealistic assumption that a Germany united under totalitarian control would be capable of accelerating the production of armaments more easily than a democracy like Britain, the Air Ministry increased its behind-the-scenes activities to encourage Britain's leading designers, Mitchell and Camm of Hawkers, to meet the inevitable challenge from Messerschmitt, Heinkel and Junkers.

After a final fling with biplanes and accepting that his Hart and Fury designs were capable of little refinement, Camm set about designing Hawker's "Fury Monoplane". Recognising that the existing tooling and expertise that had been employed on his famous biplanes could not be simply swept away, he concentrated on developing the internally braced structures used in the Hart and Fury variants. Though guessing that Mitchell would concentrate on a stressed skin development of the Supermarine 224, Camm knew that any attempt to emulate his rival's practice would be prohibitively expensive and time consuming.

On July 26, 1934, seven days after the

government approved the Air Ministry's scheme to expand the fighter defences by a further 41 squadrons before March 1939, Mitchell's redesign of Type 224 was revealed. Gradually, the Spitfire contours last seen on the S6 began to reappear and specification No. 425, as it was called, was submitted for Air Ministry consideration. Unlike the Type 224, the new design featured a straight wing, enclosed cockpit and retractable under-carriage. Now known as the Type 300, the design received a lukewarm reception from Whitehall; still powered by the rather clumsy Goshawk engine, a speed advantage of only 30 mph over the Type 224 was all that could be promised.

It was activity at Rolls-Royce which prevented the Type 300 from remaining firmly on the drawing-board and which in turn gave Sydney Camm the means of significantly improving the theoretical performance of his new monoplane. After their great success with the Schneider Trophy "R"-type engines, Rolls-Royce engineers were confident that they could mass produce a high-performance engine capable of the proven reliability shown by the company's trusty Kestrel. In 1933 the company started utilising its wealth of recent experience and started work on a private venture – an engine suitably titled PV12. With 1,000 hp as their target, Rolls-Royce's engineers ironed out a multitude of problems which resulted from attempting to produce a lightweight engine capable of such great power. Renamed "Merlin", the PV12 was developed into a power unit which added the final ingredient to Mitchell and Camm's new fighting aircraft.

Both designers had been encouraged by their employers to persevere with their respective plans, because it was widely assumed that massive rearmament would eventually be required. Also, Rolls-Royce's development of the PV12 was no secret and both designers knew that should 1,000 hp be achieved the performance of both fighters could surpass Air Ministry requirements. As work proceeded, and spurred on by the growing threat from Germany, a succession of Air Ministry specifications were written to enable each of the private ventures to benefit from official assessments of future armament and performance requirements. The two final specifications – F36/34 for Hawker's fighter and F37/34 for Supermarine's machine – required level speeds of 320 mph and 330 mph

respectively, but both aircraft exceeded these speeds when they initially entered service.

Hawker's "High-Speed Monoplane" was the first design to take to the air. The prototype of the fighter which would soon be named "Hurricane", and which would bear the brunt of the fighting during the Battle of Britain, first flew on November 6, 1935. Like its Fury and Hart predecessors it was painted silver, its polished engine cowlings gleaming brightly against the overcast skies. The Merlin "C" engine of 1,025 hp drove an enormous Watts two-bladed wooden propeller and succeeded in powering the aircraft past the 300 mph barrier during a shallow dive. It was clear to all those present that Camm had produced a solid and stable fighting plane of first-rate quality.

In developing a stressed skin aircraft Mitchell had chosen a more difficult and unproven path. Desperately ill with cancer but relentless in his pursuit for a radical new plane, he quickly amended his designs to incorporate the PV12 engine. As a result the Air Ministry issued a contract for a prototype. Once the details of specification F37/34 were ironed out development of the new Type 300 fighter gained momentum. Had it not been for the timely arrival of Rolls-Royce's PV12 into the arena of aircraft design, however, it is possible that the Spitfire might never have seen service. Only by utilising the new power-plant could Mitchell guarantee a performance that would at least match the achievements of rival designs.

The Supermarine Type 224 did not go into production, but the originality and sophistication of Mitchell's engineering ability is clearly shown in this sectionalised view of the prototype. To prevent the 660-hp Goshawk engine overheating the entire wing leading edge and undercarriage spats formed one gigantic cooling system.

A NATION ALONE

ABOVE A row of brand-new Boulton Paul Defiant "turret fighters" is paraded outside the company's factory.

RIGHT The prototype Hawker Hurricane first flew on November 6, 1935, at Brooklands, with Flight-Lieutenant P. W. S. Bulmann achieving a top speed of 315 mph.

BELOW The Supermarine Spitfire prototype first took to the air four months later than its larger rival. Its revolutionary design made possible a top speed of 349 mph during its test flight on March 5, 1936.

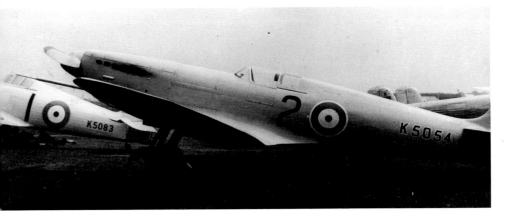

Bearing little resemblance to the final draft submission of Type 300 the prototype fighter, F37/34, gradually began to take shape. Although it incorporated a two-bladed propeller, straight canopy and flush-mounted exhaust stubs, it was already every inch a Spitfire. On March 5, 1936 the prototype of the classic fighter bounced across the grass runway at Eastleigh near Supermarine's Southampton workshops – and at last Mitchell's dream became a reality.

Though he would not live to see the Spitfire enter full production Mitchell must certainly have realised that he had created a world-beater. Certainly Supermarine's test-pilot "Mutt" Summers must have thought so as he put the neat little fighter with its characteristic elliptical wings through its paces during a 15-minute first flight. Having identified no significant snags, Summers was confident that the RAF would warm to Supermarine's

design for the aerial defence of Britain.

Yet even he could not have hoped for such a positive reaction from the aircraft's service scrutineers. Before the fighter had completed seven days of trials at RAF Martlesham Heath near Ipswich and prior to receiving any formal report on its performance, the Air Ministry issued a production contract for 310 aircraft. The Supermarine Spitfire was born.

Although the Hurricane prototype had flown some four months before the Spitfire, Hawker's did not receive their production contract until June 1936. The Air Ministry had been faced with a complicated revision of its procurement programme and had naturally been reluctant to finalise a production order with Hawker's until the clear results of Supermarine's activities were known; but on June 3, 1936 some 600 monoplane fighters were ordered. The increased number reflects the straightforward construction of Camm's type, compared to the Spitfire; and on June 27th the name "Hurricane" was officially approved by Whitehall.

The Hurricane and Spitfire were not the only monoplanes ordered during the RAF's mid-1930s expansion programme, though they were the most successful. A third monoplane was also ordered, one which would also see action during the Battle of Britain.

The Boulton Paul Defiant was an attempt to emulate the success of the First World War two-seat Bristol Fighter. At a time when investigations into multiple machine-gun armaments were in their infancy the Defiant appeared to offer a solution and provide concentrated fire in a new powerpack format. Mounting four .303-inch Browning machine-guns in a power-operated turret situated behind the pilot's cockpit, the Merlin-powered Defiant was capable of barely 300 mph. But perhaps seduced by the turreted French "multiplace de combat" aircraft and deluded by interwar theorists like Douhet (who predicted the ascendancy of "battle planes"), the Defiant's designers had failed to provide any forward-firing armament.

Although it was not far behind the Hurricane in performance, and was initially mistaken for Camm's design by German pilots unfamiliar with its configuration, the Defiant was defenceless against head-on attack – a weakness soon exploited by Luftwaffe pilots after they had recovered from the initial shock of discovering its rear-facing gun. The Defiant would see only limited action in the Battle of

DESIGNS FOR WAR

Although a later variant than the type that fought in the Battle of Britain, this Spitfire Mk IX displays the unmistakable lines of the thoroughbred. R. J. Mitchell's attention to detail and technical fluency helped produce a classic of aeronautical design.

Britain, but it went on to more respectable things when employed as a night fighter during the Blitz.

Two major developments distinguish the prototype Hurricane and Spitfire from the versions that did battle for the RAF in 1940. The first concerned the flying capabilities of the aircraft. Before the Battle of Britain all Hurricanes and Spitfires had been equipped with two-pitch propellers. These required the pilot manually to adjust the pitch (or angle of the three propeller blades) in order to control the "bite" of the propeller and maximise performance at different altitudes and airspeeds. Although a great improvement over the two-bladed Watts fixed-pitch propellers, the "two-pitch" versions were still a compromise solution and did not exploit the full potential of the new Merlin engines.

Early in June 1940 Flight-Lieutenant McGrath, an engineer at RAF Hornchurch in Essex, contacted De Havilland's propeller division at Hatfield to enquire about the possibility of fitting a new "constant-speed", variable-pitch propeller to one of the Spitfires there. De Havilland duly sent a team to Hornchurch and carried out a trial conversion. The result of their efforts was astonishing: an extra 7,000 feet was added to the service ceiling of the Spitfire and the aircraft's handling, both during take off and landing and at altitude, was greatly improved. The constant speed unit was linked via a governor directly to the engine and the pitch of the propeller blades consequently varied as the engine revolutions were altered.

Immediately the results of the conversion were known Fighter Command asked De Havilland's to fit constant-speed units to all its front-line squadrons, and with no written contract the company set about converting up to 20 fighters a day. By August 15, 1940, a total of 1,051 Hurricanes and Spitfires had been altered and Fighter Command had dramatically increased its ability to meet the challenge of Luftwaffe fighters already equipped with

Armourers check the gun-bays of a Spitfire of 19 Squadron at Duxford. The eight .303-inch Browning machine-guns could be accessed from both above and below the wing, and RAF regulations stressed the need to remove all panels; but due to the pressure of battle canny armourers soon learned to cut corners and found the knack of rearming from underneath — with a trusty forage cap the final aid in cocking the weapons.

VDM constant-speed propellers. The improvement in performance was to prove crucial when RAF Spitfires clashed with Messerschmitts at altitude above southern England and the waters of the Channel during the forthcoming battle of the skies.

The second important post-prototype development concerned armament. While the original specifications had called for four machine-guns to be incorporated into the new fighter designs, it was becoming alarmingly obvious that even this increased number might prove insufficient for modern air-to-air combat. The new monoplane bombers were capable of relatively high speeds and a fighter pilot could not be certain of more than a fleeting pass at such targets. With high-speed interception allowing only a short firing pass many more hits would be required to inflict lethal damage on the new all-metal structures. A burst of fire from four guns may have been more than adequate to smash a slow fabric covered biplane to pieces, but it was doubtful if the same weight of fire would destroy a high-speed monoplane.

Furthermore, as the machine-guns were intended to be wing-mounted they could not be re-cocked in the time-honoured manner by the pilot either tugging at the trusty Bowden cable or slamming the breech-block with a wooden mallet. A jammed feed on even a single gun would reduce the weight of

ammunition discharged by a quarter.

Squadron-Leader Ralph Sorley, in charge of the Operational Requirements Department of the Air Ministry in 1933, recognised these problems and is widely regarded as the man chiefly responsible for the decision to fit eight guns into both Hurricane and Spitfire. He calculated that a two-second burst was the most an average pilot could expect to manage while holding his target steady within the ring of the aircraft's gun-sight. An eight-gun installation reduced the effect of stoppages and he explained that, "Even if one or two did stop, there were plenty left." Yet a two-second burst from all eight guns still only delivered an eight-pound weight of shot towards the target.

After extensive trials during 1934 a new machine-gun, the American Browning, was selected for RAF service. It had a high rate of fire of 1,200 rounds per minute, a muzzle velocity of 2,440 feet per second, and its stoppage rate was dramatically lower than any other equivalent weapon available. Once the .300-inch American model had been converted to fire British .303-inch ammunition a production licence was sought and Vickers were given the contract for producing the gun to RAF specifications.

In service the gun could be armed with either standard ball ammunition, armour-piercing shot, tracer-rounds or the new De Wilde explosive bullets. The De Wilde bullet,

DESIGNS FOR WAR

though not as formidable as traditional cannon shells, nevertheless proved immensely useful in bringing down heavily armed bombers. Developed by a Belgian chemist only months before hostilities commenced, it gave an extra dimension to the rifle calibre Browning machine-guns and the delayed reaction effect of de Wilde rounds flickering and dancing across enemy airframes as the incendiary charge detonated is a familiar memory to veterans of the air battles of 1940.

The eight guns were equipped with 2,400 rounds of ammunition linked together in belts stowed next to the breeches within the aircraft's wings. The amount of ammunition carried was sufficient for approximately 14 seconds of continues firing, though of course only short bursts of fire would in reality be employed. Required to operate in temperatures as low as − 40° Centigrade the guns were heated by diverting warm air from the aircraft's radiators through ducts into the gun-bays. The simple addition of sticking patches of linen tape over the gun-ports prevented moisture from entering the gun's muzzles. On firing the tape was immediately blown away and the guns were unimpaired.

Access to the guns was achieved via removable panels above and below the wings. A quarter turn of the patent fastenings securing them released the panels and exposed guns and magazines to the scrutiny of the squadron armourers. Rearming the eight guns took only ten minutes on Spitfires after armourers had discovered an ingenious method of reloading the guns from below the wing by pulling the first round of each belt into the breech with a piece of webbing.

To ensure pilots used their impressive battery to good effect Fighter Command equipped all its aircraft with modern reflector gun-sights. These new sights consisted of a calibrated housing which projected a gun graticule sight onto an oval glass plate positioned above the instrument panel and directly in the pilot's line of sight. By setting the known wingspan of his target the pilot was able to adjust the sight mechanism so that, once suitably positioned within the illuminated ring, the target was within range.

The guns were powered by compressed air and fired by a gun-button mounted on the pilot's control column. As all eight Brownings simultaneously discharged their ammunition the whole aircraft would shudder as the airframe recoiled from the effect of 160 cartridges detonating every second. Spent cartridge cases were ejected from apertures in the underwing surface. It was the rattling of used cartridge cases across rooftops and on the

The close grouping of the Hurricane's eight Browning machine-guns – four in each wing-bay – produced a very stable gun-platform and provided a concentrated "cone-of-fire" at short range.

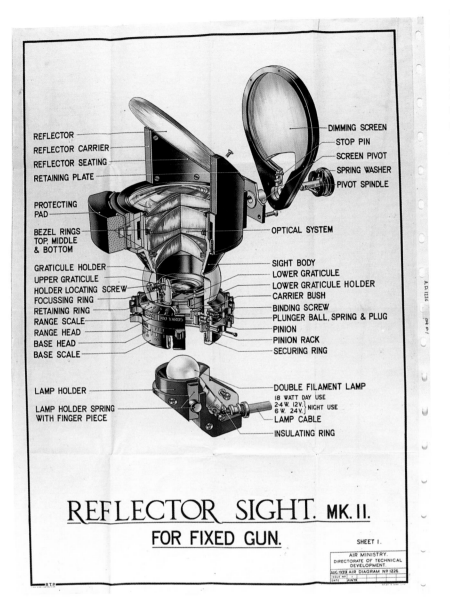

REFLECTOR SIGHT. MK. II.

FOR FIXED GUN.

SHEET 1.

REFLECTOR
REFLECTOR CARRIER
REFLECTOR SEATING
RETAINING PLATE

PROTECTING PAD

BEZEL RINGS TOP, MIDDLE & BOTTOM

GRATICULE HOLDER
UPPER GRATICULE
HOLDER LOCATING SCREW
FOCUSSING RING
RETAINING RING
RANGE SCALE
RANGE HEAD
BASE HEAD
BASE SCALE

LAMP HOLDER

LAMP HOLDER SPRING WITH FINGER PIECE

DIMMING SCREEN
STOP PIN
SCREEN PIVOT
SPRING WASHER
PIVOT SPINDLE

OPTICAL SYSTEM

SIGHT BODY
LOWER GRATICULE
LOWER GRATICULE HOLDER
CARRIER BUSH
BINDING SCREW
PLUNGER BALL, SPRING & PLUG
PINION
PINION RACK
SECURING RING

DOUBLE FILAMENT LAMP
18 WATT DAY USE
2·4 W. 12V.} NIGHT USE
6 W. 24V.}
LAMP CABLE
INSULATING RING

AIR MINISTRY.
DIRECTORATE OF TECHNICAL DEVELOPMENT.
AUG 1939 AIR DIAGRAM Nº 1226.

The Mk II reflector gun-sight was standard equipment in RAF Hurricanes and Spitfires. After dialling in the wingspan of the target the pilot waited for the enemy aircraft to frame itself within the graticule sight on the reflector plate; when in range he could unleash a two-second burst of .303-inch machine-gun fire at a rate of 160 rounds per second from a total of 2,400 rounds stored in the wing-mounted ammunition boxes.

pavements of suburbia which led to many of the rumours of German aircraft randomly machine-gunning civilians during the battle.

Once a fighter-pilot had exhausted his ammunition supply the dull thud of the compressed air operating empty breeches would signal a rapid retreat from the battlefield. To prevent being caught by surprise from lack of ammunition, tracer rounds were often included as the last few rounds on ammunition belts. The glow of their arcing flight provided a clear indication that it was time to rearm – and probably also to refuel.

Since 1940 there has been much debate concerning the lack of cannon armament in Battle of Britain fighters. Certainly the Air

Ministry had been aware of the developments in larger calibre weapons. In 1935 plans were considered which suggested installing Oerlikon cannons into Hawker's "High-Speed Monoplane Interceptor" – the prototype Hurricane. These were finally disregarded and instead Westland's Whirlwind was chosen as the first purpose-built cannon-armed fighter. By 1937 Hispano-Suiza had been granted a licence to produce 20 mm Oerlikon cannons in England. During the Battle of Britain some Spitfires were modified to carry such weapons but the results were uninspiring. Jamming was a frequent problem and the vibration caused by discharging 20 mm cartridges greatly impaired accuracy. The weapons were large and cumbersome and not ideally suited to installation within the thin wings of the new monoplanes. Unlike machine-guns the early cannons carried a limited number of rounds; magazines were rapidly emptied, leaving the aircraft unarmed often before a lethal hit had been achieved. Lastly, until improved methods of closing the breeches of cannons during the firing cycle could be found, muzzle velocity was still far from impressive.

Machine-guns, on the other hand, were reliable and rugged and squadron armourers were familiar with their maintenance and operation. Reflecting on the carnage caused in the trenches during the Great War, when a single machine-gun firing at a slower rate than the RAF's Brownings was able to decimate an infantry battalion, it is not surprising that great faith was held in the ability of combined fire from eight wing-mounted machine-guns. Six Hurricane or Spitfire fighters attacking in formation were able to bring 48 rapid-firing guns to bear, enough (it was thought) to dispatch even the most persistent foe.

Thus armed, both the Hurricane and the Spitfire were ready to do battle. Clad in the dark earth and dark green camouflage of wartime and dispersed in "E pens" to prevent a repetition of the calamity that befell the neatly parked rows of aircraft in France, the two fighters prepared to take their turn on history's stage.

Unlike their British counterparts German designers had with great difficulty managed to install cannon armament into their front-line fighter – the Messerschmitt BF109E. The BF109E was equipped with a modified version of the Swiss 20 mm Oerlikon gun then being considered by the RAF. After shortening the

DESIGNS FOR WAR

weapon's barrel and altering the breech-block to facilitate automatic operation utilising the expanding gas caused by each discharge, two guns were squeezed into the slender wings of the 109E. Although it had a low muzzle velocity (due to the need to operate the firing mechanism by syphoning off some of the explosive force of each round), the weapon generally performed well. Its explosive 20 mm shells relied for success on detonation within or against an airframe, so its low velocity was not a significant problem. Against the stressed skin of the Spitfire the weapon could be devastating, having the same effect as bursting a balloon with a sharp pin.

Curiously the more old-fashioned Hurricane fared better when caught in the sights of cannon-armed Messerschmitts. Sydney Camm's tubular steel framework, with its multitude of wires, formers and stringers, often remained undamaged as the force of a cannon shell exploding was dissipated through the fabric covering or unstressed panelling. It was not uncommon for Hurricanes to return from such engagements with great swathes of powder-burned fabric hanging torn and shredded but revealing intact framework beneath.

Like all early cannons, the German weapon had a low magazine capacity (only 60 rounds per gun) and a low rate of fire. Due to its slow operating cycle, often only one or two rounds would strike the target. The quality of the ammunition also left a lot to be desired and RAF fighter pilots often landed to discover undetonated cannon rounds embedded in their airframes. Most veterans of 1940 are satisfied that if their eight-gun armament was brought to bear accurately, and within range, their Hurricanes and Spitfires were a match for any German aircraft.

During the 1930s the RAF not only underwent radical re-equipping; it also reorganised itself dramatically. Most of the changes that occurred during the interwar period were as a direct result of Lord Trenchard's far-sighted re-evaluation in 1919 of the air force and its role as a component in Britain's armed forces. Realising that the RAF would survive as an independent body only if it adapted to the new postwar situation, Trenchard set about creating an organisation that was as efficient and technologically sophisticated as possible.

Although he argued for (and was frequently promised) a dramatic expansion of the RAF,

the fact that successive defence cuts and naïve attempts at multilateral disarmament starved it of rapid growth was a blessing in disguise. Faced with the painful reality of a small Royal Air Force, Trenchard was able to concentrate on improving its character and quality in a manner that would have been impossible had it been up to its "ideal" and much larger establishment. While the RAF was relatively small it was malleable, and Trenchard was able to shape it into the form that proved highly suited to the requirements of air-fighting in 1940.

Between 1920 and 1925 Trenchard established an extremely practical training and induction network for the RAF, beginning with the founding of the Royal Air Force College at Cranwell in 1920. Here aspiring officers would be schooled in the art of leadership and instilled with service discipline. Above all, of course, they would be prepared for their future involvement with the *raison d'être* of the RAF – flying either fighter or bomber aircraft, as well as developing their new abilities in navigation, engineering and armaments. Actual flying training was carried out at Upavon's Central Flying School and at other training schools that provided specialist instruction in wireless telegraphy, gunnery and reconnaissance duties.

However it was not uncommon for a pilot with many hours' training on bomber aircraft to end up on fighters, or vice versa. The strength of Trenchard's scheme was that it

It was crucial that pilots were aware of the need to maintain the operating efficiency of their precious armament by ensuring a plentiful supply of compressed air to the guns' breech-blocks. This Air Diagram graphically explains the point.

encouraged versatility and flexibility – all fliers were encouraged to keep abreast of the latest developments in aviation and most were able to pilot a wide range of aircraft. The wisdom of such practical yet relatively relaxed attitudes is evinced by the comparative ease with which pilots were able to adapt from one type of fighter to another under pressure during the Battle of Britain.

In 1922 a staff college for officers was established at Andover in Hampshire. This provided a more comprehensive and selective form of instruction for officers in mid-career who demonstrated a potential for higher command. The same year a network of technical colleges for groundcrew training was set up, the most famous being at Halton in Buckinghamshire. Here "Trenchard's Brats", the stalwarts of the RAF, were trained. The fitters, riggers and armourers that technical colleges at Halton, Flowerdown and Cranwell produced became the unsung heroes of the Battle of Britain. Labouring day and night, often going many hours without sleep or rest and frequently under fire, the groundcrews worked miracles and kept precious Spitfires and Hurricanes flying in circumstances which in peacetime would have been unthinkable.

To ensure the RAF attracted the broadest cross-section of officer candidate, the Short Service Commission was introduced in 1924; this enabled a man to join at 18 or 19 and serve only five years in the RAF. Officers who joined on Short Service Commissions and left after five years to pursue alternative careers were encouraged to keep abreast of future developments in aviation. Each year trained officers were able to return to the RAF for additional flying practice and were kept up to date with new techniques. As a result, a trained reserve was established which proved of great value when the deteriorating international situation requird rapid expansion of the RAF prior to the Second World War.

The Royal Air Force Volunteer Reserve, the creation of a reserve of air force officers, the Civil Air Guard, the Auxiliary Air Force and the University Air Squadrons were all part of Trenchard's initial plan and further provided the peacetime RAF with an immediately available source of reinforcement should war be imminent. During the Battle of Britain the "weekend fliers" of the AAF, RAFVR and the UAS would soon distinguish themselves in the air alongside their regular counterparts.

Trenchard had established a sound and secure base upon which the RAF was to be built and expanded. Having saved it from the ignominy of being reabsorbed into the Army and the Navy, he proceeded to adapt it to the increasingly pertinent role of home defence. After the reckless dismantling of all three services directly the guns on the Western

The forerunners of today's computer-controlled flight simulators, the mechanical Link trainers of 1940 were an essential step along the route to flying proficiency.

DESIGNS FOR WAR

Front fell silent in 1918, strategicians began to reconsider the plans for Imperial Defence, especially aerial defence, which had been gathering dust in the corridors of power.

Postwar France, ironically, was considered to pose the greatest threat to British security and her air force, within striking distance of London, was the yardstick for RAF expansion. As long as Trenchard's force matched the "Armée de l'Air" in size and capability, Britain's security was guaranteed. At least that was the theory. In practice the Air Ministry's 1922 proposal for metropolitan defence fell far short of equipping the RAF with the 600 or so aircraft it would require to counter the French striking force. In fact less than half this number was proposed and of the 23 squadrons that would be charged with home defence 14 would consist of bomber aircraft – the theory being that offensive action would prove the only adequate defence.

The following year, 1923, the Salisbury Committee suggested the establishment of a Home Defence Air Force consisting of 52 squadrons. Unfortunately the actions of Sir Eric Geddes' infamous axe and the implementation of the ludicrous "Ten-Year Rule" prevented any possibility of expansion and Trenchard was forced to spread his meagre resources thinly. The same year further thought was given to the deployment of the few aircraft that actually existed and another committee was convened and requested to study the problems of air defence.

Its report was the first step along the path of reorganisation which led to the group and command structure which proved so successful in 1940. The report proposed a system of defensive belts arcing south-east around London and protecting the capital from direct attack from across the Channel. The outer coastal belt consisted of an Artillery Zone whose purpose was to disrupt enemy formations as they headed inland. Behind this was the so-called Air Fighting Zone containing the squadrons tasked with interception.

Although three squadrons were situated on coastal airfields and would have first-hand knowledge of an approaching raid, the other inland squadrons relied on the sightings from advanced observer posts and sound locators. Sound locators were mobile arrangements of devices similar in appearance to gramophone trumpets which were trained in the likely direction of an attack and manned by army operators who strained their ears attempting

to detect the tell-tale drone of aero-engines. In ideal conditions, and only if the attacking formation was flying at right-angles to the detector, aircraft just outside earshot could be picked up on the operators' headsets.

In general use mechanical locators and later permanent acoustic detectors were useless. Squadrons would in practice receive very little warning of an enemy attack and consequently would have been unable to climb to combat altitude in time to effect a successful interception. It is not surprising therefore that little faith was shown in the possibility of fighter aircraft preventing devastating aerial bombardment. Until raids would be detected by more practical means and fighters could claw their way more quickly to altitude, the arguments in favour of retaliation seemed convincing.

As a final gesture of defiance an Inner Artillery Zone enveloping London formed the last line of defence. Here, it was hoped, bombers that had fought their way through the two outer zones would be picked off by heavy artillery. In reality of course it is highly likely that a raid reaching the coast unobserved would be more or less intact once it reached London. Hence the fears of the prophets of doom who predicted a metropolitan wasteland minutes after an air-raid raid had passed.

By 1940 advances in technology were having a positive influence on both the efficiency of the RAF and the security of its aircrews. To enable ground controllers to guide pilots to successful interceptions it was important that the aircraft's radio equipment functioned properly. RAF technicians worked around the clock maintaining aircraft R/T installations and replacing damaged units.

WILLS'S CIGARETTES

ANTI-AIRCRAFT GUN

WILLS'S CIGARETTES

HEIGHT FINDER

THE HEIGHT FINDER is an essential part of the equipment of the Anti-Aircraft Gun Section, for on the skill of the men working it the whole success of the shooting rests. Our picture shows an instrument with a base length of 9 ft. being operated by its crew of 3, who are wearing gas masks. This is a modern instrument and is being issued in considerable quantities to Territorial Anti-Aircraft Units for Home Defence. (No. 49)

AN ANTI-AIRCRAFT GUN must have a high rate of fire and be capable of following the movements of the fastest bombing aircraft. The 3-inch gun shown in the picture is mounted on a mobile platform for use with the Field Army. It can throw a 16 lb. shell to 20,000 ft. in 23 seconds and can fire 20 rounds in a minute. This gun has a crew of 8. It is towed by a tractor and has a road speed of 20 miles per hour. Territorial Units for Home Defence are equipped with this gun on a fixed platform. It is, however, now being replaced by larger and more powerful equipment. (No. 50)

Wills's cigarettes reflected the general concern of the public about the need for efficient air-raid precautions, and for a while wartime worries edged out the more familiar collections of film stars and sportsmen.

In 1925 the structure of national defence was altered yet again with the introduction of a co-ordinated command known as the Air Defence of Great Britain (ADGB). ADGB consisted of a series of geographically allocated areas under the command of a single air officer commanding-in-chief. The first such AOC-in-C was Sir John Salmond. ADGB comprised five separate areas: Western Area, with eight heavy bomber squadrons; Central Area, with 11 squadrons of light bombers; Fighting Area (Southern England), with 14 fighter squadrons; Inland Area (army co-operation and training); and Coast Area, consisting of one torpedo bomber squadron and four flying-boat squadrons. Cranwell and Halton were their own commands.

By 1934, although it had not been officially revealed to the world, it was obvious that Germany had been building a mighty air force, and the government had little option but to accept the need urgently to expand the Royal Air Force. At last the plan for enlarging the service which had been tabled over ten years before was initiated, and on July 19, 1934 the government decided to increase the RAF by 41 squadrons over five years.

Predictably the programme was not fully completed in time for the Battle of Britain – but a start had been made.

In July 1936 ADGB was replaced by a new command structure which was to survive not only throughout the Second World War but indeed for a long time afterwards. Four commands – Bomber, Fighter, Coastal and Training – were established, each with its own commander-in-chief. The first C-in-C of Fighter Command, and the man responsible for its operation during the Battle of Britain, was Hugh Dowding, the 58-year-old son of a prep school headmaster.

After graduating from the Royal Military Academy at Sandhurst, Second Lieutenant H. A. C. Dowding joined the Royal Garrison Artillery and served with them in Gibraltar, Ceylon and Hong Kong. On his return to Britain he attended the Staff College at Camberley, and while there he became attracted to the century's newest thrill, flying, then an activity still in its infancy. Fortunately Camberley was conveniently situated close to the tiny airfield within the Brooklands racing circuit and following not a little intrigue Dowding enrolled for flying lessons before

WILLS'S CIGARETTES

WILLS'S CIGARETTES

ANTI-AIRCRAFT SEARCHLIGHT

WILLS'S CIGARETTES

REPRESENTATION OF BALLOON BARRAGE FOR DEFENCE OF LONDON

ANTI-AIRCRAFT SOUND LOCATOR

ANTI-AIRCRAFT SEARCHLIGHT. The duty of anti-aircraft searchlight units is to find and illuminate enemy aircraft so that they can be attacked by our own fighter machines or fired at by anti-aircraft guns. The searchlight has a glass paraboloid reflector 36 in. in diameter and an electric arc lamp which gives a light of many millions of candle power. In fine weather the searchlight has a range of over 5 miles. The complete searchlight detachment consists of 10 men who work the searchlight, a sound locator (illustrated and described on Card No. 48) and a generating plant which provides the necessary power for the arc lamp. (No. 47)

REPRESENTATION OF BALLOON BARRAGE FOR DEFENCE OF LONDON. The balloon barrage forms an important part of the co-ordinated scheme—consisting of guns, searchlights, fighter aeroplanes and balloons—for the air defence of London. In time of war, the balloons would be disposed in a rough circle round the perimeter of London. Each balloon is attached by a steel cable to a winch on the ground by which it can be let up or hauled down to the required height. The balloon cables form a "death trap" to any enemy aeroplane colliding with them. The balloons are organized in flights and squadrons, the squadrons being on an auxiliary basis manned by volunteers with a small nucleus of fully trained regular personnel. (No. 46)

A·R·P

ANTI-AIRCRAFT SOUND LOCATOR. One sound locator is an essential part of the equipment of an Anti-Aircraft Searchlight Detachment and is used for directing the searchlight beam on to a target which can only be heard. It is manned by a crew of 3. Two of these are listening numbers, one uses the pair of trumpets which gives the horizontal direction of the target, the other uses the pair which gives the vertical direction. The third member of the crew uses the sight which makes an allowance for the speed of the target; this member telephones instructions to the searchlight controller, who then moves the searchlight beam so that the target is illuminated. Large numbers of these sound locators are used in the Air Defence of Great Britain. (No. 48)

starting work each day at the college. After only an hour and 40 minutes off the ground he gained a prized Royal Aero Club Certificate and became a fully accredited aviator.

The Royal Flying Corps was the natural next step for an officer with Dowding's abilities, and soon he was in France and in action. Characteristically, he was shortly involved with the technical aspects of military aviation as a flight commander in what was then known as "the wireless squadron". Radio was still a novelty as far as air-to-ground communication was concerned, but its applications fascinated Dowding. Prophetically, in view of its later involvement with advanced early warning and communications equipment, Dowding and technology were further wedded when, subsequent to promotion to captain, he was given command of the RFC's new wireless school at Brooklands. When the armistice was signed in 1918 Dowding was a brigadier-general. Peace severely restricted the fledgeling RAF's development and Dowding continued in his distinguished but somewhat unspectacular career.

By 1930 he was in command of "Fighting Area" of Air Defence of Great Britain (ADGB). For the next ten years he was to have an intimate involvement with the nation's defences and would ultimately become the chief architect of a system which survives to this day, but his first priority at ADGB was to improve the organisation's communications. From January 1930 onwards Dowding concentrated on ensuring sufficient land-lines and exchanges were available to relay operational orders from headquarters to the squadrons under wartime conditions. His previous experience with radio was put to good use as new equipment was at last reaching the RAF to improve its ability in ground-to-air communication.

In September 1930 Dowding was posted to the Air Ministry and appointed to the Air Council as Member for Supply and Research. His first priority was to ensure that metal replaced wood as the principal material in aircraft production. With his encouragement the Hurricane and Spitfire fighters were ultimately developed and aircraft armament was increased from a mere two machine-guns to eight. He also initiated the RAF's fruitful involvement with radio direction finding (RDF), later to be called radar.

Air Chief Marshal Sir Hugh Caswell Tremenheere Dowding (later Lord Dowding of Bentley Priory), unsung architect and quiet mastermind of the RAF's remarkable victory in 1940.

A vegetarian, non-drinking bird-watcher and amateur spirtualist, Dowding was very different from the typical RAF officer. His rather solitary and austere lifestyle gave rise to the nickname "Stuffy", a term affectionately used by all who knew him or served under his command. Those who did not know him well considered his rather brusque manner and indifference to socialising a pretention towards aloofness and a desire to set himself apart from his fellow men. In fact Dowding was sensitive to such criticism but more determined to achieve the difficult targets he had set himself if he was to fulfil his responsibilities.

When Fighter Command was created in 1936 Dowding was appointed its first commander-in-chief. Having been involved in every aspect of the development of Britain's new air defence network, he was in the fortunate position of deciding how best it should be used. Under his guidance the command was forged into a tempered instrument of war, and there was not a detail in which Dowding did not personally involve or interest himself.

When concrete was not forthcoming to provide all-weather runways for his squadrons Dowding personally investigated the most suitable grass seed to sow on his airfields. Later, as it became obvious that his fighter aircraft would need increased protection from the effects of multi-gunned enemy aircraft, he pushed for the application of armoured glass windscreens for Hurricanes and Spitfires. His argument to the Air Ministry has become famous: "If Chicago gangster can have bullet-proof glass in their cars I can't see any reason why my pilots should not have the same." Frequently he got his own way but, as so often, not before a fight. Sadly, Dowding's career was characterised by a mutual misunderstanding with Whitehall.

Not all his remonstrations to the Air Ministry were successful, however. He immediately realised the inadequacy of the Boulton Paul Defiant and pointed out the senselessness of building a fighter that had no forward armament and weighed nearly half a ton more than the similarly powered Hurricane. Dowding was not consulted about the decision to proceed with the Defiant production and none of his arguments could prevent its implementation into squadron service. He thought the aircraft was fit only for training purposes and proposed such use "where they will do least harm".

Dowding's responsibilities at Fighter Command extended far beyond the control of interceptor aircraft; the Observer Corps, Balloon Command and Anti-Aircraft Command all came under his operational control. In July 1939 General Frederick Pile became Commander-in-Chief of Anti-Aircraft Command and moved into a small house in the grounds of Fighter Command's headquarters at Bentley Priory in Stanmore, Middlesex.

Pile came to know Dowding well, meeting with him virtually every day. He considered Dowding "the outstanding airman I met in the war . . . a man who knew more than anybody about all aspects of aerial warfare." Pile witnessed Dowding's daily requests to Beaverbrook for increased aircraft production, urging the business magnate-cum-national quartermaster with the words "what

DESIGNS FOR WAR

we want is more revs". Pile recalled that Dowding spoke only after careful consideration and had a habit of pacing his office and issuing instructions or advice as if delivering a lecture. A self-opinionated man, Dowding even managed to lecture the Queen for over half an hour without pause at a lunch during the royal visit to Bentley Priory during the Battle of Britain.

Whatever his faults Dowding's capabilities far outweighed them. He was one of the greatest commanders of the Second World War and one of the few immediately to grasp the vast potential of new inventions and techniques.

Of all the developments introduced during Dowding's tenure at Fighter Command, by far the most innovative and ultimately decisive was Radio Direction Finding, better known later as radar. Its origins can be found among the scores of dissertations resulting from prewar research into the new fields of radio energy and electro-magnetism.

Most people were familiar with X-rays and ultra-violet light as used in hospitals, and many had read about medical research into the use of short-wave radiation to raise the body temperatures of patients with muscular disorders. Scientists had even developed a method of pest control which used radio energy literally to shake parasitic insects to pieces. However, no means had been found to amplify the low-power output of existing devices and all equipment in use relied on close contact with a subject that was exposed to radio emissions of very long duration. The facts notwithstanding, there appeared also a growing curiosity into the possibility of a death-ray which could be used to destroy infantry, tanks or even aircraft at the flick of a switch or touch of a button.

The fascination with death-rays was somewhat contagious – even the government was drawn towards investigating the phenomenon. Though eschewing the more fantastic predictions of the popular press the Air Ministry was mildly concerned that if experiments made by professors had succeeded in stopping car engines then perhaps RAF fighter aircraft might suffer magneto malfunctions and their pilots be subjected to nausea if exposed to such theoretically implausible weapons.

With this in mind the Air Ministry's Defence Committee instructed its Director of Scientific Research, Dr Harry Wimperis, to

investigate the possibility of death-rays. Late in 1934 Wimperis wrote to Robert Watson-Watt, the Superintendent of the Radio Research Station at Slough, an outstation of the National Physical Laboratory, and asked his opinion on the likelihood of "destruction by radio".

Watson-Watt then requested one of his scientists, Arnold Wilkins, to investigate. As a yardstick he was to calculate how much radio energy would be needed to raise a man's blood to fever heat within a specified distance. Wilkins considered that as the power requirements were well beyond the capabilities of contemporary physics, destruction by radio was out of the question. Keen to help the Air Ministry, Watson-Watt asked Wilkins if there was indeed any potential in the RAF utilising radio for defensive measures, and Wilkins recalled a report from the Post Office which detailed interference to an experimental VHF radio signal caused when an aircraft crossed the path of the transmission.

Having completed further calculations based around a 50-metre wavelength, a beam width then able to be successfully transmitted by high-power equipment, Wilkins was now confident that aircraft could be detected by the signal they re-radiated from their metal structures. Indeed the return from an aircraft with a wingspan corresponding to the average bomber's size was calculated to be much stronger than expected. Wilkins suggested using a Heyford bomber as a suitable target as its wings would act as a 75-foot half-dipole aerial for a 50-metre signal, and although fabric covered its metal skeleton it would prove an effective radio reflector.

To ensure it discharged its responsibilities to the Air Defence of Great Britain (ADGB) as effectively as possible, the RAF held many peacetime exercises to train its pilots in rapid-response techniques. Here pilots of No. 111 Squadron scramble from their crew-room at Northolt in 1938.

A NATION ALONE

Once Wilkins had assimilated his figures and Watson-Watt had checked them they were submitted to the Air Ministry on February 12, 1935 in a document entitled "Detection and Location of Aircraft by Radio Methods". The findings impressed the Air Ministry and especially its Air Member for Research and Development, then a certain Air Vice-Marshal Dowding. Within just a few days an experiment was planned.

On the cold, damp morning of February 26, 1935 one of the RAF's ageing Heyford biplane bombers took off from Farnbrough to fly a carefully plotted course which would take it between the BBC's powerful short-wave transmitter at Daventry and a mobile laboratory mounted in the back of a Morris van in a field not far away at Weedon. The van was crammed full of cumbersome but for then highly advanced equipment. Wilkins and his assistant were squeezed in among an assortment of "black boxes" that included a large receiver and a very early example of a cathode-ray oscilloscope. The Daventry transmitter was chosen because its 49-metre wavelength was roughly twice the wingspan of the Heyford then en route to its rendezvous. Watching the experiment was an anxious Watson-Watt and A. P. Rowe, an observer from the Air Ministry.

There was no need for any nervousness, since Wilkins had been correct with his predictions. As the Heyford bomber passed between the transmitter and the receiver there was a rapid oscillation of the "blip" on the cathode-ray screen. The oscillation was due to the phase difference between the time the direct signal from Daventry took to reach the receiver and the time the re-radiated one took to reach it after being bounced off the Heyford. As the relative position of the aircraft changed during its flight a rough approximation of its distance from the receiver could be gauged by studying the variations in oscillation visible on the screen.

The experiment was a resounding success, showing that radio detection was not only possible but practical. Perhaps the bomber would not always get through – radio's invisible eye could spot it long before it reached its target. Watson-Watt was pleased: it is claimed he turned to Rowe and said, "Britain is once more an island."

Although the Heyford had been detected at a range of no more than eight miles Watson-Watt was confident that with available technology it would be possible to detect aircraft at distances of over 100 miles. The immediate implications of such a revelation were obvious: enemy aircraft could be detected as they crossed the Channel and at least 30 minutes' warning of an impending attack could be gained by studying the returns of transmitted signals.

The Air Ministry immediately allocated £10,000 to support further research. The term "Radio Direction Finding" (RDF) was used as it implied investigation into the familiar area of radio beacon navigation. An RDF team under the direction of Watson-Watt was established at Orfordness on the Suffolk coast at a site codenamed the new Ionospheric Research Station, and work continued at a furious pace. Within days transmitters and receivers were in place and very soon the "Islanders" (as they were dubbed by locals) had erected a 75-foot radio mast.

All the while progress was monitored by an Air Ministry committee under the chairmanship of a well-known physicist, Henry Tizard. Early on Watson-Watt recognised the need for two separate systems to detect both high-altitude and low-flying intruders. To provide the best results for long-distance detection 200-foot masts were proposed. These would form the basis for the distinctive Chain Home network that ringed Britain – though in operation they would in fact soar to an impressive 350 feet in height.

In July 1936 Churchill was appointed to the Imperial Defence Sub-Committee on Air Defence. Though a stern critic of Stanley Baldwin's handling of national defence issues, he promised not to reveal any details regarding the new RDF investigations. What he did do, however, was insist that Professor Lindemann should join Tizard's committee. Churchill greatly trusted his close friend's judgment on all scientific matters and would employ him as scientific adviser throughout the war.

Though an eminent man Lindemann frequently clashed with Tizard, for he was more interested in infra-red detection than in Watson-Watt's RDF. His other pet project was a parachute bomb which could be sown in the path of enemy bomber fleets, thereby fouling the aircraft's propellers. Tizard felt that anything which detracted from radar was an unnecessary extravagance, and due to Lindemann's influence he and another member of the committee resigned. It was only after the committee had been reinstated –

DESIGNS FOR WAR

ABOVE & LEFT Dowding's office at Bentley Priory, the forbidding architectural curiosity which served as Fighter Command's headquarters during the Battle of Britain, has been preserved very much as it was in 1940. Today the huge country house is still at the heart of Britain's air defences, situated within the modern RAF's No. 11 Group Command complex.

without Lindemann – that research could continue smoothly.

It should be noted that the man responsible for coaxing the rather temperamental scientists to work for the Air Ministry in the first place, and who was responsible for sorting out the early differences of opinions, was Lord Swinton, who had been appointed Secretary of State for Air in 1935. Without Swinton's guidance Britain may have followed a similar path to Germany and allow its military and scientific communities to pursue separate strands of research in isolation. For five years before the Battle of Britain the RAF was able to benefit from the advice of some of Britain's most brilliant scientists, a combination which proved crucial to the nation's survival.

Gradually the researchers at Orfordness were able to increase the range of their apparatus and on July 24, 1935 managed to identify a formation of three aircraft. Height and bearing calculations were proving difficult, however, and they would still prove the least satisfactory aspect of radar during the Battle of Britain.

Only seven months after the first experiments, aircraft at ranges of nearly 60 miles

were detected. Understandably impressed, the Committee of Imperial Defence immediately recommended the establishment of a chain of radar stations from the Tyne to the Solent. Soon the scientists moved to a more suitable site close to Orfordness at Bawdsey, which would become an operational station and an integral part of the radar network. Watson-Watt was in turn transferred to the Air Ministry's payroll.

When Dowding became C-in-C of Fighter Command in 1936 his job in research and development was taken by Sir Wilfred Freeman and radar continued to be given priority. In 1937 the RAF started working alongside the scientists at Bawdsey and a radar-training school was established.

Watson-Watt had found that women proved extremely adept at the difficult task of radar interpretation. Although initially sceptical, the Air Ministry relented and women operators were accepted onto the training programme. In 1940 WAAF operators were to discharge their duties with determination and courage, fully vindicating Watson-Watt's faith in them.

By May 1937 Bawdsey had become the first

A NATION ALONE

RIGHT When the Battle of Britain started there were 21 Chain Home (CH) stations presenting an invisible shield to the enemy. Chain Home had a range of 120 miles but could only "look" seaward and not inland. While the huge 350-foot transmitter masts might have presented ideal targets, their lattice construction was extremely good at dissipating the effects of blast.

BELOW At 50 miles, the range of the Chain Home Low (CHL) radar was much shorter than the larger CH equipment, but the 30 CHL stations were capable of detecting low-flying raiders trying to slip under the standard CH curtain.

fully operational Chain Home (CH) station. Work on the 19 others designed to complete the network continued at an accelerated pace as it became clear that Germany was rearming. Five overlapping stations were soon in operation – at Dover, Dunkirk (near Canterbury), Canewden (near Southend), Great Bromley (near Colchester) and Bawdsey. All the sites were near the coast and positioned on land sloping towards the sea. Topographical obstructions were avoided as these produced irritating permanent echoes.

The five-station network was put to the test during the air defence exercises of August 1938. Although the weather was poor the equipment worked well and detections were consistently achieved. However, low-flying aircraft were able to slip through the net and a more precise system was now sought as an alternative to the broad-beamed Chain Home method of detection.

The RDF team at Bawdsey produced a solution to the problem by adapting an experimental directional gun-laying radar array employed as a showpiece for visiting officials. The gun-laying radar consisted of a 1.5-metre aerial system which was fully rotatable and could thus be directed at an individual target. Intended for Admiralty service, the set had amazed visitors to Bawdsey by continuously tracking ships at sea with unfailing accuracy – the apparatus could accurately measure the range of vessels to within 20 yards.

The Air Ministry reasoned, correctly, that

DESIGNS FOR WAR

the 1.5-metre wavelength was what they required to solve the problems of detecting low-flying intruders. Soon Chain Home Low (CHL) aerials resembling modern radar scanners were paired with the existing Chain Home masts to plug the gaps in the system beneath the existing radar curtain. In simple terms the CH radars radiated a floodlight beam while the CHL equipment formed a searchlight able to pinpoint a target with much greater accuracy.

To prevent confusion from returns by friendly aircraft, IFF (Identification Friend or Foe) transmitters were fitted to RAF aircraft. These sets produced a characteristic blip on radar station oscilloscopes, enabling operators to distinguish between RAF and enemy aircraft. Both these devices, in the form of Radar and Transponder, continue to ensure the safety of air traffic today.

As the storm clouds gathered on the continent, Britain's radar chain was switched on early in 1939 to provide 24-hour coverage of the coastline. The system identified its first intruder in May 1939 when one after another radar stations along the east coast picked up the returns from an extremely large target. However, the unusually large blip on the cathode-ray tubes was caused not by a squadron of German bombers but by a solitary object of a kind which had once been a familiar if unwelcome visitor to British skies – the Zeppelin.

LZ130, the famous airship *Graf Zeppelin*, had slipped its moorings in Germany and set out on the world's first electronic eavesdropping mission. The curious lattice-work towers that had sprouted along the British coastline were the subject of its investigations and the airship carried no less a passenger than the head of the Luftwaffe Signals Branch, General Wolfgang Martini. German observers were intrigued by the tall radar masts but could only guess their true purpose. German scientists were busily developing short-wave radar and could not believe that Britain had built a workable network based on the longer wavelengths suggested by the towers.

As the Zeppelin drifted serenely up and down the coast, Luftwaffe operators on board were unable to pick up anything other than static on their receivers. No trace of any radar pulses could be found among the centrimetric wavelengths their equipment was designed to search. General Martini deduced that the British had not yet managed to implement a

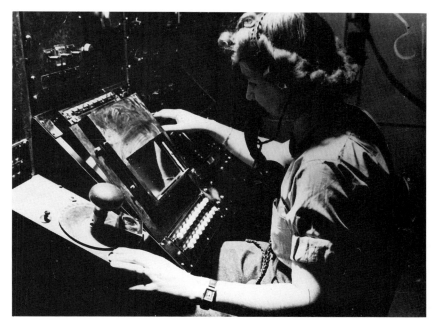

radar system of any kind since no indication of its presence had been detected on any of the sensitive electronic equipment that filled the airship's gondola.

If the Luftwaffe signals staff had been able to search wavelengths other than the UHF bands they then assumed were essential for practical radar, they would have realised that all along their every move had been observed by their RAF counterparts. A further foray by the Zeppelin again revealed no trace of radar pulses and the Luftwaffe analysts concluded that Britain possessed nothing worthy of consideration in this field. Perhaps the most critical strategic error the Luftwaffe ever made had occurred before a shot had been fired in anger.

As far as the public was concerned radar was an unknown quantity. Indeed in 1939 the government had discreetly asked the Radio Society of Great Britain not to publish letters in its *Bulletin* from "hams" who were curious about the strange pulse signals picked up on the 10-metre band of their receivers. In his *Modern Armaments*, published in 1939, Professor A. M. Low wrote: "Another suggested form of the death-ray is ultra-sound . . . The weapon would be all the more deadly in that it would be perfectly silent. But methods of producing high frequencies that will travel any reasonable distance have to be developed and the beam difficulty we find with wireless would arise. Moreover, unless the sound were restricted to a narrow path, it would affect the users as much or more than

Women's Auxiliary Air Force personnel (WAAFs) spent long hours crouched over the dimly flickering cathode-ray tubes in the RDF receiver huts, and they soon became expert at judging the value of a particular "blip" and gauging whether the approaching raid was, for example, 50-plus or 100-plus. By passing her information on to a "converter", a calculation was made which helped determine the height and bearing of the plot.

A NATION ALONE

Aircraft identification was a national pastime that assumed great importance once hostilities had started. Though countless books and identification aids were produced, some of which are illustrated here, accurate recognition of different aircraft types was a hit-and-miss affair that anti-aircraft gunners, Observer Corps personnel and even pilots found hard to master for most of 1940.

the enemy." For over four years prior to the publication of his book, British scientists had been successfully directing beams over great distances with effects that would have startled the venerable professor.

British writers were not alone in their ignorance of radar and its significant properties. Their German counterparts were none the wiser. In 1939 the Right Book Club hastily translated a work by the London correspondent of *Deutsche Allgemeine Zeitung*, Count Pückler, entitled "How Strong is Britain?". The book was a sweeping criticism of Britain and her chauvinistic attitude towards the rest of the world. The once-strong nation had become flaccid and out of touch with reality, argued Count Pückler. It could no longer rely on isolation for protection. Its author confidently pointed out that "the development of the modern air-arm has created a new and supplementary threat. The narrow arm of water which separates her from France is no barrier to an air fleet, whilst the wide stretch of sea surrounding her other coasts is on the whole more favourable to the raiders than to the defenders because it protects the raiders against premature discovery."

In fact the wide stretch of sea provided an ideally uncluttered horizon for the new radar transmitters to search, throwing into clear relief any raider that dared approach the British coast. Count Pückler cannot be blamed for not knowing this, though the enormous

radar masts could not of course be disguised and their appearance gave rise to much speculation about their purposes. The observers of Mass-Observation filed one report, dated June 6, 1940, that unwittingly revealed some typical anxieties about the function of Chain Home towers. In the small village of Shingle Street, close to the radar station at Bawdsey, rumour was rife that the wireless masts in the neighbourhood could be used for stopping enemy aeroplanes by rays. On April 29 a middle-aged woman exclaimed: "My mother doesn't like those masts. They're supposed to stop the Germans, but she's afraid they'll land here. There was a seaplane up a little while ago and it came down near here and the people inside were killed. My mother thinks they were testing and turned the rays on too strong. She says they died to make us safe. Of course we don't know really, but there was nothing about it in the papers, was there?"

A small boy, the son of a gamekeeper, was equally intrigued: "That's the secret station over there. It's full of spies round here, trying to get at it and blow it up. It stops the engines of aeroplanes, that's what it does. You wouldn't think wireless could do that, now would ye?"

DESIGNS FOR WAR

In fact the existence of RDF remained a closely guarded secret throughout most of the war. The official Air Ministry account of the Battle of Britain published in 1941 stated ". . . something must be said about or methods of defence, although it is not easy to do this without giving away State secrets". All it would reveal was that information regarding the approach of the enemy was obtained by a "variety of methods".

As the locals who lived close by the sinister looking radar stations speculated on the purposes of the 350-foot wooden masts that dwarfed surrounding villages and the tallest trees, the RAF began to learn to use its invisible eye to good effect. Most of the tactical research was carried out at Biggin Hill under the direction of Henry Tizard. Radar had eliminated the need for wasteful "standing patrols" and Tizard was confident that enough warning would be given to enable fighter pilots to wait on the ground in readiness until the order to scramble towards an interception was given.

An early problem was the time it took to calculate the correct point of interception using co-ordinates that were often "out of date" once they had been relayed to airborne pilots. Much academic thought was given to the matter, without success, and it was the Station Commander at Biggin Hill, Wing Commander E. O. Grenfell, who solved the problem by employing an educated guess based on an awareness of the flight characteristics of bombers and fighters.

His rough and ready judgment was refined by Tizard into the "Principle of Equal Angles", a simple calculation predicting the point at which interceptor and intruder would meet. The calculation became known as "the Tizzy Angle" and was an invaluable aid to controllers when, during the heat of battle, they were forced to make snap decisions as to the likely point of interception.

If the radar system was to work effectively pilots had to be confident that they could interpret the instructions relayed to them by controllers in operations rooms many miles distant, and the RAF thus employed ex-operational pilots as controllers to help reassure their airborne charges. Britain and its coastal waters became a giant chessboard across which the aircraft of Fighter Command were moved like gaming pieces by controllers who had a complete picture of the unfolding contest with its many feints, attacks and counter-attacks. The pilots in the air enjoyed no such overview and relied instead on accurate guidance from the ground – and their own ability to fly along a given co-ordinate.

To help its pilots grasp the complexities of the new system Fighter Command devised some ingenious training methods. Perhaps the most bizarre took place at RAF Uxbridge, where the station's sports field was given over to the requirements of interception practice. Aspiring fighter-pilots were seated on ice-cream vendors' tricycles; they wore headsets and their vision was obscured by an all-enveloping hood. A compass was mounted on the tricycle's handlebars alongside a three-speed gear which simulated the trottle quadrant of a fighter. One tricycle was assigned as the enemy, the other played the part of a Fighter Command interceptor. The object of the exercise was obvious: by following instructions received through his headset the "fighter" pilot had to manoeuvre his tricycle using compass bearings until a successful interception was achieved and both tricycles collided!

As a sergeant, Desmond Fopp underwent training at Uxbridge and recalled with a smile his many sorties astride the RAF's three-wheeled fighter! "You had a three-speed bike with 'normal cruise', 'buster' and 'gate' on the handlebars. If you were in gate you were travelling at full pedal and you were given a course to steer to intercept the other character. He would be trundling along minding his own business when he would suddenly get hit if you did things right!"

This somewhat surreal solution to the problem of successful interception was a success and pilots left Uxbridge having learnt the new radio procedures that were employed and with an improved ability to fly by instruments, not instinct. But although they were told that the position of enemy aircraft was to be passed to them by a variety of means – and many pilots made educated guesses about the purpose of the conspicuous radar masts – they were not told exactly how the system worked.

By early 1940 the radar network provided complete coverage in all the directions from which it was thought the Luftwaffe was likely to attack. Once it became obvious that France would fall, plans to extend the network further were accelerated to close the gaps through which enemy aircraft operating from airfields along the Channel coast could pass. If the

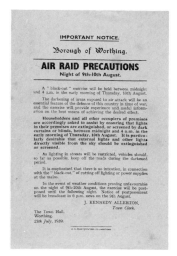

Local authorities co-operated with the military to ensure that effective black-out contingencies would work well should war break out, and the Munich crisis of 1938 no doubt served as a suitable catalyst for immediate civil defence improvements. This leaflet was distributed around Worthing, in West Sussex.

A booklet governing the establishment of Observer Corps posts, published in 1938.

A typical Chain Home (CH) receiver room; the console is on the right and the receiver is on the left. Raids were termed "Hostiles" and given a number – for example "Hostile 25". RAF fighters were identified as "Friendlies" as they carried "Identification Friend or Foe" (IFF) transmitters which automatically revealed their position to the defences.

Sandbagged revetments were common sites for isolated Observer Corps posts in 1940. The man with the earphones and chest microphone would relay any relevant information on to Fighter Command. The cap badge bears the motto "Forewarned is forearmed" and includes an emblem of an Elizabethan lookout from the days of the Armada. The Corps certainly did their duty during the Battle of Britain, and richly deserved the "Royal" prefix added to their name the following year.

radar masts and aerials were the eyes and senses of the new defence system, the brain and nervous system which received the information from radar and processed it into operational orders for the waiting fighter squadrons was equally impressive.

The 120-mile range of the Chain Home system was sufficient to detect the build-up of enemy bomber and fighter formations as they circled and formed up on each other at pre-arranged assembly points above their captured French aerodromes. As the cathode-ray tubes linked to the radar aerials and receivers flickered into life, WAAF and RAF operators sat crouched over the dim green oscilloscope

screens in the "receiver huts" at the base of the tall masts, scrutinising the increasingly active displays for information regarding the strength, altitude and direction of the forthcoming attack.

An ingenious electrical calculator dubbed "the fruit machine" was employed to convert the height, position and bearing of each plot into a series of co-ordinates which could be readily transferred onto the standardised grid of Fighter Command's plotting tables. Once information had been assessed and converted the radar operators used secure land-lines to telephone their information direct to the Filter Room at Fighter Command headquarters in Stanmore.

The Filter Room was a clearing house for all incoming radar plots from both the CH and CHL networks. There WAAF plotters used battery-powered electro-magnetic croupiers' rakes to push coloured markers indicating radar plots onto a gridded map of the British Isles and its environs.

Each plot was classified friendly, hostile or doubtful and was given a number and a time identification based on updates at five-minute intervals denoted by colours which matched divisions on the Filter Room clock. A filter officer checked the accuracy of each plot and removed any duplicated or extraneous information from the plotting table.

Immediately next door to the Filter Room in Stanmore's underground complex was the Fighter Command Operations Room. Verified plots that had been filtered and classified

DESIGNS FOR WAR

were passed to the Operation Room staff and positioned onto a main map table spread out below a viewing balcony which housed the controller, his staff and representatives from Anti-Aircraft Command, Balloon Command and the various civil defence organisations.

From the balcony the controller enjoyed a grandstand view of the unfolding air activity and was able to make considered judgments concerning the necessary steps required to deal with a particular situation. For example, instructions could be relayed to Air-Raid Precautions officials to enable them to sound the air-raid sirens in time to give the public a chance to take cover. Equally, decisions were taken about shutting down BBC transmitters if it appeared that Luftwaffe pilots were using them as homing beacons.

Essentially the Command Operations Room was the forum for the strategic control of the UK air defences, the place were Dowding learnt to interpret the intentions of his German adversaries and take the steps necessary to prevent them from achieving their goals. The key to the system was its ability to provide a continuously updated picture of events which allowed the strategists at Stanmore to devolve direct responsibility for the application of the fighter resources to a second tier of command involved in the "battle zone".

Those fighter groups were flexible divisions of the total command structure with administrative control over a number of sector and satellite airfields. By mid-July in 1940 Britain was divided into four fighter groups comprising a total of 20 sector stations: No. 10 Group, Headquarters at Box, near Bristol, responsible for the air defence of the South-West; No. 11 (Uxbridge) for the South-East and London; No. 12 (Watnall near Nottingham) for the Midlands and East Anglia; and No. 13 (Newcastle) for northern England, Scotland and Northern Ireland.

Each of the fighter group headquarters had operations rooms almost identical in pattern to the central one at Stanmore. At the group operations rooms information received from the Command Filter Room was added to the map tables, which differed from Stanmore's version only in that they covered the group area and its surroundings and not the country as a whole.

Group operations rooms were constantly manned by one or more duty controllers who studied the indications of approaching enemy

aircraft and considered the best means of achieving an effective interception. A "tote board" was mounted on the wall opposite the controller's gantry showing, at a glance, the location and state of readiness of all squadrons within the group. Electric lights signalled whether a squadron was "at standby", "at readiness", "detailed to raid" or "ordered to land".

The groups were divided into a number of sectors, each with a principal airfield or sector station which also possessed an operations room. Forward or satellite airfields were controlled by individual sector stations. Group controllers gave orders directly to sector stations and liaised with adjoining gun operations rooms to ensure that barrages did not fall on friendly aircraft.

Sector operations rooms relayed the orders from group headquarters by land-lines and loudspeaker systems directly to the dispersal points where pilots on duty awaited the order to "scramble". A radio-telephone (R/T) transmitter was linked into the sector command network to allow controllers to talk directly to pilots and thereby provide them with the necessary target co-ordinates deduced from careful interpretation of the map tables. To prevent the R/T transmitters from revealing the location of sector operations rooms they were usually situated some distance away from the control centre.

From Fighter Command headquarters, through group and finally sector commands to the pilots in the Hurricanes and Spitfires, a complete overview of developments was

The Operations Room – or "the Hole" as it was better known – at Fighter Command's HQ at Bentley Priory. The controller and his staff and members of Anti-Aircraft Command look on as WAAF plotters push and pull croupiers' rakes across the huge map table. Information was received from an adjacent Filter Room and from the various Observer Corps representatives attached to each fighter group.

available allowing the slender resources of the RAF to be husbanded in a way that would have been impossible before the timely advent of RDF.

Once airborne, pilots were told exactly where to go by means of compass bearings or vectors. A system of codewords was used to enable clear instructions to be heard above the crackling static of flying helmet earphones. Messages, when transmitted, were directed to the squadron leader. "Angels" denoted height in thousands of feet, "Bandits" meant hostile aircraft and "Tally-ho" signalled the fact that a squadron was about to commence an attack; "Buster" meant full-throttle, a "Bogey" was an unidentified aircraft and "Pancake" warned the airfield ground-crews and services to expect an emergency landing.

Although the IFF transmitters carried by fighter aircraft were capable of identifying them as friendly, and clearly distinguished the Hurricanes and Spitfires from enemy aircraft on radar screens, they did not provide an accurate fix of their positions. For controllers to establish accurately the location of RAF fighters a separate direction finding (DF) system had to be incorporated into the air defence network.

In association with the Marconi organisation, the RAF Signals Branch had successfully experimented with high-frequency direction finders in the early 1930s. The result of these efforts – the Chandler Adcock Short-Wave Direction Finder – worked well when fitted to Bristol Bulldog and Hawker Hart fighters and the decision was taken to refine the equipment for future inclusion into the new breed of fighters being planned.

By 1940 high-frequency direction finding (HF/DF, or "Huff Duff" as it was more generally known) was a firmly established part of the RAF's detection and interception organisation. A device known as "Pipsqueak" was fitted to fighters and its intermittent transmissions were used to gain an accurate bearing on the aircraft's position. Although new VHF radio sets (designated TR 1143) were hastily being installed into fighter aircraft immediately before the Battle of Britain, it was not until September 1940 that a substantial section of Fighter Command's aircraft had been converted. During most of the Battle the old high-frequency (HF) sets had to suffice.

The "Pipsqueak" device was linked to both HF and VHF sets and automatically transmitted its signal for 14 seconds in every minute. Should pilots wish to use their radio telephones within such a period a manual override was fitted to enable them to speak through the microphones of their canvas facemasks. Each sector within Fighter Command possessed three direction-finding stations which received the individual Pipsqueak transmissions and converted them into map references, figures that could then be passed to the sector operations room and added to the information already established on the plotting tables. Not surprisingly this system, in common with RAF procedure, was awarded its own codename – "Cockerel". If a pilot had inadvertently left his radio-telephone on manual override and thus unwittingly turned off Pipsqueak, his controller would remind him to put matters right by enquiring: "Is your cockerel crowing?"

RDF was a crucial factor in the defence of Britain. Its ability to deliver early warning of impending attack reversed the perilous situation in which the nation found itself during the early 1930s. Yet its usefulness was limited by its inability to provide inland as well as seaward coverage. In 1940 the problems associated with ground returns and the clutter caused by natural obstacles had not been ironed out, and the all-seeing eye of radar could look in one direction only – to the front. Once aircraft had passed directly overhead of the installation they escaped its penetrating stare. As they disappeared from view on the receiver-hut oscilloscope screens, enemy formations had to be tracked by more conventional methods. Fortunately a very well-established organisation existed which was able to fill in.

The Observer Corps was an organisation of trained volunteers who spent a great deal of their time looking skywards in search of enemy aircraft that had crossed Britain's coastal perimeter. The origins of the Corps can be traced to Major-General Ashmore's control and reporting network incorporated within the London Air Defence Area (LADA) of 1917, when the threat from German Gotha and Staaken bombers was partly countered by improved air defences built around a co-ordinated information processing system.

As the politicians gradually reappraised Britain's air defences in the early 1920s the files containing Ashmore's strategy were dusted off and thought was given to reimplementing a method of visual identifi-

DESIGNS FOR WAR

With RDF ("Radio Direction Finding", later "Radar") on the secret list the public were led to believe that air defence still relied on traditional methods of detection and interception. This cover was from *Modern Wonder* in July 1939.

cation of airborne raiders. Ashmore was invited to resume his investigations into aircraft observation and plotting, and during 1924 the first of a series of proving exercises were held in Kent.

The RAF supplied a Sopwith Snipe for the trials and Ashmore's observers, special constables, had no difficulty in identifying the aircraft and plotting its course. The results were so successful that two groups of observers were established – one with its headquarters in Maidstone, the other in Horsham – the object being to provide coverage of the vulnerable airspace over Kent and Sussex.

On October 29, 1925 the network was officially recognised as the Observer Corps (though it did not receive the "Royal" prefix until 1941). In 1929 the RAF took over control of the growing organisation and a command centre was created. By 1940 the Observer Corps had swollen to more than 30 group reporting centres, each linked to a handful of the 1,000 observer posts. Each post comprised up to 20 operatives who took turns in either observing, calculating or reporting identified plots. An ingenious instrument called the "Micklethwait Height Correction Attachment" was fitted to a circular plotting table which covered an area of some ten miles radially from the post. Either by remembering recognition doggerels or by consulting a variety of identification booklets and charts, observers would pass on information concerning the identity of a particular aircraft type and the height and direction information calculated via the plotting instrument to group reporting centres. It was essential that information thus established quickly reached the necessary authorities, and to this end the GPO network linked the isolated observer posts directly to their command centres. Camouflaged observer posts could often be identified by the sudden termination of a series of telegraph poles in the middle of an apparently deserted field.

Each Observer Corps group reporting centre was in touch with its local RAF sector station, which processed the information received and added it to the data already displayed on the "ops room" plotting table. Sector information was relayed to the relevant Fighter Command Group HQ, where it was collated and passed on to Dowding's Command Centre at Stanmore via the Observer Corps liaison officer on the staff of Air Commodore Warrington-Morris, the Corps Commander.

Information gleaned from radar and the Observer Corps was supplemented by intelligence gathered from a variety of different sources. On November 5, 1939, for example, an anonymous courier deposited a mysterious parcel at the British consulate in Oslo. Its contents were a revelation. On page after page of neatly typed manuscript secret details of a variety of German research programmes were revealed. As a means of authenticating the text the deliverer of the windfall had included an example of a new German proximity fuse intended for use by Hitler's flak regiments.

The Oslo Report, as it was subsequently

Anti-aircraft defences had been badly neglected during the interwar years. Most "ack-ack" guns like this one were barely capable of hurling shells high enough to reach the enemy's operating altitude and rarely scored direct hits. They were, however, an important morale-booster, helping to encourage the feeling that Britain was hitting back at the hated raiders.

DESIGNS FOR WAR

Barrage balloons were flown high above vulnerable targets from small, mobile winch lorries. Their benign appearance belied their danger to low-flying bombers, and they succeeded in pushing enemy aircraft to greater heights, so disrupting their aim.

called, included details of a new Luftwaffe high-speed dive-bomber, the Junkers Ju-88, and outlined the development of German radar and radio navigation aids. As a catalyst for increasing the scrutiny of German technical and military developments the report was without equal, revealing how a raid by Wellington bombers on the port facilities at Wilhelmshaven in the early days of the war had been tracked and intercepted by radar guidance. Clearly the Luftwaffe possessed the means for waging war on a grand scale against Britain and every effort had to be made to gain as much information about its intentions as possible.

This was a special case, of course. Principal among the RAF's intelligence operations was its series of wireless listening posts known as the "Y-Service", which had been established by the Air Ministry Intelligence branch during the 1930s. The original station was at Cheadle in Cheshire and was responsible for intercepting medium- and high-frequency radio traffic from German bomber, training, transport and reconnaissance aircraft. Other stations were established at Fairlight in Sussex and Hawkinge in Kent and concentrated on intercepting radio-telephone transmissions from German aircraft.

The main radio-telephone interception centre was soon moved to Kingsdown in Kent since Hawkinge, being an operational RAF station, was vulnerable to attack. All the listening posts were staffed by a dedicated team of WAAF operators, each of them fluent in German. Their interception of Luftwaffe plain-language transmissions often yielded significant information about the Luftwaffe's order of battle.

The Luftwaffe operated their medium-frequency safety service for the take-off, approach and landing of its aircraft, and once picked up by the Y-Service these transmissions helped to build up a fairly accurate picture of increasing enemy air activity. Before the start of operations Luftwaffe wireless operators would often engage in dummy radio exchanges in order to calibrate their sets to the high frequencies used in combat. The code used during such exercises had been broken by British crypto-analysts and the transmissions were a further indication that operations were about to start. However the daily unit call-signs were not cracked until the Battle of Britain was well under way, and so confirmation of exactly which unit was about to take-off was not available early on in the conflict.

This Air Diagram illustrates the colour schemes applied to the newly acquired Bristol Blenheim in 1936. The aircraft provided a useful workhorse for the RAF until the advent of more powerful fighter-bombers like the Beaufighter and the Mosquito, and was the first plane to be equipped with airborne radar.

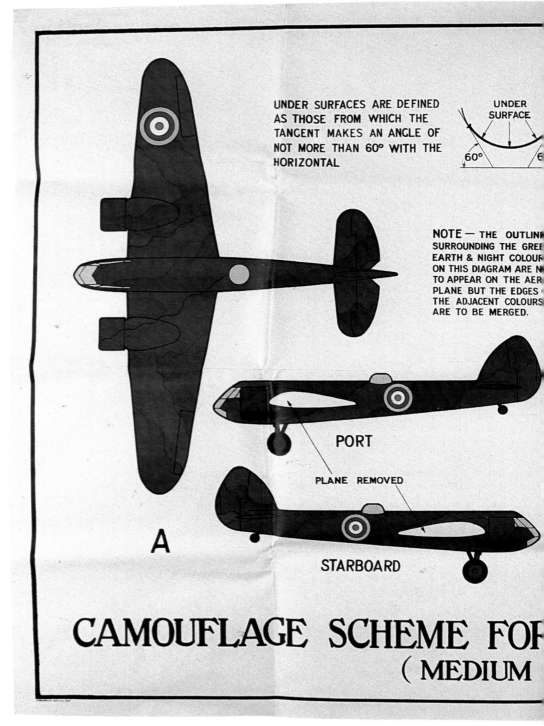

UNDER SURFACES ARE DEFINED AS THOSE FROM WHICH THE TANGENT MAKES AN ANGLE OF NOT MORE THAN 60° WITH THE HORIZONTAL

UNDER SURFACE

60°

NOTE — THE OUTLINE SURROUNDING THE GREE EARTH & NIGHT COLOUR ON THIS DIAGRAM ARE N TO APPEAR ON THE AER PLANE BUT THE EDGES THE ADJACENT COLOURS ARE TO BE MERGED.

PORT

PLANE REMOVED

A

STARBOARD

CAMOUFLAGE SCHEME FOR (MEDIUM

A further RAF radio interception station was established at Chicksands and was responsible for gathering information from the most secret source available – Ultra. This was the code-name given to top-secret intelligence gathered from decoding the German's Enigma enciphering machine. Ironically the Enigma apparatus had been available on the commercial market for years, but it was the German Intelligence Service which converted the device, resembling a compact typewriter, into an apparently unbreakable encoding machine. Fortunately for British intelligence an example of the German Enigma had been smuggled into Britain by the gallant efforts of the Polish Secret Service, and soon a team of crypto-analysts at Bletchley Park in Buckinghamshire

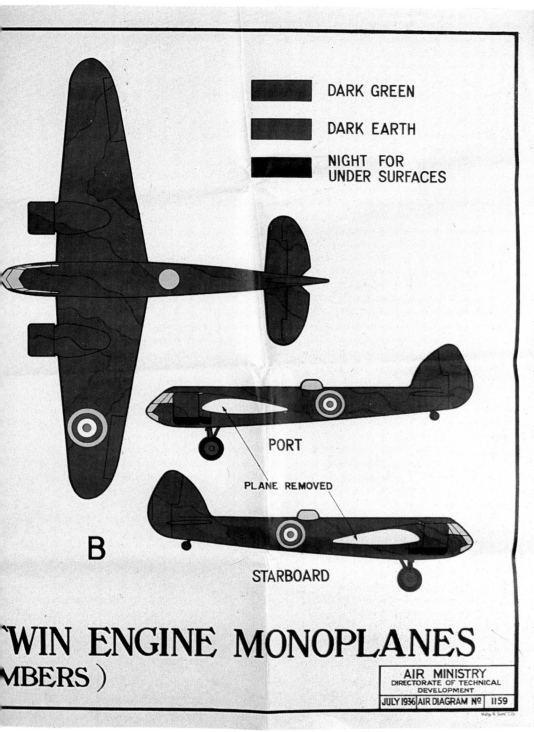

DARK GREEN

DARK EARTH

NIGHT FOR
UNDER SURFACES

PORT

PLANE REMOVED

STARBOARD

B

TWIN ENGINE MONOPLANES
MBERS)

| AIR MINISTRY |
| DIRECTORATE OF TECHNICAL DEVELOPMENT |
| JULY 1936 | AIR DIAGRAM Nº | 1159 |

were engaged in constructing primitive computers or "bombs" which could decipher the German codes or keys.

British intelligence cracked the Luftwaffe's Enigma keys – blue for practice use and red for operational and administrative purposes – between January and March 1940. It was a colossal breakthrough but Ultra intelligence, though valuable, was not as useful to Dowding as it was to other British commanders later in the war. The main reason was that after the fall of France the Enigma transmissions by Luftwaffe units began to dry up as high command directives were transferred to secure land-lines which had hastily been installed once captured airfields had been repaired and occupied by the victorious Fliegerkorps.

A NATION ALONE

The Heinkel 111 was the staple bomber of the Luftwaffe's 1940 air-fleets. Here a machine is rolled out of its hangar for inspection prior to take-off.

On June 23, however, Enigma suggested that some Luftwaffe units were resting and refitting in preparation for activity over England from northern France and the Low Countries. This information was confirmed by the high-flying Spitfires of the Photographic Reconnaissance Unit (PRU) which returned from sorties over France with photographs of new runway extensions. On June 25 Enigma was again activated, and this time the "bombs" decoded information which revealed that Stuka dive-bombers were assembling at airfields in the same area.

At the end of June Enigma "decrypts" showed that Hitler had cancelled his victory celebrations in Paris, further indicating that something big was about to occur from which German forces could not be diverted. The PRU Spitfires returned with photographs of huge railway guns which had been moved to emplacements directly across the Channel coast from Dover. On July 4 the Combined Intelligence Committee informed the War Cabinet that the Luftwaffe should have completed refitting by mid-July and that invasion could be expected immediately after that date.

However, no signs of landing-craft nor invasion shipping had yet been detected in the German-occupied Channel ports. Once Germany began assembling a suitable invasion fleet the PRU Spitfires could supply further vital information regarding the likely direction of attack. On July 24 pictures of the Bordeaux area indicated no significant change in the use of French ports and harbours, thereby almost ruling out the possibility of an invasion of the south-west coast of England. It was not until the end of October, though, that Spitfires capable of flying the longer return journey to Scandinavia also ruled out an attack from German bases in Norway.

In June 1940 the Air Staff had been told that the Luftwaffe was at a front-line strength of 5,000 aircraft, 2,500 of which were bombers, and had in the region of 7,000 reserves. It was calculated that this formidable armoury could deliver 4,800 tons of bombs a day over England. The actual strength of the Luftwaffe was about 2,000 aircraft, of which between 1,500 and 1,700 were bombers. Thanks to Enigma intercepts and the refusal of Churchill's scientific adviser Lindemann to believe the inflated figure the estimate was corrected to 1,250 bombers.

It was this realistic estimate, confirmed by the intelligence sources, which gave Dowding a much more precise picture of the Luftwaffe's strength and encouraged his belief that it could best be defeated by gradually wearing it down.

Probably the biggest intelligence coup of the period occurred after a solitary Heinkel 111 of Kampfgeschwader (Bomber Group) 26 had been shot down during a nocturnal foray over England in March 1940. Inside the twisted wreckage RAF technical intelligence officers salvaged a scrap of paper which included a reference to a navigational aid known as "Knickebein". Another crashed bomber and interrogation of captured aircrew revealed that Knickebein, or "crooked leg", was a method of target marking which used intersecting radio beams to pinpoint a specific objective. Intelligence sources had already established that the Luftwaffe possessed a navigational system known as X-Gerät; was this and Knickebein one and the same thing?

Enigma once more provided the answers. On June 5 a message was intercepted which after analysis revealed the location of one of Knickebein's elusive transmitters. After much detective work by Professor R. V. Jones of Air Scientific Intelligence and Group Captain Blandy of the RAF "Y" Service, the technical aspects of Knickebein were worked out and its frequencies discovered.

It was soon realised that Knickebein was an advanced modification of the prewar Lorenze Instrument Landing System (ILS); and for Knickebein to work, two transmitters were needed in order to provide a signal intersection which marked the point at which bombs were to be released. Scrutiny of documents taken from Luftwaffe aircraft before Dunkirk identified the second transmitter and indicated that Knickebein was ready for operational use.

DESIGNS FOR WAR

The system would provide amazing accuracy at night as pilots merely had to fly along an equi-signal which they could hear in their earphones, and should they veer off course a series of dots or dashes indicated that they were flying to the left or right of the true course. Once a pilot detected the equi-signal of the second beam he knew it was time to release his bomb load. If Knickebein could not be jammed its accuracy would mean that a single raid could destroy any of the vital production centres desperately needed to supply Britain's war machine.

The race to discover a solution to the Knickebein threat received direct encouragement from Churchill himself. Soon an RAF Avro Anson had detected the elusive beam and found that it passed directly over the Rolls-Royce aero-engine factory at Derby, then engaged in turning out the Merlin engines for Fighter Command's Spitfires and Hurricanes. An RAF Radio Counter-Measures unit officially known as 80 Wing but code-named "Headache" was quickly estab-lished and, using medical diathermy sets concealed in country police stations, proceeded to try to jam the German signals. Eventually more powerful jammers known as "Aspirins" were used and VHF receivers sited at several radar stations were employed to track the frequencies used by the Luftwaffe signals organisation.

The Luftwaffe had been extremely careless in testing out its Knickebein over enemy territory and for keeping the signals switched on for such long periods. Had they kept it a secret until they unleashed their massive "Eagle Attack" during the Battle of Britain no counter-measures could have been employed quickly enough and the system's accuracy would have resulted in the destruction of strategic targets such as factories, shipyards and airfields.

As it was the RAF was able to confuse the German bomber crews into misinterpreting Knickebein's signals and little precision bombing was achieved. Furthermore a myth gained currency among Luftwaffe crews

The streamlined birdcage nose of the Heinkel 111 provided plenty of all-round visibility for the aircraft's crew – but did little to dispel the feelings of vulnerability once an RAF fighter was glimpsed through the flimsy Perspex glazing. At this stage of the war the commander in most German bomber crews was not the pilot but the bomb-aimer, observer and nose-gunner who operated at the front of the aircraft.

Fighter-pilots epitomised the spirit of the age, with chivalry and modernism combined. It was therefore fitting that manufacturers reflected the positive attributes of the airman in their products – here "Squadron Leader Tobacco", circa 1940.

which was based on an imaginary fear that British night-fighters were riding the beams and understandably morale was much affected. Although jamming did not prevent mass bombing raids and the beams were never bent towards dummy targets, as has often been suggested, the RAF's early discovery of Knickebein was a significant victory which added to the Luftwaffe crews' strong feelings of uncertainty while operating over Britain.

Later X-Gerät was found to be an improved method of Knickebein which allowed for the automatic release of bomb-loads once an aircraft was directly over its target. This in turn was subjected to radio counter-measures and jammed by a new transmitter known as "Bromide". Sadly the effectiveness of X-Gerät's sophisticated technology was clearly demonstrated on the night of November 14, when Coventry received a massive raid before accurate jamming had been achieved.

To further confuse Luftwaffe bomb-aimers and navigators a more passive form of deception was practised. Dummy airfields and factories were constructed adjacent to real ones in an attempt to lure the Germans away from vulnerable targets. The fake airfields were known as "K-sites" and were often constructed by technicians seconded from the various film studios in South-East England. Their skill and experience was put to good use and resulted in convincing imitations of fighter and bomber aircraft tied to the ground outside canvas hangars and dispersal huts.

At night dummy flarepaths, "Q-sites", were illuminated to simulate airfield runways. Airmen were sometimes employed to ride bicycles sporting landing-lights up and down to mimic the landing and taxiing of operational aircraft. During bombing raids huge fires known as Starfish were lit to further encourage enemy airmen to deviate from their original course.

General Pile, the Commander of Anti-Aircraft Defences, was situated in close liaison with Dowding at Fighter Command Headquarters in Stanmore. Since September 1939, Pile's AA guns had been situated within a 25-mile deep belt stretching from Newcastle, around London, to Portsmouth. This arrangement was known as the Couverture System and included 960 searchlights, 288 guns, 1,000 officers and 22,000 other ranks.

Between September 1939 and the end of June 1940 AA Command had accounted for 13 aircraft destroyed and a further 15 intruders damaged. Its gunners had provided moral support for the apprehensive population and suffered the privations of a vigilant watch of the cold night skies. One of the least pleasant experiences its men endured was attack from fearless Luftwaffe pilots who dived directly down the searchlight beams and sprayed the vulnerable arclight and its operators with machine-gun bullets.

Although Dowding could summon the resources of the radar network designated as No. 60 Group, Observer Corps, Anti-Aircraft Command, Balloon Command and a variety of intelligence sources, it was ultimately the Hurricanes and Spitfires of Fighter Command that would determine whether Britain's defences were to be breeched.

By the time of the French capitulation on June 22 the RAF had lost a total of 1,025 aircraft during operations over the Western Front and in Norway; 509 of these were precious fighters, mostly Hurricanes. The home defences had been reduced to 331

DESIGNS FOR WAR

Hurricanes and Spitfires backed up by 150 second-line fighters – Blenheims, Defiants and Gladiators. Fortunately arms manufacture, under Beaverbrook, was on the increase and in June 1940 some 309 Hurricanes and 135 Spitfires rolled off the aircraft industry's production lines.

Trained pilots were however in desperately short supply as 435 of them had been either killed or captured during the Battle of France; 58 pilots were transferred from the Royal Navy to the RAF and Bomber, Coastal and Army Co-operation Squadrons were combed for men capable of adapting to the rigours of fighter combat.

Fighter Command's human resources were supplemented by trained pilots from the Dominions, Belgium, France and, perhaps most notably, 200 men from Poland and Czechoslovakia. Having narrowly escaped the German onslaught of their homelands the Poles and Czechs were determined to even the score with the Luftwaffe. Initially they

appeared to Dowding an ill-disciplined mob but he did not doubt their fighting spirit. During the Battle of Britain the Eastern Europeans were to prove formidable opponents of the Luftwaffe and fought with a tenacity and determination which astounded their regular RAF superiors.

Americans, too, joined Fighter Command after skilfully evading the US Embassy's efforts to prevent them breaking American neutrality. Eventually an American Squadron, No. 71 Eagle Squadron, was formed, its pilots displaying the same dash and glamour which were to characterise the 8th Army Air Force when it operated from British bases later in the war.

Though Dowding tried to trim as much time off the RAF's pilot training programme he soon realised that he would have to fight the forthcoming battle with the pilots already on the Command's strength. The training machinery designed for a peacetime requirement simply could not be accelerated fast

The tenacity of ordinary young men caught up in extraordinary situations is movingly demonstrated by the log book and accompanying letter belonging to Flying Officer J. R. Whelan, a Blenheim pilot of 18 Squadron (B.E.F.), injured in combat during the Battle of France. Whelan later went on to achieve the rank of Air Commodore with the RAF after the war.

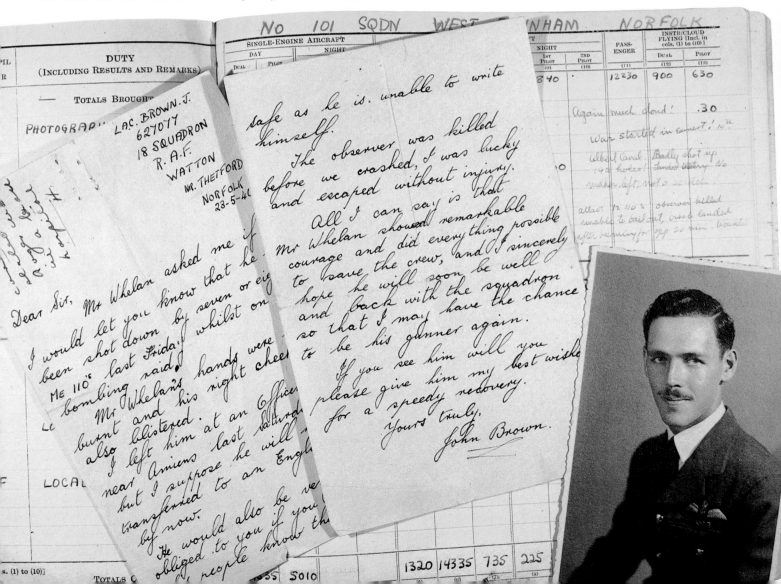

Air Vice-Marshal Trafford Leigh-Mallory, Commander of No. 12 Group during the Battle of Britain, was a passionate advocate of offensive tactics.

troops with a mixture of arsenic, trioxide and copper acetate known as Paris Green. Plans to attach a terrifying weapon called the Paraslasher to Tiger Moths were also seriously considered in June. The Paraslasher was, as its name implies, a means of killing parachutists by shredding their canopies with scythes attached to the wings of the innocent-looking biplanes.

More seriously the Miles company, used to providing trainers for the RAF, was asked to consider producing a cheap and easily built fighter constructed round the Merlin engine. Although the result, the Miles M20, was faster than the Hurricane and the prototype was produced in record time, the idea was not pursued when it was realised that production of Hurricanes and Spitfires would probably prove sufficient.

On July 1, 1940 Fighter Command's order of battle stood at a total of 639 fighters spread among its three groups: Nos 11, 12 and 13 (Number 10 Group was not established until mid-July). Of this total 346 were Hurricanes, 199 were Spitfires and the remainder Blenheims and Defiants. Additionally there was a total of 439 fighters in RAF storage units, though not all of them were available for immediate issue.

To help Dowding fight the imminent battle he relied on the support of his group commanders, the men who wielded executive control of Fighter Command's thinly spread squadrons. Once the Luftwaffe had taken control of French forward airfields along the Channel coast it was obvious that No. 11 Group would bear the brunt of the fighting over South-East England.

This was commanded by Air Vice-Marshal Keith Park, an officer of outstanding ability who had served at Bentley Priory as Dowding's Senior Air Staff Officer (SASO). The two men had grown to like and respect one another and Park, as the C-in-C's right-hand man, was frequently taken into Dowding's confidence.

With 20 years' experience in the RAF behind him, Park was able to apply a good deal of wisdom to his responsibilities while on Fighter Command's staff. He was particularly adept at understanding the realities of modern high-speed fighter combat and was attuned to the difficulties involved in controlling and directing aircraft once such conflicts had commenced.

Park was quick to grasp the fundamentals of

enough significantly to add to existing budgets and resources.

In an attempt to augment the RAF's front-line strength desperate remedies were considered. Advanced trainers had machine-guns installed in their wings; Flying Training Command received orders to implement an operation codenamed "banquet" if an emergency situation developed, a scheme involving the use of obsolete and ill-equipped aircraft in a last-ditch attempt to prevent an enemy bridgehead; 350 Tiger Moth and Magister trainers were fitted with rudimentary bomb-racks and were intended to drop 20 lb bombs on enemy formations when they were ordered aloft.

More bizarre last-minute plans included fitting mustard-gas dispensing containers to Lysanders, Battles, Blenheims and Wellingtons and converting Tiger Moths into human crop-sprayers capable of dousing enemy

DESIGNS FOR WAR

Dowding's new operations policy. He agreed with his mentor that tactical command had to be dispersed to the fighting areas and could not be totally directed from the confines of Stanmore's underground control complex. To the chagrin of more traditional staff officers he enthusiastically endorsed Dowding's plan to delegate more responsibilities to group and even sector commanders. Fighter Command headquarters, he argued, served a more useful purpose if it concentrated on the overall direction of air defence and involved itself with broad policies of engagement rather than day to day or hour by hour interference with the handling of local events.

However, Park's efforts were not directed exclusively towards the implementation of Dowding's grand strategy or the issuing of revised operational directives covering the minutiae of Fighter Command's business; he also deeply involved himself in the basics of air-fighting. Having learnt his trade during the Great War, when he accounted for 20 German aircraft, he was well qualified to voice an opinion but was wise enough to realise that the principles of dog-fighting and bomber interception had to be brought up to date if the new generation of fighter-pilots were to have a chance of surviving lethal encounters at breakneck speeds against heavily armed adversaries. With this in mind he busied himself with the tactics of aerial combat between the up-gunned monoplanes and their rivals and ensured that, when relevant, his ideas were disseminated to the squadrons.

After studying the relative armament of opposing fighter aircraft he strongly recommended the use of larger weapons than the rifle-calibre .303-inch machine-guns then considered suitable for use. Park suggested that heavier .5-inch machine-guns were more suitable as their high rate of fire and larger bore would produce devastating results against the complex structures of modern metal aircraft. Events over England would later prove him right; the Luftwaffe's larger calibre weapons were found to be more lethal than those of the RAF.

Some of Fighter Command's new tactics were put into practice during the final peacetime air exercises operated in conjunction with Bomber Command. Confusion concerning the capabilities of radar – and a reluctance on Bomber Command's part to commit more than a token force to the role of "enemy" – prevented a full and proper testing

of the defences, but even so some useful information was gathered.

The most alarming discovery was the inability of the system to detect low-flying raiders that regularly slipped through the defensive net. Dowding and Park were also alarmed that 12 Group's C-in-C, Air Vice-Marshal Trafford Leigh-Mallory, consistently overreacted to "enemy" attack and deployed too many fighters for local airfield defence duties rather than using them to protect the key objectives of the opposing force – the vulnerable industrial belt in the Midlands.

On one occasion Leigh-Mallory actually evacuated his operations room at Watnall during a "raid" – a move which resulted in a stiff note of censure from Dowding ordering all ops room staff to remain at their posts unless their equipment was damaged beyond use. Although the new RDF system negated

Air Vice-Marshal Sir Keith Park, Commander of No. 11 Group, which bore the brunt of the Luftwaffe's bludgeoning attacks during 1940, adhered rigidly to Dowding's decisive defence policy.

95

the use of standing patrols, Leigh-Mallory still relied on this costly expedient rather than scrambling his fighters at the optimum moment.

To his own surprise, and especially to that of Leigh-Mallory, Keith Park was given command of 11 Group in April 1940. Leigh-Mallory, senior to Park and in line for the appointment, felt slighted by Dowding's apparent snub. He had never really got on with Park, or Dowding for that matter, and considered the latter's selection to be an example of obvious favouritism towards a loyal staff officer.

Park's posting to Uxbridge merely added fuel to a fire which had long smouldered. As early as October 1938 Leigh-Mallory demonstrated his determined resistance to Dowding's new devolutionary methods by submitting a plan for the redeployment of Fighter Command's resources which would leave only 12 squadrons protecting London –

the principal target of any enemy. Dowding was dismayed that Leigh-Mallory's ideas showed a complete disregard for even the basic principles of the new defence system, with its emphasis on the properties of RDF and improved radio communications, meaning that fighters did not need to be situated directly adjacent to enemy objectives in order to protect them.

So the stage was set for the ensuing battle. Dowding sat in command, flanked by the willing Park and the recalcitrant Leigh-Mallory, who between them controlled the cream of the total of 52 squadrons which Fighter Command possessed to meet the threat to its very existence. Across the Channel its opponents in Hitler's Luftwaffe had all but completed their own preparations and were keen to demonstrate their superiority. Britain would not have to wait long to see whether Dowding's long years of toil had been in vain.

Chapter Four

"Since England, in spite of her hopeless military situation,
shows no signs of being ready to come to an understanding,
I have decided to prepare a landing operation against
England and, if necessary, to carry it out."

Adolf Hitler,
"Directive No. 16", July 16 1940

A SEA-LION STIRS

By mid-July 1940 Luftwaffe crews had familiarised themselves with the tactical aspects of Operation Sea-lion – codename for the invasion of Britain – and bomber units prepared for offensive operations over England. This promotional postcard was produced by the Heinkel works.

Early in the evening of June 28, 1940 the people of Jersey and Guernsey detected the curious throb of unsynchronised aero-engines drifting towards them on the light summer breeze from the direction of the Cherbourg peninsula. As the steady drone grew louder the anxious Channel Islanders, unprotected since the recent military evacuation of their territory, resigned themselves to an imminent German landing.

Yet as the flights of Luftwaffe Heinkel 111 bombers, some as low as 3,000 feet, sped towards the harbours of St Helier and St Peter Port, it soon became clear that they carried a cargo more volatile than companies of stormtroopers. Within a few seconds, their machine-guns blazing and high-explosive bombs tumbling from yawning bellies, the sinister black-crossed shapes flashed over-head, unleashing a hail of death and destruction on the defenceless islanders.

As the aircraft wheeled about and headed back towards their airfield bases the only note of defiance sounded from a single weapon on board the elderly mail-steamer *The Isle of Sark*. Behind them the aircrews of Luftflotte 3 (Airfleet 3) had, for the cost of only 180 bombs, left 44 civilians dead and many more injured from the effects of shrapnel. Confident that the lines of lorries on the quaysides they hit were army vehicles (in fact they carried the island's vegetable harvest), the pilots brought their aircraft back undamaged from what they thought was a successful military engagement. And although history has recorded that the air-fighting off England's south coast a fortnight later was the beginning of the German offensive, the smoke that spiralled high above the Channel Islands on June 28 signalled that the Battle of Britain had begun.

In fact the tragedy of the Channel Islands could easily have been avoided. Just why the British government had not clarified their demilitarised status sooner is one of the minor

Bomben auf Engelland

Lied aus dem Film der Luftwaffe „Feuertaufe" von Hans Bertram
Worte: Wilhelm Stoeppler   Musik: Norbert Schultze

3.
So wurde die jüngste der Waffen im Feuer getauft und geweiht!
Vom Rhein bis zum Meer das fliegende Heer, so steh'n wir zum
Einsatz bereit!

Kehrreim:
Kamerad! Kamerad! Alle Mädels müssen warten!
Kamerad! Kamerad! Der Befehl ist da, wir starten!
Kamerad! Kamerad! Die Losung ist bekannt:
Ran an den Feind! Ran an den Feind! Bomben auf Engelland!
:/: Hört ihr die Motoren singen: Ran an den Feind!
Hört ihr's in den Ohren klingen: Ran an den Feind!
Bomben! Bomben! Bomben auf Engelland! :/:

Propaganda like this postcard, with its stirring verse entitled "Bombs on England", dispels the myth of German indifference towards the prospects of a successful campaign against Britain.

stepping-stones in their retreat from France, and once the last military personnel had been evacuated, the Home Office could have prevented subsequent loss of life by informing the Germans of the peaceful status of the islands. The Chiefs of Staff had long recognised that they were almost undefendable and of little strategic value, but the laggardly treatment of the Channel Islands by Britain's politicians was symptomatic of the poor service the loyal islanders had received from their guardians since the German offensive in France had commenced.

While the German 216 Infantry Division finalised its preparations for an assault on defences still thought to be manned by a well concealed garrison, the actions of a single Luftwaffe pilot reduced the situation almost to the level of farce and cleared the way for an unopposed occupation. On the morning of June 30 Hauptmann Liebe-Pieteritz was detailed to carry out a routine reconnaissance of the Channel Islands, but he was surprised to observe that the airfield at Guernsey appeared deserted and decided to test the inactive defences by attempting a landing. As he touched down on the small runway he achieved the honour of being the first German to "invade" the islands.

Although his visit was abruptly interrupted by the timely arrival of a flight of RAF Bristol Blenheims operating from airfields in England, it was obvious that the Islands were passively awaiting the inevitable. The same evening a platoon of Luftwaffe soldiers was dropped on Guernsey, apparently vindicating Reichsmarschall Hermann Goering's boast that the Luftwaffe was capable of winning territory without the help of either the army or the navy. The following day, July 1, Jersey succumbed to a similar fate and by July 4 both Alderney and Sark were in German hands, thereby completing Hitler's minor triumph.

The loss of the Channel Islands, though not a serious strategic setback, was a further humiliation for a country now beset by evacuation and retreat. For the first time since the Norman Conquest part of the British Isles had fallen to the might of an invader. Of course for Hitler the unopposed occupation was a great propaganda victory, a further demonstration of his prowess as Germany's supreme commander. However he was careful not to provoke the British into further condemnation of his achievements and the Islanders were treated with a surprising

mysteries of the Second World War. By June 20 the *SS Biarritz*, sailing from Guernsey, and the *SS Malines*, from Jersey, had evacuated the remaining garrison and the islands had been stripped of all their offensive and defensive armament. A press notice detailing the evacuation of the islands and their subsequent demilitarisation was prepared on June 22, but for some reason it was not released until six days later – the evening of the German raid.

Obviously Britain did not want to offer an open invitation to Hitler to occupy the Channel Islands; but after the BEF and RAF had finished using Jersey and Guernsey as

A SEA-LION STIRS

Denn wir fahren gegen Engelland.

(Matrosenlied)

Heute wollen wir ein Liedlein singen,
Trinken wollen wir den kühlen Wein,
Und die Gläser sollen dazu klingen,
Denn es muß, es muß geschieden sein;
    Gib mir deine Hand,
    Deine weiße Hand,
Leb wohl, mein Schatz, leb wohl,
Denn wir fahren gegen Engelland.

Unsre Flagge und die wehet auf dem Maste,
Sie verkündet unsres Reiches Macht,
Denn wir wollen es nicht länger leiden,
Daß der Englischmann darüber lacht;
    Gib mir deine Hand,
    Deine weiße Hand,
Leb wohl, mein Schatz, leb wohl,
Denn wir fahren gegen Engelland.

Kommt die Kunde, daß ich bin gefallen,
Daß ich schlafe in der Meeresflut,
Weine nicht um mich, mein Schatz, und denke,
Für das Vaterland da floß sein Blut;
    Gib mir deine Hand,
    Deine weiße Hand,
Leb wohl, mein Schatz, leb wohl,
Denn wir fahren gegen Engelland.

Hermann Löns

Another patriotic German postcard, this one headed "When we sail for England", fancifully depicts a sailor's farewell to his girl as he sets off to join Hitler's invasion flotilla.

degree of fairness. Although the new symbol of authority on the streets of St Helier and St Peter Port was the silver gorget of the Feld-Polizei there were no mass round-ups or deportations. And though the helpless population was on the receiving end of an increasing number of official pronouncements which chipped away at the freedoms they had long cherished, life during the first weeks of occupation went on much as usual.

The reason for such suspicious benevolence on the part of the occupying forces was Hitler's intense desire to be seen by the world as a statesman of vision rather than a totalitarian conqueror. His armed forces had achieved more in a shorter time than he had ever believed possible. It was inconceivable, some weeks earlier, that German troops might reach the Channel coast with such ease, and the opportunity of invading Britain so early in the war had never been seriously entertained by the Führer. Now it had arisen and only a narrow strip of water separated the ill-prepared British from his mighty war machine, he hesistated about continuing the offensive. Uncharacteristically, Hitler did not want to push his luck; he still sought a negotiated peace with Britain.

As France sued for an agreeable armistice Count Ciano, Mussolini's son-in-law and Italy's Minister for Foreign Affairs, noted in his diary: "Hitler is now the gambler who has made a big scoop and would like to get up from the table risking nothing more." Germany's own Foreign Minister, Von Ribbentrop, was equally nervous about continuing the war and

was eager to secure a peace treaty, his staff busily exploring diplomatic channels via neutral Sweden. As late as July 20, after the Luftwaffe's assault on England had been under way for ten days, Ciano returned from a conference with Hitler and remarked on the German leader's persistent desire to find an alternative to head-on confrontation: "He would like an understanding with Great Britain. He knows that war with the British will be hard and bloody, and knows also that people everywhere today are averse to bloodshed."

Yet even if Hitler had serious misgivings about demolishing the British Empire and considered Britain to be an important factor in maintaining world equilibrium, he still fashioned an elastic attitude. Should Britain refuse to resign herself to the role of spectator in European affairs, it was at least prudent to make preparations for an invasion of the country. One way or another – "so oder so", to use one of Hitler's favourite phrases – the British would come to terms with German superiority, and if they chose a fight then his field-marshals would be urged on to one more victory before they turned their attention towards the real enemy, Russia. Where diplomatic pressure failed military might would prevail. So as the world looked on and nations one by one wrote off Britain's chances of surviving a clash with Europe's mightiest power, Germany's military commanders went through the motions of examining the possibility of an all-out assault on Britain.

Surprisingly it was the navy, not the army,

A NATION ALONE

ABOVE The Channel Islands were regarded as a great prize by Hitler and as such were quickly and effectively fortified, using slave labour controlled by the Organisation Todt. It is interesting to speculate how quickly the Wehrmacht would have consolidated its bridgehead on British soil had the proposed amphibious assault been successful.

ABOVE RIGHT German gun emplacements and reinforced concrete bunkers were virtually impregnable against anything other than a direct hit from large naval guns.

RIGHT Germany's victory in France netted huge caches of war spoils. Here a Renault tank turret has been shipped to Jersey and ingeniously incorporated into a defensive bunker.

ABOVE RIGHT By the end of the war German military engineers had succeeded in completing a ring of steel around the Channel Islands. Many of the observation towers like this one and much of the bunker complex remains to this day; attempts at demolition would be prohibitively expensive – and not necessarily successful.

which had prepared the first draft proposals. Hitler had made it clear to Grand-Admiral Raeder that the principal function of the Kriegsmarine was to apply an impenetrable blockade on Britain. At a conference in May 1939 he stressed that she could be defeated only by economic warfare since her "geopolitical safety, mighty fleet and brave airforce" made direct military victory untenable.

Dependence on imports was the one chink in such inviolable armour. Once Britain's vulnerable supply lines had been severed, capitulation would be inevitable. Such speculation was not unreasonable. In 1917 the Kaiser's U-boat fleet had almost succeeded in strangling Britain into submission, and Hitler was confident that the new generation of submariners would prevail where their forebears had failed. The navy's top-secret magnetic mine would further supplement the activities of the U-boats and complete the envelopment of Britain. Indeed subsequent

events nearly proved Hitler right, for until the Royal Navy developed a suitable submarine-hunting short-wave radar system and invented a method of countering the effects of the lethal mines, Britain's shipping losses accelerated to critical levels.

Once the 1939 offensive had commenced Raeder and OKM (OberKommando der Kriegsmarine), the German Navy's high command, began to direct their thoughts towards improving the prospects of naval warfare against England. At the same time as his planners considered the acquisition of German bases on the North Sea and Atlantic coasts to facilitate improved operations against British shipping, Raeder gave an order for "the possibility of invading England to be examined". By the end of November 1939 his staff had come to the conclusion that a seaborne invasion across the North Sea was a practical way of forcing Britain to sue for peace. This initial plan was prepared without

With the Channel Islands occupied by the Wehrmacht the people had to adapt quickly to the strictures of martial law. Soon the full panoply of Third Reich militarism was on display in the streets. The photograph shows a collection of contemporary Third Reich insignia including [bottom left] a gorget of the Feldgendarmerie (Military Field Police). The "chained dogs", as the German military police were known by their comrades because of their insignia, were responsible for the immediate enforcement of Hitler's wishes on captured territory prior to the arrival of the security police, Gestapo and intelligence services. The diving golden eagle is a Fallschirmjäger (paratroops) badge. The eagle and two shields are army national insignia while the death's head badge would have been worn by a member of the SS. The brass door-plate belongs to a department of the Reichsarbeitsdienst (National Labour Service) which was involved in the organisation of skilled labour. The small book is a popular souvenir recounting Hitler's conquest of Poland. The Nazi armband is the finial from a flag standard belonging to a German infantry division.

any reference to either the army command, OKH (OberKommando des Heeres) or to OKW (OberKommando der Wehrmacht), the high command of the German armed services.

The navy plan was approved by Raeder on November 29. It outlined certain pre-requisites that were essential for a successful operation. First, British naval forces had to be eliminated or contained; second, coastal forces in the vicinity of the landings (then envisaged to take place along Britain's east coast) had to be put out of action; third, strong anti-submarine measures would have to be taken and dense minefields sown to form a protected channel for the invasion fleet; finally, the RAF would have to be completely destroyed before the invasion flotillas set sail. If all these conditions were fulfilled, the report con-cluded, the strategy would "in all probability result simultaneously in the complete collapse of her [Britain's] will to resist; thus a landing, followed by occupation, will scarcely still be necessary."

In December OKH began to take an interest in the invasion scenario. The navy planners received a memo from the army C-in-C General Von Brauchitsch on the 13th stating that he had "ordered an examination of the possibility of a landing in England". The resulting plan was to be called "North-West", a rather unimaginative name given to the invasion plans until "Sea-lion" was coined in July 1940.

The OKH plan was not the product of a visionary determination on the part of the army general staff to impress their Führer but rather a realistic extension of the plans for the proposed campaign in the West which, if successful, would yield port facilities in the Low Countries and among the Dutch estuaries from which a seaborne assault could be launched. The army plan was more complex than the earlier naval one as it involved the use of an element of surprise as well as the application of paratroops and an elaborate disembarkation schedule. However it too concluded that the assault ought to be on England's North Sea coast. The Kriegsmarine was sceptical about the OKH plan and pointed out the difficulties of protecting the enormous armada from the attention of the Royal Navy. OKM was especially curious about the army's elaborate transportation scheme and was fascinated to know where the proposed shipping would be acquired.

The Luftwaffe were equally unenthusiastic about "Study North-West", maintaining that

In an effort to present the occupation as fair and just the Germans ensured their own troops stayed on the straight and narrow. Day passes (Tagesausweis) were required for almost anything and tokens were issued for use in German establishments like Soldatenheime (soldiers' rest homes) and for civilians to regulate the amount of produce they were permitted to grow.

without absolute air superiority the proposed airborne force would be cut to pieces. Furthermore unless surprise could be guaranteed they would be unable to sustain an effective aerial umbrella above the sea-going force, leaving it vulnerable to any RAF aircraft that had escaped their attention and especially the Royal Navy's strong surface forces.

Clearly a measure of inter-service rivalry was responsible for the Kriegsmarine's apparent about-face, but the Luftwaffe's lukewarm reception served to pour more cold water on the invasion idea. Nevertheless the army had at least investigated the possibility and was satisfied that a contingency existed should Hitler request a feasibility study.

However by early 1940 the high command was more concerned with the forthcoming attack against France and its allies. This was by no means guaranteed to succeed, and more than a few of Hitler's generals feared the possibility of a repetition of the stagnant trench warfare that beset the Great War. With preparations for the 1940 version of the Schlieffen Plan foremost in their minds the German planners soon shelved thoughts of invading England and Study North-West was consigned to the filing cabinet.

It was not retrieved until May 21, 1940, when Hitler asked to see the Kriegsmarine's invasion proposals for the first time. With Von Rundstedt's armoured divisions regrouping on the Channel coast at the mouth of the Somme it was perhaps an appropriate time for the Führer to consider capitalising on his unexpected windfall and pressing on towards England while the BEF remained isolated in Flanders. But Hitler appears to have been unimpressed with the results of his navy's deliberations. Rather than pursue the war against Britain by a direct assault he urged Raeder to intensify the naval blockade and endorsed the admiral's proposal for an increase in U-boat production.

On June 20 Raeder up-dated Hitler on the preparations for invasion which the Kriegsmarine was undertaking as a contingency against a sudden change of plan, but the supreme commander remained uncommitted to the possibility, preferring instead to discuss a hare-brained scheme for invading Iceland! Undaunted by the Führer's indifference, Raeder continued provisionally to earmark shipping for amphibious operations and ordered his staff to start collating topographical intelligence about the south coast of England – a likelier target than the more familiar east coast due to the potential exploitation of Germany's newly won territory in France.

As their troops assembled along the Channel coast Hitler's generals could clearly see England laid out before them through their field-glasses. Across the narrow stretch of water the English cliffs shimmered and sparkled in the warm haze like jewels waiting to be plucked from an azure crown. In a matter of weeks they had achieved the impossible, and it was not unnatural they should reconsider an invasion of the now-vulnerable islands that lay before them.

Hitler's thoughts, however, were elsewhere. With the British Army kicked out of France and clearly unable to offer serious resistance he expected to receive peace proposals at any time. So confident was he of an end to the fighting that he reduced his army by one fifth to 120 divisions and sent the demobbed soldiers back to their factories and farms. He was acutely aware of the risks involved in large-scale amphibious operations and was as pessimistic as ever about the chances of successfully invading Britain.

In addition the German people and its industries had been on a war footing for years and Hitler was keen to deliver the benefits of his many victories to a Reich eagerly awaiting a conclusion to the war. As all his peace attempts were rebuffed by the belligerent British and "the gangster Churchill", Hitler became increasingly annoyed that his desire to achieve a negotiated peace was frustrated.

On July 2, 1940 OberKommando der Wehrmacht, the co-ordinating authority for the German armed forces, issued an order headed "The War Against England". It stated that "the Führer and Supreme Commander has decided . . . that a landing in England is possible provided that air superiority can be attained and certain other necessary conditions fulfilled." No target date was included but preparations were to commence at once "on the basis that the invasion is still only a plan, and has not yet been decided upon." This note of indecision was characteristic of all subsequent proposals issued by OKW and lends credence to the generally held view that at no stage did Hitler ever seriously entertain the possibility of invasion.

On July 10 Hitler ordered that all heavy ordnance should be moved up to the Channel coast to provide covering fire for the invasion

A SEA-LION STIRS

fleet. Accordingly gun emplacements were hastily constructed between Calais, Cape Gris Nez and Boulogne and the heaviest weapons in the German armoury were brought forward and trundled into position.

Two days later, on July 12, OKW began to firm up its invasion plans, and in a study titled "First Thoughts on a Landing in England" the Chief of the Wehrmacht Operations Staff, General Jodl, attempted to address some of the problems that might be encountered. The threat from the Royal Navy, it stated, could be contained by operating solely in Channel waters which were too narrow for Britain's capital ships and which could be successfully mined.

Jodl was more concerned with the threat from Britain's shore-based defences, recognising that a mobile reserve could be rapidly moved to cover the invasion area once its location had been identified by the direction of the assault ships. To counter this danger Jodl suggested a landing across an extended front so that no single point received a concentration of attention from the defenders.

However it is clear from the terminology employed that OKW underestimated the difficulties in store and merely equated the Channel crossing to fording a river on a grand scale. "The landing must therefore take place in the form of a river crossing in force on a broad front," wrote Jodl. "In this operation the role of artillery will fall to the Luftwaffe . . . and in place of bridging operations, a sea-lane completely secure from naval attacks must be established in the Dover Straits." When the German troops had taken to their rubber dinghies during their successful crossing of the Meuse in May, machine-guns on the German bank provided effective support fire

ABOVE & BELOW Even before the Battle of Britain began in earnest the occasional German raider was intercepted in the skies above Britain. This beached Heinkel 111 was shot down off the south coast of England on June 19, 1940.

Auftrag 8.Pz.235

Auftrag 11.Pz.235

Ansammlungen!

Belegung!

151.Div.

J.R.21

21.3.Angriffsbeginn
6.Pz.Div.

11.Pz.Div.

Weitere Deutsche Kräfte

Teile 18 Div.

170

45. Div.

J.R.11

3.A.102

Batl.
I.R.32

I.R.32

I.154

3.A.209
III /A.R. 158
IV /A.R. 158
I. Pi. 158
Teile N.A.158

209

158

I.220 C

J.R.220
I./A.R.158
Teile II.A.158

A.A.158.3.Pz.mot
Pa.Jg.Abt.

• Lage 21.5. früh
• Lage 22.5. abds.

LEFT Operation Sea-lion required careful planning. Although the Wehrmacht approached the problem of mounting an invasion without much co-ordination and forethought, military planners rapidly furnished the services with overprinted copies of British Ordnance Survey maps such as this one. It clearly displays the proposed routes by which the army's Panzer divisions were to smash through Sussex and Kent towards London.

ABOVE & BELOW Assembly points, observation points and locations where bridges were to be captured or rivers forded were all carefully indicated. The term "Angriffe Beginnen" (Attacks Begin) marks a proposed start line from which regrouped infantry and Panzer divisions would press on towards their next objective – London.

and the Panzer grenadiers and sappers were able to reach the opposite bank unopposed. It is clear from the muddled logic of Jodl's proposal, and Hitler's directive that heavy guns should be positioned along the French coast, that both men were under the delusion that the unpredictable English Channel was nothing more than an unhelpfully exaggerated river.

On July 13, at his mountain retreat, the Berghof, Hitler conferred with his generals and approved their latest plans, code-named "Lion". He made one minor amendment: henceforth Lion would be known as "Sea-lion", a name more befitting the amphibious nature of the undertaking. Three days later he issued his famous directive No. 16, a document so secret that only seven copies were ever made.

After stressing that Sea-lion was a last resort in the face of British intransigence Hitler explained the main thrust of the exercise: "The landing will be in the form of a surprise crossing on a wide front from about Ramsgate to the area west of the Isle of Wight. Units of the air force will act as artillery, and units of the navy as engineers."

The Führer ordered that all preparations had to be completed by the middle of August. These were the elimination of the RAF, the clearance of mine-free channels, the sealing off of the flanks of the attack from intrusion by the Royal Navy, the protection of the sea-route by coastal artillery, and, lastly, the containment of the British Mediterranean Fleet by units of the Italian Navy.

The day after Directive No. 16 was issued detailed operational plans were finalised and 13 hand-picked divisions were moved up to the coast for use as first-wave troops. Sea-lion was indeed an ambitious plan. Under Von Rundstedt's command, six divisions of General Busch's 16th Army would cross from the Pas de Calais and come ashore between Ramsgate and Bexhill. At the same time four divisions of General Strauss's 9th Army, crossing from Le Havre, would land between Brighton and the Isle of Wight. Three divisions of Feldmarschall Reichenau's 6th Army, embarking in the Cherbourg peninsula area, would support the offensive by landing between Weymouth and Lyme Regis.

In all 90,000 men could wade ashore during the initial assault, and reinforcements would increase the total to 260,000 men by the third day of the campaign. Airborne troops would also be used to secure key targets north of Lyme Bay and on the Hampshire coast. Furthermore the first wave would be rapidly supported by six panzer divisions and three motorised ones. Once all the units earmarked for Sea-lion had been committed a total of 39 divisions and two airborne divisions would be involved in the operation.

After the bridgeheads had been secured and gun positions established to further protect the build up of reinforcements from seaward attack, the mobile troops would hurry forward to their next objective. Their task was to hold a line running along the North Downs from Gravesend to Southampton but, for the moment, stopping short of London. Once Luftwaffe engineers had patched up RAF airfields captured during the initial attack the Stukas and Junkers 88 dive-bombers would be able repeatedly to attack key targets north of this first stop line.

Although fighting was expected to be tough OKW was confident that the blitzkreig techniques of combined ground and air operations which had proved so successful in Poland and France would result in an advance towards the second objective – a line stretching from Malden in Essex to Gloucester and the Severn. While London was surrounded armoured units would race ahead to other major industrial and commercial targets in the Midlands and the North. The entire operation was confidently predicted to take no more than a month once London and the principal garrisons had surrendered – and what was left of the British administration had sued for peace.

The German Navy did not share the army's optimism. On July 17 Raeder informed Feldmarschall Von Brauchitsch of his misgivings and explained that he simply did not have enough resources to meet the requirements of Sea-lion. Raeder pointed out that it would not be a simple river crossing "but the crossing of a sea which is dominated by the enemy". Mindful of the Kriegsmarine's recent savaging at the hands of the Royal Navy during the Norwegian campaign, when half of Germany's destroyer fleet was sunk, he envisaged the balance of his tiny navy meeting a similar fate in the restricted waters of the Channel. However the die had been cast and reluctantly Raeder proceeded to apply himself to the impossible task of accumulating the miscellany of landing-craft, transports and barges that would be required to transfer the

invading army from one coast to the other.

In June the OKM Merchant Shipping Division was given the job of procuring the vessels necessary for invasion. Sea transportation representatives were sent to all the major Channel ports between Amsterdam and Boulogne and began scouring the quaysides and slipways for suitable tonnage, and any sea-going or coastal craft capable of completing the crossing was considered. Since some 400 medium-size steamers and a large collection of auxiliary vessels and barges were sought, many examples would have to be specially constructed and others converted into the role of landing-craft.

The job was made all the more difficult by the heavy use of all available tonnage for the key transportation of coal and iron-ore to Germany's hungry power-stations and foundries. Nevertheless work began on assembling the makeshift navy and soon the ports of occupied Europe were hives of activity as labourers sweated to adapt the rusting barges for their new role. Ramps were added to enable horses (which still pulled much of the German Army's field-guns and supply wagons) to scramble over the side of each barge towards the safety of land. Once underway the huge flotilla of unpowered barges would be dragged at a leisurely five knots towards the enemy coast.

As the line of barges was expected to extend to a length of 12 miles even the poorly trained gunners manning Britain's coastal batteries would have been unlikely to miss such a target. The hardened stormtroops in the vanguard of the German assault would have fared little better than their colleagues aboard the barges, for although they were equipped with impressive sounding vessels called Sturm-boote these were in reality little more than modified river craft, unarmoured and capable of carrying only a handful of lightly armed troops. There had been some successful experiments involving the addition of brea-thing apparatus or "schnorkels" to tanks to aspirate their engines while partially sub-merged, but the fact remained that during disembarkation from the hastily improvised barges, now assigned as tank landing-craft, the Panzers would be exposed to anti-tank fire for an unacceptably long time.

Although the Kriegsmarine patiently went about the business of requisitioning the

Observer Corps posts were usually spartan affairs. Often isolated from built-up areas, the damp and dingy dwellings were linked to regional headquarters via the corps' own tele-communications network.

The advent of food rationing and the paradoxical need for increased energy intake to sustain the longer working hours led to many ingenious recipes and home economics schemes. This reconstruction shows typical wartime domestic ephemera including grocery bags on recycled paper, ration coupons and Ministry of Food dried milk.

merchant vessels of French and Dutch masters it continued to voice its disquiet with the newly energised plans, pointing out that the task was out of all proportion to its strength. The naval staff were equally upset to discover that the retreating Allied armies had vandalised the port and harbour facilities before they fell into German hands. What had not been demolished had received the unhelpful attention of the RAF, leaving the German Navy's engineers with a mammoth repair job before they could even begin to commence fresh construction work. Hitler brushed aside his navy's fears but suggested that the army estimates would definitely need to be increased to a minimum landing of 40 divisions rather than an unrealistic 25, which the generals had hoped might be enough for the initial assault.

Curiously, although Hitler appeared to be tackling the question of an invasion of England with renewed vigour, he further demonstrated his inconsistency by withdrawing his military headquarters from the Franco-German border to deep within the

heart of Germany at Ziegenberg. It was hardly appropriate for a supreme commander to transfer his staff far behind the front line if he was serious about embarking on a decisive campaign. During the fighting in Poland, France and the Low Countries Hitler had positioned his headquarters close to the front to be able to wield day-to-day control over the battlefield. How could he hope to successfully conclude an offensive against Britain which, by its very nature, was many times more complicated than anything that had gone before, if he languished in a mountain retreat far to the rear?

On July 19, three days after Directive No. 16 was issued, Hitler returned to Berlin to address the Reichstag and reward his loyal military commanders for their services to the fatherland. During a long and at times rambling speech to the party faithful the Führer made his famous "last appeal to reason", imploring Britain to grasp his outstretched olive branch and avoid the crushing defeat which would result if she continued the folly of resisting Germany's superiority.

A SEA-LION STIRS

Most of the speech consisted of an account of the recent German victories in Poland, the Low Countries and France, and according to the speaker the successes were due largely to his own foresight and unequalled military prowess. On each occasion he had proved that he could back up his threats with action, and on each occasion the Reich's enemies had been contemptuously brushed aside by its ruthlessly efficient war machine.

Reference to the peace offer came at the end of the carefully prepared text: "Herr Churchill ought perhaps for once to believe me when I prophesy that a great empire will be destroyed – an empire which it was never my intention to destroy or even to harm."

It was soon apparent that Britain was unimpressed by Hitler's entreaties. On the same day as the address to the Reichstag, Count Ciano noted in his diary: "I believe that his desire for peace is sincere. In fact, late in the evening, when the first cold British reactions to the speech arrive, a sense of ill-concealed disappointment spreads among the Germans."

In fact Britons treated the peace offer either as an insult or, more commonly, a joke. Although *The Times* ran a bold headline, "Hitler's Threats to Britain", few people took them seriously. Churchill had long been sceptical about the risk of Germany successfully invading Britain – and especially now, after so long a breathing space.

The official British response to Hitler's speech was delivered on July 22 by Lord Halifax, Churchill's Foreign Secretary who, after comparing Hitler to the anti-Christ, said that "the peoples of the British Commonwealth, along with all those who love truth and justice and freedom, will never accept this new world of Hitler's. Free men, not slaves! Free nations, not German vassals! A community of nations, freely co-operating for the good of all – these are the pillars of the new and better order that the British people wish to see. And I hope that our country, which leads the fight today to prevent the immeasurable human tragedy which Hitler's victory would mean, will be the one to point the way for all peoples to a better life . . ."

The text of Halifax's speech did not mark the end of Hitler's peace attempts, for on the evening of August 1, 1940 thousands of copies of his Reichstag address floated down out of the night sky over Britain, littering the quiet countryside below.

THRIFTY WAR-TIME RECIPES — Good Housekeeping Book of

Economical Vegetable, Fish, Meat & Game Dishes Soups and Salads

Approved by the MINISTRY OF FOOD

6D

As Britain's supply lines were put under increasing pressure by Hitler's marauding U-boats the need for "Thrifty War-Time Recipes" grew ever more obvious. This *Good Housekeeping* booklet was published in 1940.

Perhaps he thought that Britain's leaders had withheld the full extent of his "last appeal" from the people, and as he had always hoped for a popular revolt against Churchill's aggressiveness perhaps he thought a direct appeal to the population might pay off. He would not have been pleased to discover that copies of his oratory received little serious attention, most of them being put to good use in countryside privies or raffled as curios at village fêtes! But his dismay soon turned into a stubborn resolve to finish things once and for all and punish the British for their continual impudence. "Sea-lion" would go ahead.

The Kriegsmarine was still deeply concerned about the operation's chances of success. After a succession of delegations were dispatched to OKW's headquarters at Giessen in order to point out some of the technical problems that worried the navy, Raeder finally received an opportunity at the end of July to submit a revised plan to Hitler. The new proposal suggested scaling down the operation and selecting a single landing zone in the vicinity of Dover. The previous scheme required large amounts of fully sea-going shipping which not only was proving difficult to find but would also be too vulnerable to fire from the shore defences of Britain as it lay at anchor for up to 36 hours while troops, vehicles and stores were unloaded.

If the new, shorter crossing was accepted then stronger counter-measures like mine channels, anti-submarine defences and sur-

As this letter from Lord Beaverbrook at the Ministry of Aircraft Production shows, the government was grateful for fund-raising efforts, however small they were, to help meet the enormous cost of supplying Fighter Command with expensive modern monoplanes.

face escorts could be provided to protect the invasion flotilla and reduce the risk of dislodgement once a bridgehead had been secured. Raeder told Hitler that if the new scheme was adopted preparations would be completed by September 15. Under increasing pressure from Raeder, Hitler finally relented and accepted this revised plan, which was subsequently sanctioned in a directive dated August 27.

Alongside the main assault between Folkestone and Beachy Head a secondary landing was to take place at Brighton, consisting of an assault unit of 7,000 men supported by 4,500 paratroops who would tumble from a fleet of Junkers 52 transports and land on the ridge of the South Downs behind the town, thereby securing the high ground and covering the route of any breakout north towards London.

It now seems inconceivable that OKW could sanction a new strategy which employed a greatly reduced force (the number of divisions had been culled from the previous minimum of 40 to 13) at a time when the enemy had benefitted from over three months' grace to improve its defences. The unexpected stay of execution had enabled Britain to replace the aircraft lost in France, scrape together a reserve of pilots, rearm the divisions saved at Dunkirk and improve shore defences beyond recognition.

By mid-July, shortly before he was replaced as C-in-C Home Forces by Alan Brooke, even the cautious Edmund Ironside was becoming more confident about Britain's chances of repulsing a German attack. "Three days' hard work at inspecting," he wrote on July 16. "Things are much better and every day makes a difference . . . I noticed no defeatism at all." A day later, he noted that "We have reached another morning without any active operations by the Bosches. It does not seem that he can go on allowing us to bomb him so badly without much return from him."

Bomber Command, though ill-equipped, had nevertheless maintained a night offensive against Germany since the aborted Norwegian Campaign. Its targets were principally shipping and port facilities, even if casualties were high among the aircrews of their Whitleys, Hampdens, Wellingtons and Blenheims.

On July 19, the day that Ironside retired, he was satisfied enough with the state of Britain's defences to start formulating a plan for a separate Home Army to free the more experienced men of the Field Army from their restrictive defensive duties. "We still have an immense amount of work to do to get the coast defences in order, but we are well on the way towards it. When that is finished we can arrange the local reserves . . ."

The lull before the storm had provided enough time for the people of Britain to get over their initial shock at Germany's rapid continental triumphs and replace it with a cheery resolve. The clatter of metal against metal identified the location of huge dumps where aluminium ironmongery was deposited in answer to Beaverbrook's claim that "we will turn your pots and pans into Spitfires and Hurricanes, Blenheims and Wellingtons . . ." Although scrap merchants argued that their own yards were full, and it is unlikely that the scheme yielded very much useful material, the pots and pans drive and the more sensible "Spitfire Funds" which were started all over the country had enormous value in unifying the people against a common foe.

It was not until August 9 that Enigma decrypts revealed the term "Adler Tag" or "Eagle Day" and hinted that a massive attack was being prepared. Yet as early as July 14 Churchill began to suspect that the ominous calm cloaked final preparations for the air assault that would be an essential preparation for any invasion attempt. After breakfast at Chequers on that Sunday, he confided to his

A SEA-LION STIRS

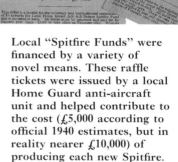

private secretary John Colville that "der Tag" might be imminent and repeatedly said, "Hitler must invade or fail. If he fails he is bound go to east, and fail he will."

In fact the Sea-lion planners had selected a suitable day for the Eagle Attack or "Adleranagriff" as it was known to the Luftwaffe. Adler Tag would take place on August 13, 1940, triggering an all-out assault on the RAF which, Goering boasted, would be smashed to pieces within four days and completely eradicated in two to four weeks.

By the middle of July the strategic deployment of the Luftwaffe in the occupied territories had been completed. Three massive Luftflotten had been transferred from bases in Germany to new airfields in France, the Low Countries and Scandinavia. Feldmarschall Kesselring, from his headquarters in Brussels, commanded Luftwaffe 2, which operated from the Low Countries and northern France; Feldmarschall Sperrle (HQ in Paris) commanded Luftwaffe 3, operating from north-western France; and General Stumpff (HQ in Stavanger) commanded Luftwaffe 5, the most distant of the Luftwaffe airfleets, operating from bases in Norway and Denmark.

In command of the combined force of over 800 single-engined fighters (Bf-109s), 220 twin-engined fighters (Me-110s), 260 dive-bombers (Ju-87 Stukas), and 990 bombers (He-111s, Do-17s and Ju-88s) that were ranged against the 650-plus RAF fighters was Hitler's named successor, Reichsmarschall Hermann Goering.

In 1940 Goering was 47 years old. In Germany he was known as "Der Eiserne" (the Iron Man) because of his apparent strength and military bearing. In Britain a book published in 1940 entitled "Goering – Germany's Most Dangerous Man" likened the rotund leader to a pathological criminal, and certainly Goering was a man of extremes. At times he displayed a dynamic charm and an intense political conviction, at others he appeared a buffoon given to displays of childish temper and bloated by an extravagant lifestyle unequalled in the Reich.

During the Great War he was an accomplished fighter-pilot, good enough to lead Jagdgeschwader 1, the famous and admired "flying circus" after its legendary commanding officer Manfred Von Richthofen had been killed. After repeated acts of bravery over the Western Front Goering was awarded the highest accolade, the Blue Max.

By 1940 he was at the pinnacle of his prestige and after Hitler he was possibly the most famous man in Germany; indeed a portrait of a noticeably leaner Reichsmarschall was one of the most popular postcards on sale in the Reich. As his much-vaunted Luftwaffe finalised their reorganisation throughout the conquered lands of Europe, Goering transferred from his opulent palace "Karinhall" to equally sumptuous accommodation on board his special train *Asia*, which was moved to sidings at Beauvais in France to enable the Reichsmarschall to view the imminent air battles in style and comfort.

Although the all-out attack on Great Britain was not scheduled until mid-August aerial activity over southern England had been steadily increasing since early July as the Luftwaffe units became operational. British histories traditionally give the date of July 10, 1940 as the start of the Battle of Britain, but Luftwaffe operations beginning now were more an extension of Hitler's policy for destroying Britain's economy by disrupting the nation's trade rather than the initial phase of Operation Sea-lion which, as we now know, was not ratified until later in the month. Nevertheless the period did mark an intensification of the challenge to Britain's air defences which, though continually tested throughout the previous winter, did not until the summer of 1940 have to deal with any large-scale threat.

The Luftwaffe organised its fighter and bomber forces in a distinctive and structured

Local "Spitfire Funds" were financed by a variety of novel means. These raffle tickets were issued by a local Home Guard anti-aircraft unit and helped contribute to the cost (£5,000 according to official 1940 estimates, but in reality nearer £10,000) of producing each new Spitfire.

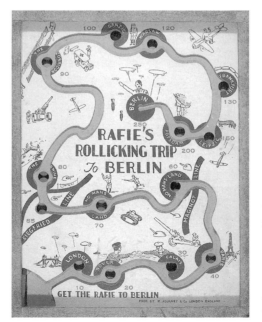

This rather bizarre boxed game reminds us that throughout the Battle of Britain Bomber Command struck deep within German territory to give Hitler a taste of his own medicine – and provide a tonic for the population at home.

way. The principal unit was the "Luftflotte", which was in fact a complete and self-contained air force consisting of fighter, bomber, reconnaissance, ground attack and support units. The smallest operational unit was the "Staffel" which, commanded by a "Staffelkapitaen", usually comprised nine aircraft, either bombers or fighters depending on the type of unit. Three Staffeln and a "Stab" (headquarters flight) made a "Gruppe", the basic Luftwaffe operational flying unit; this was generally centred on its own airfield, but on occasions more than one Gruppe operated from a single base.

Usually commanded by a "Gruppekommandeur", a Gruppe could consist of up to 150 aircrew and over 500 groundcrew for bomber units, though less for fighters. Three such "Gruppen" resulted in a single "Geschwader"; with over 90 aircraft at its disposal it was the largest individual flying unit and commanded by a "Geschwader Kommodore", usually the rank of major. Each Geschwader was generally assigned a single role, either fighter or bomber operations, for example.

Accordingly the Luftwaffe added a series of prefixes to denote the responsibilities of individual Geschwader. Fighter units were called "Jagdgeschwader" (JG), bomber units "Kampfgeschwader" (KG), dive-bomber units "Stukageschwader" (StG) and the rather optimistically named Me-110 "destroyer units" "Zerstoerergeschwader" (ZG). Other units, designed for reconnaissance, transport or development duties were given their own corresponding prefixes.

Fighter Staffels were usually broken up into a combat pair called a "Rotte" when in action. The Rotte was a superior fighting unit to its RAF equivalent as it enabled the leader ("Rottefuehrer") to concentrate on his offensive duties as his wingman ("Katchmarek") looked out for trouble and covered the attack. Two "Rotten" made up a "Schwarm" of four aircraft which flew in a staggered formation, like the outstretched fingers of the hand, with the leading Rotte flying slightly ahead and to one side of the other.

This formation had first been successfully used by Germany's Condor Legion during the Spanish Civil War and earlier by Oswalde Boelke during the Great War. It provided the maximum protection for each pilot yet enabled the unit easily to perform complex manoeuvres. Against the RAF's rigid fighting

area attacks, which were performed to rule-book precision at the call of a specific number like "fighting area attack number one", the Schwarm was markedly superior as it encouraged aggressiveness and dispensed with the need for strenuous formation flying.

The Luftwaffe aircrews were equipped with a varied assortment of aircraft, varying from the inadequate Stuka to the excellent Messerschmitt 109. In the early 1930s the "illegal" German Air Force had relied largely on obsolete biplane designs which were poorly armed and under-powered. Once Hitler came to power steps were taken to put things right.

In October 1935 comparative flight tests were carried out to select a new front-line fighter for the Luftwaffe and four companies entered the competition – Arado, Focke-Wulf, Heinkel and Bayerische Flugzeugwerke. Bayerische employed a brilliant designer called Willy Messerschmitt at their Augsburg headquarters and his submission, the Bf-109, was a compact little fighter that sat high on its two stalky undercarriage legs and which mounted small, extremely thin wings. It beat the competition hands down and was ordered into production.

The following year at Rechlin Ernst Udet, famous Great War fighter-ace and postwar stunt flier, now head of the Luftwaffe's technical supply department (Technisches Amt), organised a series of trials to choose a precision dive-bomber for the Luftwaffe. While touring the USA he had been greatly impressed by demonstrations in dive-bombing carried out by Curtiss Helldiver aircraft, and after careful scrutiny a suitable candidate was found in the unlikely shape of the gull-winged Junkers 87 – the large, ungainly monoplane which later achieved infamy as the "Stuka".

The appearance of its cranked wings and the shrill sound of its screaming sirens would come to strike terror into the hearts of ground troops and refugees alike all over Europe. Its successes in Spain, Poland, the Low Countries and France appeared to justify Udet's faith in the aircraft, but unfortunately for its unwitting crews it was to prove less than deadly over England.

The one gap in the Luftwaffe's inventory, the factor that plagued it throughout the Second World War and which to a great extent restricted its operations during the Battle of Britain, was the lack of any heavy bombers. In 1934 Colonel Wever, the German Air

A SEA-LION STIRS

Ministry's Chief of the Air Command, had foreseen this huge deficiency and issued a specification for a four-engined heavy bomber. Two prototypes were built, the Dornier 19 and the Junkers 89.

Goering visited the Junkers factory in the spring of 1935 and was unimpressed; the War Minister, von Blomberg, visited the Dornier factory and was impressed. After Wever's death, however, all development work on both prototypes was brought to an abrupt end as a result of a direct order from Goering. A lack of suitable engines had meant that neither bomber was likely to be capable of anything more than 175 mph, an inadequate speed given the performance of enemy fighters then known to be in the pipeline. Also, it must be said, Germany's new leaders were keen to amass a large air force for prestige and propaganda reasons – and fighters and medium-bombers could be produced more cheaply and in larger numbers than complex heavy bombers. Another factor was that two engines instead of four gave a 50% increase in available motors if bombers were kept light and twin-engined.

As a result of its failure to develop an operational four-engined bomber the Luftwaffe had to make do with a trio of twin-engine variants. The Heinkel He-111 had a cigar-shaped fuselage sporting an extensively glazed birdcage nose. Its performance was acceptable by the standards of the day but its bombload of only 2,134 lbs with full tanks was unimpressive. Its hand-operated 7.9 mm machine-guns were not easily brought to bear on fast-moving targets and its glazed nose, though providing excellent visibility, encouraged an acute feeling of vulnerability among the aircrews.

The Dornier Do-17 bomber, nicknamed "the flying pencil" because of its slim fuselage, was a development of a high-speed mail courier. It was marginally faster than the He-111 but carried a smaller bombload; it too was inadequately armed during the Battle of Britain and suffered accordingly.

The Junkers Ju-88 was the best bomber in Luftwaffe service during 1940 and later proved the most adaptable when it achieved great success as a night-fighter over Germany against the Allied bomber offensive. It had in fact been built to a tougher specification than either the He-111 or Do-17 and, unlike its older counterparts, could bomb horizontally or in a spectacular dive. In dive-bombing trials in 1937 the Ju-88 demonstrated its superior performance by planting 50% of its bombs within a target measuring only 150 feet in diameter. It was able to outperform the Blenheim twin-engined fighters which during the Battle of Britain had the misfortune to try and intercept Ju-88s, and its top speed was only about 30 mph slower than a Hurricane's

The backdrop to this photograph is a rare Home Guard flag belonging to the 8th Battalion, City of London Home Guard. On the left is a battledress blouson of a Home Guard "ack-ack" gunner; on the right an officer's greatcoat. Home Guards were equipped with the British Army's standard anti-gas respirator. The rifle is in fact a swift target-rifle which fired a pin into a target card mounted at the end of the "barrel". Due to the scarcity of weapons after Dunkirk such improvised training aids at least enabled Local Defence Volunteers and later Home Guards to get the feel of a gun. The two hand-weapons in front of the target-rifle are entrenching tool-handles fitted with converted bayonets in a brave effort to supply volunteers with stop-gap weaponry.

A NATION ALONE

ABOVE The Messerschmitt Bf-109 provided the claws of the Luftwaffe. Its pilots, many battle-hardened by the Spanish Civil War, were an élite combat force confident in their ability to meet RAF defence head on. Unfortunately for German airmen the combination of the 109's short range and its allocation to bomber defence would reduce enormously its tactical value.

BELOW The Messerschmitt Me-110, Goering's beloved "Destroyer", was a paper tiger when challenged by Spitfires. However, its concentrated nose armament and acceptable performance for its size meant that Hurricane pilots always approached it with respect.

operational "fighting" average of 320 mph.

In 1939 the Luftwaffe supplemented its growing armoury of Bf-109s with the addition of another fighter from Willy Messerschmitt's stable. Unfortunately his new machine, the twin-engined Bf-110, did not match the performance of its illustrious brother. Goering considered his Bf-110 crews to be an élite and the aircraft was honoured with the title "Destroyer"; but although the large two-man fighter packed a formidable punch with its concentrated nose armament of four machine-guns and two 20 mm cannon, it was a structurally weak (in the tail assembly) and unmaneouvrable aircraft – no match for a skilfully flown Hurricane or Spitfire.

The Luftwaffe's superiority in numbers tended to compensate for its deficiencies in overall quality. Where it mattered in fighter-to-fighter comparisons, the two sides were evenly matched in terms of performance. The Messerschmitt Bf-109 was marginally faster than the Spitfire and could easily outrun a Hurricane, but it was less maneouvrable than either aircraft. Its one great advantage was its impressive fuel injection system which enabled it to escape from trouble by immediately putting its nose down and diving towards the ground. Due to their unsophisticated float carburettors RAF fighters had to perform half-rolls before they dived to swill petrol into the engine to prevent it from cutting for a few vital seconds.

In terms of armament, the Bf-109 had more punch because it carried cannons, but these were low-powered and had to be brought to bear accurately before they did serious damage. Many RAF pilots survived encounters with Bf-109s and landed to find unexploded cannon shells embedded in their aircraft or damaged areas that did not prove fatal due to the low velocity of the German weapon.

By early July 1940 the preparations and equipment of both the Luftwaffe and the RAF began to be tested. German activity in the Channel began to increase and Goering's bombers accelerated their mine-laying activities in Britain's coastal estuaries; Luftwaffe reconnaissance aircraft started to appear with suspicious regularity, many of them converted high-altitude types whose pilots wore special

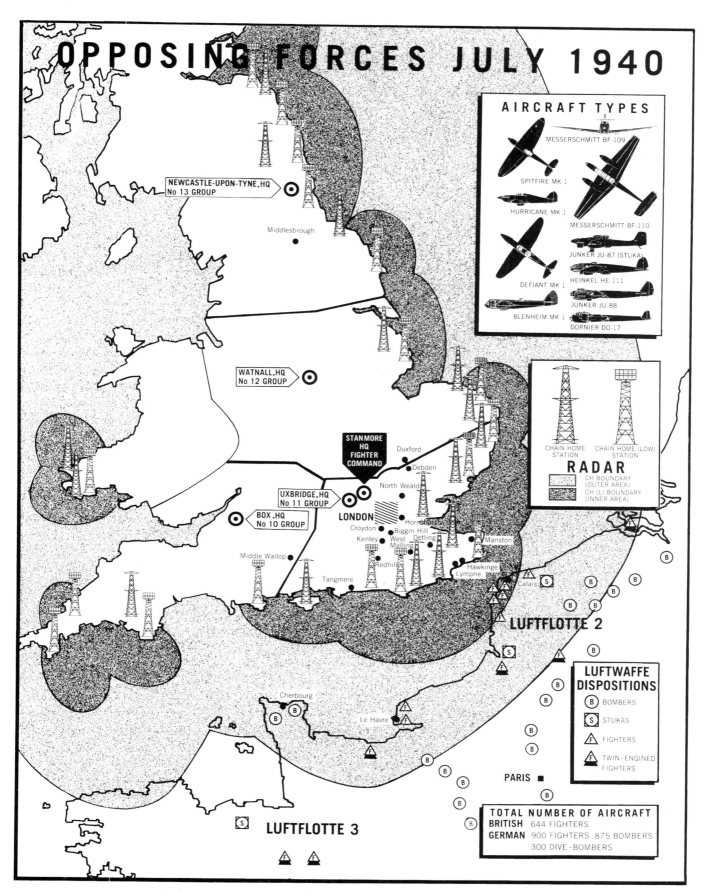

OPPOSING FORCES JULY 1940

AIRCRAFT TYPES

- MESSERSCHMITT BF-109
- SPITFIRE MK 1
- HURRICANE MK 1
- MESSERSCHMITT BF-110
- JUNKER JU-87 (STUKA)
- DEFIANT MK 1
- HEINKEL HE-111
- JUNKER JU-88
- BLENHEIM MK 1
- DORNIER DO-17

RADAR

- CHAIN HOME STATION
- CHAIN HOME (LOW) STATION
- CH BOUNDARY (OUTER AREA)
- CH (L) BOUNDARY (INNER AREA)

NEWCASTLE-UPON-TYNE.HQ
No 13 GROUP

Middlesbrough

WATNALL.HQ
No 12 GROUP

STANMORE HQ FIGHTER COMMAND

Duxford

Debden

North Weald

UXBRIDGE.HQ
No 11 GROUP

LONDON

Hornchurch

BOX .HQ
No 10 GROUP

Croydon
Biggin Hill
Kenley West Detling
Malling
Manston

Middle Wallop
Redhill
Hawkinge
Tangmere Lympne

Calais

LUFTFLOTTE 2

Cherbourg

Le Havre

LUFTWAFFE DISPOSITIONS

- B BOMBERS
- S STUKAS
- F FIGHTERS
- F TWIN-ENGINED FIGHTERS

PARIS ■

TOTAL NUMBER OF AIRCRAFT
BRITISH 644 FIGHTERS
GERMAN 900 FIGHTERS 875 BOMBERS
300 DIVE-BOMBERS

LUFTFLOTTE 3

up to battle. At the same time Bf-109s would be let loose on "Freijagd" or free-hunt missions – individual fighter sweeps intended to probe Britain's defences and cause as much trouble as possible for Dowding and his commanders.

To emphasise Germany's determination to seal the Channel to British shipping – thereby clearing it so that mine-laying and preliminary activities needed to prepare the way for the invasion flotilla could be carried out without interference – a special command was created. Johannes Fink, Geschwader Kommodore of KG2, was appointed Kanalkampfführer and ordered to close the Channel to British shipping. For operational and administrative reasons each of the three Luftflotten facing Britain was divided into Fliegerkorps (Air Corps). Kanalkampfführer Fink belonged to General Lörzer's 11 Fliegerkorps which, as part of Luftflotte 2, was stationed on the Pas de Calais.

In addition to his own Dornier bombers of KG2 Fink was given two Stuka Gruppen and two Bf-109 Jagdgeschwader to help him carry out his orders and gain air superiority over the Channel. Two of Germany's greatest fighter pilots, Major Adolf Galland and Major Werner Mölders, led the fighter element of Fink's force, Galland in JG 26 and Mölders in JG 53. Both pilots had learnt their trade during the Spanish Civil War and though they were great friends their competitive spirit drove each to victory after victory in an effort to accrue the highest personal score during the Battle of Britain, earning admiration of friend and foe alike.

ABOVE The pilot of the He-111 enjoyed superb visibility from his position to the left of the aircraft's centre line. His controls convey a mixture of German engineering and proficiency and a curious "ersatz" crudity consisting of a jumble of clumsy levers, push-rods and unprotected cables.

BELOW The He-111 displayed at the RAF Museum at Hendon.

breathing equipment and which flew too high to be intercepted. On July 7, however, Fighter Command managed to shoot down three reconnaissance Dornier 17s as they flew over the south coast.

Later in the evening, after a day of sporadic fighting, a strong formation of Dornier bombers found and attacked a convoy off Folkestone. One ship was sunk and three were damaged. "Kanalkampf", the Luftwaffe's Channel offensive, had commenced. Over the next few weeks the Luftwaffe would intensify operations intended to disrupt British shipping, hinder port activities and draw the RAF

July 8 and 9 witnessed further sporadic fighting over the Channel; more reconnaissance aircraft were intercepted and Channel convoys were again continually harried. Wednesday July 10, the day officially designated as the start of the Battle of Britain, in fact dawned overcast and showery. Radar detected some long-range Focke-Wulf Kondor aircraft heading out towards the Atlantic on a meteorological reconnaissance, but they were too high and too far to the south-west to offer the chance of a worthwhile interception.

Later in the morning a heavily escorted Do-17 reconnaissance aircraft was intercepted by Spitfires from RAF Coltishall in Norfolk and was damaged. The Do-17 had been shadowing the large convoy of merchant ships codenamed "Bread" which was making steady progress through the Straits of Dover. On the

A SEA-LION STIRS

Pas de Calais the bomber and fighter crews completed their briefings and climbed aboard their aircraft ready for the order to take-off and seek out this vulnerable and slow-moving target. At about 1.30 pm the luminous green cathode-ray tubes of Britain's Chain Home network began to dance up and down in response to an alarming build-up of enemy activity behind Calais. It appeared to Fighter Command's controllers, watching events unfold on the plotting tables before them, that Germany's hammer blow was about to be struck.

The 20 Luftwaffe bombers and 50 fighters flashed past, above the heads of their admiring ground-crews, and crossed the coast to the cheers of Flak crews and bathing Wehrmacht infantrymen. Soon it became clear that their target was not England herself but the convoy peacefully meandering along the Channel. And before the six unsuspecting Hurricanes patrolling close by the convoy could come to its rescue the German bombers were upon it; 24 RAF fighters were scrambled to the scene to help protect the convoy, and soon a tremendous dog-fight broke out. A huge spiral of aircraft turned and twisted above the convoy – Bf-109s on top, Bf-110s in the middle and Do-17s below. One Hurricane from No. 111 Squadron collided with a Dornier and lost a wing; its pilot baled out but died as a result.

The Hurricane pilots were surprised by the readiness the Bf-110 pilots showed in adopting tight, mutually protective circles of defence, the idea being that each aircraft was covered by the rear-gunner of the 110 in front. But it was a clear indication of the type's unsuitability for fighter-to-fighter combat. For all the activity only one 700-ton freighter was sunk, the rest of the ships reaching their destinations scarred but intact. During the engagement the Luftwaffe lost four fighters against three RAF machines.

On the same day over 60 Ju-88 bombers attacked Falmouth and Swansea, killing 30 people, damaging ships, a power station and railways, and demonstrating the Luftwaffe's ability to extend its operations to other areas of Britain. By sunset the RAF had suffered a loss of six aircraft, the Luftwaffe 13.

On July 11 Goering's staff issued a directive concerning the "Intensive Air War Against England". Orders were issued for preliminary attacks against Channel shipping targets and for raids on a number of specified targets.

Goering's basic directive formed the basis for a series of more detailed briefings which were distributed from individual Luftflotte head-quarters to the Geschwaders under their control. On the 13th Luftflotte 5 distributed an order stating that "as the prerequisite condition of a successful air war against England it is envisaged that the enemy's air armaments industry and the enemy's air force will be destroyed at the earliest possible moment by the first blows of the attack."

The bombs carried in Heinkel 111s were stored vertically in racks within the fuselage. The result was a cramped interior in what was a relatively small bomber – especially considering its intended role as leveller of cities.

It is not difficult to imagine the vulnerability felt by the Heinkel's bomb-aimer. Lying flat on a narrow "bed" which projected forward of the cockpit and left the airman's head hanging, seemingly in space, within the hemisphere of the nose-fairing, he must have felt very detached from the crew behind him.

A NATION ALONE

On the 21st Goering assembled Kessel-ring, Sperrle and Stumpff as well as Feld-marschall Erhard Milch (the Luftwaffe's Inspector General and effectively its chief architect/administrator) to a conference at Karinhall. Goering proceeded to update his senior commanders with the latest plans for air activity against Britain. Headed simply "Air War Against England", the new directive made two amendments to the earlier orders of July 11, both additions being results of OKW's recently accelerated planning for Operation Sea-lion.

A new target, the Royal Navy, was given to the Luftflotten commanders, and they were instructed to ensure that the fleet anchorage at Portsmouth was put out of action to hamper the Royal Navy's ability to operate in the familiar waters of the Channel. However, certain other harbour facilities were to be left undamaged so that they could be used by the

Due to its astonishing ability to achieve a near-vertical dive the Ju-87 Stuka was capable of frightening accuracy during the blitzkrieg in Poland and France . . .

A SEA-LION STIRS

German forces once they had crossed the Channel. Finally, Goering cautioned his commanders against sowing mines in areas where they could in turn damage his own invasion fleet.

As the conference was brought to a conclusion Kesselring, Sperrle and Stumpff left to prepare their own amended directives. Kesselring wanted to attack London at an early stage in the battle, so as to draw the RAF defenders away from their exposed airfields; this would enable the Luftwaffe to concentrate all its forces and destroy the RAF en masse above its burning capital. But Hitler expressly forbade any attack on London and the Luftflotten were ordered to concentrate their activities against industry and the RAF.

In fact in the days since the fighting on July 10 the RAF had refused to rise to the Luftwaffe's bait, with Dowding and Park stubbornly husbanding their forces in a careful and deliberate manner. Though their use of penny-packets of fighters frustrated many Fighter Command pilots as much as it did the Luftwaffe, their action was eminently sensible. Each day a convoy was selected for attack and German aircraft were dispatched from their forward airfields to be met by a handful of aircraft whose pilots always seemed to know they were coming; and each day airmen of both sides fell to their deaths in the deceptively dangerous waters of the Channel – or limped home with aircraft torn and shattered and senses reeling.

Early on in the engagement large silver seaplanes bearing Red Cross markings entered the battle zone. The Luftwaffe employed about 30 Heinkel He-59 seaplanes to rescue their pilots from the water. If a pilot had been forced to bale out over water he released a brightly coloured dye into the sea around his dinghy to mark his position, and within minutes a He-59 would usually approach the scene making a stately entrance—surrounded by an entourage of up to 12 Bf-109s acting as close escort.

Many German pilots were rescued in this manner and later, when it was suspected that the He-59 was being used for reconnaissance purposes, Dowding ordered such rescue aircraft to be shot down regardless of the presence of Red Cross markings. Luftwaffe ground-crews then hastily applied a dull coat of camouflage to their 59s. If they were not picked up immediately by the Luftwaffe rescue service the downed German pilots could swim to one of the many floating safety islands that dotted the sea and provided temporary shelter and accommodation.

In comparison the RAF rescue operation was meagre. There were few purpose-built rescue launches (an Air-Sea Rescue service

. . . planting bombs on targets which high altitude attacks would have missed. Against a concerted fighter defence over England, however, the slow, poorly armed aircraft was an easy target for Hurricanes and Spitfires – and was eventually withdrawn from the Luftwaffe's order of battle.

Willy Messerschmitt's clever move on the 109, joining the undercarriage directly to the fuselage, made the wings more aerodynamic.

The Bf-109's cockpit was small and rather cramped for pilots of even average build. A thick armoured glass windscreen and heavy cockpit framing also reduced forward visibility.

did not come into operation until 1941), and pilots depended on a chance encounter with friendly fishing-boats and the keen eyes of a lifeboat crewman. It had been considered unnecessary to equip them with dinghies, and many pilots drowned simply because they had insufficient strength left to blow through the rubber tube to inflate their "Mae West" life-jackets. Luftwaffe pilots enjoyed the benefit of carbon dioxide canisters which, when in contact with water, automatically inflated

their jackets. Luftwaffe life-preservers became prized booty and were removed from captured German aircrews to be used as an alternative to the Air Ministry version.

On July 14 listeners to the BBC enjoyed a ringside seat at an air battle off Dover. Attacks in this area were becoming so frequent that the location became known as "Hellfire Corner". As Stukas clashed with Spitfires above yet another convoy the BBC Home Service's reporter Charles Gardner excitedly recorded

The sophistication of Willy Messerschmitt's design is evident in this Air Ministry section of the 109.

his eye-witness account of the air combat, a spectacle which was clearly visible through the heat haze and fine mist of spray which hung over the ships as a result of near misses by high-explosive bombs.

At the end of the day the RAF calculated that 593 sorties had been flown in response to the enemy activity off Dover and a separate attack on Swanage in Dorset. Throughout the night the Luftwaffe increased its pressure on the defences, which though adequate by day were largely ineffectual after dark. As the sun dropped below the horizon Goering's bombers picked their way through the blackout and successfully raided Bristol, the Isle of Wight, Kent and Suffolk. Fortunately casualties were light since the population had learnt to take ARP precautions seriously during the sporadic winter raids, and both the Anderson shelters and those provided for the general public were put to good use.

Between July 14 and July 19 Kanal-kampfführer Fink maintained his offensive against Britain's coastal installations and Channel shipping. To the irritation of his frustrated fighter-pilots Dowding was equally consistent in his refusal to dispatch large groups of aircraft to intercept the Luftwaffe's provocative action. Protecting Britain's maritime interests, especially the Royal Navy's rather exposed dock facilities, had never been part of Dowding's defence plan, and he had neither the resources nor the strategy to carry

it out. However, although heavily outnumbered, RAF fighters were regularly sent to harass the Luftwaffe raiders, flying some 313 sorties on the 16th, for example. Nevertheless Dowding stubbornly restrained the bulk of his 23 front-line squadrons – who were by now tugging at the leash, impatient for an opportunity to do battle.

Each day Luftwaffe aircraft crossed the coast in an effort to find out more about the RAF's defence measures. Although Goering later boasted to an American journalist that the early Kanalkampf operations were nothing

Unlike Spitfires and Hurricanes, the Bf-109's cockpit hood ringed to one side and thus could not be slid back to facilitate taxiing while on the ground. The armoured headshield behind the pilot protected him from small-calibre machine-gun fire from the rear.

more than armed reconnaissance missions, the Luftwaffe's intelligence gathering was woefully disorganised and its results inaccurate. On July 16 the Luftwaffe intelligence staff produced a paper – which, though wildly misleading, became the basis for all German planning prior to Eagle Attack. The report overestimated Britain's fighter resources (900 aircraft as opposed to the true figure of 600), but underestimated just about every other aspect of her enemy's defences.

In assessing the comparative strengths of each air force the survey insisted that both the Hurricane and Spitfire were inferior to the Messerschmitt 109, claimed that the Bf-110 was superior to anything less than "skilfully handled Spitfires" and discounted the Blenheim due to its poor performance. The Luftwaffe also understimated the potential of forward airfields, which were considered merely as reserve landing strips. In fact as the aerial activity increased Dowding moved more of his squadrons to important coastal airfields like Manston, Hawkinge and Lympne in Kent and Tangmere in Sussex to improve their chances of an early interception with the enemy before Goering's airfleets crossed the English coastline.

The report's great failing, however – at least from the Luftwaffe's point of view – was its inability to appreciate the extent of Britain's increased aircraft production capacity. It assumed that Beaverbrook's factories were producing between 180 and 300 fighters per month and predicted that this figure would decline dramatically under the influence of an intensified bombing offensive. Yet the "shadow factory" scheme and the further dispersal of manufacturing to furniture-makers, tube-stations and even garages had increased Britain's total fighter production to 496 fighters in July, a figure which was to remain more or less consistent in August and September despite the ferocity of the Luftwaffe's bombardment.

Interception of RAF radio traffic during the opening stages of Kanalkampf had indicated a high level of ground-to-fighter transmissions. This was mistakenly thought to reveal the inflexibility of the RAF's control system, fostering the belief that Fighter Command's pilots were tied to a rigid pattern of interception techniques. As we know, the liaison between ground and air enabled RAF pilots to benefit from advanced warning of enemy activity and greatly improved their chances of a successful interception. Based on information from their listening posts and unaware of the true purpose of the familiar radar masts, the intelligence report wrote off Dowding's command system as inflexible and outdated. It also claimed that, at intermediate levels, RAF officers had little experience of actual flying and were consequently unsuited to leadership.

The report's conclusion was a confirmation of Goering's own views and appears to justify the Reichsmarshal's contempt for the RAF's fighting capability. Summing up, the Luftwaffe intelligence staff stated: "The Luftwaffe is clearly superior to the RAF as regards strength, equipment, training, command and location of bases. In the event of an intensification of air warfare the Luftwaffe, unlike the RAF, will be in a position in every respect to achieve a decisive effect this year if the time for the start of large-scale operations is set early enough to allow advantage to be taken of the months with relatively favourable weather conditions."

Events over the Channel a few days later, on July 19, appeared to bear out the Luftwaffe's confidence. Early that morning the RAF shot down yet another reconnaissance Do-17, and later on a quartet of Dorniers evaded the defences and managed to hit Glasgow's Rolls-Royce factory. By midday nine Defiant two-seater turret-fighters of No. 141 Squadron, just transferred from Edinburgh, were in formation off Folkestone after taking off from the forward airfield at Hawkinge.

As the unwieldy Defiants climbed to their assigned height of 5,000 feet their gunners

Though it packed a fearful punch from its one-ton power-operated gun-turret, the Defiant's lack of forward armament left it easy prey for Luftwaffe pilots who sensibly avoided attack from the rear.

traversed the aircraft's power-operated gun-turret and scanned the dangerous skies for enemy aircraft. But they did not see the 20 Messerschmitt 109s which were diving at them out of the bright midday sun.

The Luftwaffe had first encountered the Defiant over Dunkirk and initially, after mistaking the type for a Hurricane, had experienced some losses after receiving fire from its four-gun turret. Soon, however, the Messerschmitt pilots discovered the Defiant was a paper tiger; a heavy aircraft, slow and unmanoeuvrable, it had no forward armament and was vulnerable to frontal assaults, rarely surviving such encounters.

As they dived towards their unsuspecting prey the score of high-speed 109s unleashed a storm of machine-gun bullets and cannon-fire on the gaggle of Defiants below them. The Defiant gunners struggled to bring their guns to bear, but it was too late. Within minutes six aircraft, shot to pieces, were tumbling earthwards. Five of them struck the cold water of the Channel; one, after temporarily regaining straight and level flight, almost made it back to Hawkinge but engine failure prevented such good fortune. The sixth Defiant smashed into a residential street in Dover, its crew unable to escape from their aircraft. In all ten aircrew were killed or listed missing.

Three Defiants made it back to base but one, damaged during the onslaught, landed minus its rear-gunner, who had baled out over the Channel. All the Defiants may have been lost had it not been for the arrival of Hurricanes from No. 111 Squadron out of

Croydon, who shot down one of the attacking 109s and shepherded the remaining two-seaters home. What was left of No. 141 was returned to Scotland, this time to Prestwick and far safer duties against the unescorted bombers of Luftflotte 5. Although it was now obvious that the Defiant was unsuitable for use against fighters, July 19 was not the end of the aircraft's front-line activity. Amazingly 264 Defiant Squadron, after moving to RAF Hornchurch the following month, was thrown into the thick of the fighting on August 24, the unit being ordered forward to protect the badly mauled airfield at RAF Manston near the Kent coast.

As 264 Squadron took off from this exposed airfield, Manston was subjected to yet another raid. Seconds before bombers threatened to destroy them on the ground, nine Defiants clawed their way upwards from the debris-strewn airfield and climbed to intercept the Junkers-88s bent on Manston's destruction. During repeated assaults on the airfield four of the nine aircraft were destroyed; three more aircraft landed, damaged but repairable. As one of the three Defiants force-landed at Manston the Very signal cartridges exploded which its pilot, Flying Officer Campbell-Colquhoun, scrambled clear. Fortunately both pilot and gunner escaped unhurt. Six aircrew were posted missing and a seventh, a rear-gunner, later died of his wounds. One of the four aircraft which failed to return was last seen chasing a Ju-88 out to sea across the Channel in brave but fruitless pursuit.

As the Channel fighting continued losses on both sides mounted steadily. By July 23 the

The Boulton Paul Defiant was a direct development of the successful First World War Bristol fighter. Unfortunately for its crews (seen here arriving for duty aboard a lorry) air-fighting had progressed enormously since the days of Albert Ball and Manfred Von Richthofen – and the Defiant proved a hopeless anachronism. The savaging of the RAF's Defiant squadrons during the Battle of Britain mirrored the destruction of the equally inadequate Fairey Battles in France.

123

RAF had lost 45 aircraft compared with the Luftwaffe's 85. Dowding was aware that worse was to come and realised that the Luftwaffe had carefully concealed its hand.

On July 25 just how potent Goering's air force could be was demonstrated off the Straits of Dover. As 21 merchantmen (mostly colliers) edged nervously through the narrow channel they were set upon by 60 bombers of Luftflotte 2; this time they were supported by nine E-boats who diverted the attention of two British destroyers, *Boreas* and *Brilliant*, assigned as the convoy's escort.

In successive waves dive-bombers plummeted towards the ships, the aircraft rearing up and climbing only after they had released their well-aimed bombs onto the heaving decks below. Five ships were sunk and six more severely damaged in this way. Both destroyers were dive-bombed as well and one suffered the humiliation of later being towed into Dover harbour.

Two days later, on July 27, two destroyers were sunk and a third damaged. On the 29th yet another destroyer was sent to the bottom, forcing the Admiralty to abandon Dover as a base for anti-invasion destroyer units. Equally alarming was the first sighting of bomb-carrying Messerschmitt-109s, a further indication of the enemy's offensive capability.

Drizzle and poor visibility hampered German operations on July 30. In scattered east coast raids Orfordness, Clacton and Harwich were attacked at a cost of five Luftwaffe aircraft, but no RAF machines were destroyed. While his planes were groping through the Channel squalls in search of suitable targets Hitler was explaining his latest plans to Goering. The Reichsmarschall was told that "immediately and with the greatest haste" he should prepare for the "great battle of the German Air Force against England". It was to begin at 12 hours' notice.

As Goering studied the OKW teleprint which contained his Führer's order he considered his next move, and the following day he issued operational orders to his air fleet commanders. The assault would begin with a huge feint attack on London to draw the RAF up to battle. As the aircraft of Fighter Command were lured from their airfields they would be annihilated by the superior numbers of German fighters weaving high above the bomber formations acting as bait.

But the Luftwaffe units involved needed more time to finalise their tactical plans. With this in mind Hitler issued a directive on August 1 which postponed the air assault until the 5th, weather permitting. The decision to initiate Sea-lion would be taken by the Führer personally between 8 and 14 days into the aerial offensive – as it became clear that the Luftwaffe had met its objectives.

On August 2 Goering issued his final directive concerning the forthcoming Adler-angriff (Eagle Attack). On Adler Tag (Eagle Day) Air Fleets 2 and 3 would combine to deliver a concentrated blow against England; Air Fleet 5 would join the attack the next day.

The reduction in Channel shipping suggested that the Kanalkampf had been won by Germany. The next phase of the plan, the task of securing air superiority over southern England within four days, was about to begin. So, as Britain waited, the eagle sharpened her talons.

Chapter Five

". . . If you are on fire do not open the hood until the last
moment, as it will draw flames into the cockpit. If your
clothes are soaked in petrol, switch off the engine switches and
leave the throttle open, otherwise as you get out sparks from
the exhaust may act like the flint in your cigarette lighter."

Air Ministry instructions to pilots on baling out, 1940

THE HAMMER
AND THE ANVIL

The radar masts at Dover
being shelled by long-range
German guns from
France – and captured by
long-range German cameras.

In terms of air battles the first week of August 1940 was unspectacular, with Luftwaffe units busy studying reconnaissance photographs and rehearsing operational procedures in preparation for Eagle Day. Between the 1st and the 7th Figher Command lost only three aircraft but succeeded in destroying 20 German machines.

Bad weather and the distraction of planning for the forthcoming all-out attack had restricted Luftwaffe activity to a minimum since the air battles of late July – and the unexpected respite enabled Dowding to continue building up his forces. Between June 30 and August 10 Fighter Command's strength had risen from 587 to 749 operationally available aircraft, and the Luftwaffe could muster 805 serviceable aircraft on August 10. The number of RAF fighter squadrons had increased, too. By August 8 Fighter Command's strength had gone from 52 to 55 squadrons with the addition of two Polish (302 and 303) and one Czech (310) squadrons. Though the Polish and Czech pilots severely tried the patience of their British superiors, with their indiscipline and scant knowledge of English, their fighting ability was never in question. After suffering the pain and humiliation of seeing their homelands fall to German domination the Poles and Czechs were keen to even the score and spared no effort in their attempts to destroy Luftwaffe aircraft. Indeed Sergeant Josef Frantisek, a Czech pilot with No. 303 Squadron, is now generally recognised as the RAF's highest scoring ace during the Battle of Britain, having destroyed 17 aircraft.

The supply of pilots available for combat had also increased, from 1,200 at the end of June to 1,434 by August 3, although this

RIGHT It was crucial that pilots thought before they reacted, and this official poster portraying an RAF fighter unwittingly providing an ideal target for Luftwaffe gunners shows. The warning was titled "Temper Dash with Discretion", while the smaller print reads: "Don't let your eagerness spoil a combined attack and incidentally make you a 'sitter' for the enemy."

RIGHT The "Sheer Carelessness" in this Air Diagram refers to the need for a full supply of oxygen when operating at altitude. It was usually the novice pilots, unsure of the complexities of high-speed aerial combat, who fell prey to careless mistakes or, more often, the keen eyes of experienced Luftwaffe fighter-pilots. The sub-line – "Neglect to check your oxygen or other equipment may bring disaster on yourself and your formation" – again stresses loyalty to fellow airmen.

RIGHT Echoing the famous adage of First World War pilots, "Beware of the Hun in the sun" speaks for itself. The planes of both sides – as in most of these warning posters – bear surprisingly little resemblance to the real things.

THE HAMMER AND THE ANVIL

impressive increase in pilot strength was not achieved without sacrifice. Churchill had become increasingly curious about the seemingly high number of pilots who possessed wings but were not operationally qualified. The Air Minister, Sir Archibald Sinclair, patiently pointed out that combat readiness required in excess of 100 hours of training after a pilot had received his wings. Professor Lindemann, Churchill's scientific adviser, was equally sceptical about the RAF's training programme and shared the Prime Minister's view that the training period could be reduced. "Are not our training standards too high?" he asked Sinclair. "The final polish should be given in the squadrons."

As a result the training period was cut from three months to one and the final polish was often brief and abrasive, usually high above the Channel at the hands of skilled Luftwaffe pilots. The "old hands" – men like Bader, Standford-Tuck, Malan and Deere – were more likely to survive than the younger pilots who lacked combat experience.

The contribution that Bomber and Coastal Command made to Britain's war effort during this stage of the battle was crucial. At night Channel ports in occupied Europe were raided, indicating what was in store for the German invasion fleet if it set sail. Goering had repeatedly assured Hitler that Germany's borders were impregnable to RAF attack and even went as far as bragging that "if a single enemy bomber flies over the Reich's territory, you can call me Meyer!"

But to his immense embarrassment the Reichsmarschall could do nothing to prevent RAF bombers from crossing the frontier in droves and scattering their unwelcome cargo far and wide throughout Germany. One anonymous character probably summed up the general feeling in Britain concerning the night bombing of Germany when she remarked to a Mass-Observation operative: "I'm glad we've started dropping a few bombs on Germany. That will wake them up a bit. Of course you can't help it if one or two civilians do get hurt – they shouldn't get in the way."

Goering grew increasingly impatient to deal the knock-out blow. All he needed was four days of good weather and the troublesome RAF would cease to exist in the skies above southern England, and now his meteorological staff pointed to a belt of high pressure which was slowly approaching from the Azores. When it came, they predicted, the Reichs-

ASKING FOR IT DO NOT LET YOURSELF BE SURPRISED BY THE ENEMY. KEEP A GOOD LOOK-OUT ALL ROUND AT ALL TIMES.

Unless a vigilant all-round lookout was observed pilots could be unaware of the split-second diving attack that was the favoured manoeuvre of the hunter – and which could spell destruction to unsuspecting prey.

marschall would have his fine weather and the full fury of his Luftwaffe could be unleashed. Until then Goering decided to resume the bombing offensive in the Channel, and he did so with a vengeance.

Under cover of darkness, early in the morning of August 8, Convoy CW9 (code-named "Peewit") slipped into the Straits of Dover. In the light of recent experience the Royal Navy was taking no chances, and alongside an escort of anti-aircraft destroyers the Admiralty had provided a flotilla of barrage-balloon vessels to protect the 25 merchantmen. Even in darkness, however, the convoy was in danger. Miles away, across the Channel, the enemy was watching its every

RAF veterans of the Battle of Britain have a healthy respect for the capabilities of Luftwaffe air-gunners. This Air Diagram, headed "Don't give the Rear-gunner a 'sitter'," warned of the dangers of negligence.

A NATION ALONE

By 1940 it seemed that most civilians were involved in some kind of Civil Defence (CD) duties. The panorama of badges shown in this photograph includes those worn by a wide variety of ARP and medical services. The Red Cross badges are notable in that they belonged to American volunteers who manned ambulances in support of the hard-pressed British medical services. Also featured (top right and bottom right, dated 1940) are those worn by Czechoslovakian troops fighting from Britain. Of the two Spitfire badges the top one was sold in aid of the "Spitfire Funds", while the "Sweetheart badge" below it was hammered out of a penny coin by a skilful and doubtless amorous RAF mechanic.

move, for high up on the cliffs at Cap Blanc Nez a German Freya radar was scanning the distant horizon for possible targets.

As the silhouette of Convoy CW9 was bounced back to the receiver equipment the Freya operators relayed their sighting to local E-boat packs and supplied the necessary target co-ordinates. The well-armed E-boats raced at speed to intercept the unsuspecting convoy; and before dawn the predators had sunk three ships and damaged two others.

The Luftwaffe was determined to finish off the scattered remnants of the convoy and by nine o'clock had despatched a force of Stukas and Bf-109s. This attack was beaten off by six RAF squadrons sent to the convoy's aid and the ragged collection of vessels limped on towards the Isle of Wight, but by midday the skies above the convoy darkened in the presence of a massive formation of Luftwaffe aircraft. Nearly 60 Stukas and three times as many fighters jostled for position above the ships, then in waves the Junkers 87s banked and dived towards the helpless merchantmen.

The Stuka was a large and clumsy aircraft but its bombing technique enabled it to achieve consistently precise results. With the throttle pulled right back and the dive-brakes opened the aircraft automatically nosed over into the dive, and by using a window between his feet for sighting the target a Stuka pilot could then judge the angle of his descent by aligning the horizon with a series of markings on his cockpit canopy.

An angle of between 30° and 70° could be selected, depending on the target. The aircraft's nose was used as the bomb-sight and the pilot applied either left or right aileron to

keep the machine on line. At a dive-angle of 90° the Stuka would quickly accelerate to over 370 mph as it dropped towards its target. After releasing the bomb, which was swung out on a cradle from its perch beneath the fuselage, a signal light on the aircraft's contact altimeter flashed when it was time to pull out of the dive. The pilot then depressed a knob on the control column and the Stuka's automatic pull-out was initiated. If this mechanism failed brute force was required to pull back the control column to right the aircraft – no easy task when pulling six "g" and with the water racing closer. Once the aircraft's nose was pointing above the horizon the dive-brakes were retracted, the airscrew pitch set to climb and the throttle opened up.

With rule-book precision the Stuka dive-bombers followed their attack procedures and struck Convoy CW9. RAF squadrons from Tangmere, Westhampnett, Middle Wallop and Warmwell were scrambled to its rescue and raced headlong towards the battle taking place south of the Isle of Wight. Soon a total of seven fighter squadrons had joined the mêlée above the shattered convoy.

Later in the afternoon 82 more Stukas and their escorts approached the scene in response to a Luftwaffe order that the convoy should be destroyed. Exhausted seamen fought to keep their vessels underway as high above them a confusion of aircraft danced to the rhythm of machine-guns and cannon. The tangled wakes of fleeing ships below were echoed in the elaborate pattern of smoke-trails that emerged and dissolved aloft.

In their battle to reclaim the convoy from the Luftwaffe's clutches many RAF pilots experienced their first encounters with the infamous Stukas. And as Hurricane and Spitfire pilots selected their targets from the mass of animated dive-bombers they soon became aware of the enemy aircraft's obvious shortcomings.

As RAF pilots jockeyed for suitable attack positions, they carefully manoeuvred their fighters to bring the eight machine-guns to bear at the optimum range and angle of deflection. Reflector gun-sights were set to project a luminous circle corresponding to the target's wingspan, and once the distinctive gull-wings of a Stuka filled the circle of the sight, "fire" was selected on the control column hand-grip. Compressed air then instantaneously operated the machine-gun breeches, firing all eight guns simultaneously

THE HAMMER AND THE ANVIL

and with such force that the aircraft shuddered under the recoil.

Patches that were stuck across the gun-ports to prevent the admission of moisture were blown to shreds as a stream of bullets sprayed from the muzzles of each weapon. As the pungent odour of cordite pervaded each fighter's cockpit, pilots fixed their stare on the ribbons of tracer that flicked towards the dive-bomber they had chosen and which was desperately jinking to evade its effect. If a pilot's aim had been true, ball ammunition would rip into the thin aluminium which clad the Stuka's airframe. De Wilde explosive bullets, if carried, would be seen to whip across wings and fuselage, leaving tiny puffs of smoke as they penetrated and blew up the unfortunate enemy machine.

Once hit, Stukas would perform their last and involuntary dive, spewing smoke and flame from their smashed engines. As the sea rushed up to meet them the Luftwaffe aircrew, usually too low to bale out, braced themselves against the inevitable impact. With its huge chin-mounted radiator and awkward spatted undercarriage the Stuka was difficult to ditch; most turned over directly they hit the water, consigning their terrified crews to a cold and suffocating end in the grey water.

One Hurricane pilot from 145 Squadron actually managed to destroy two Stukas after his engine had stopped running. With his propellor uselessly windmilling the young flight commander dived silently on one Ju-87, causing it to crash into the sea. The dive encouraged the engine of his Hurricane to fire and enabled him to shoot at a further '87 – sending it plummeting into the waves.

Short of fuel and ammunition the Stukas and their Bf-109 and Bf-110 escorts were forced to break off the attack and turn home. They left the sea awash with oil and debris after sinking four more merchant ships, severely damaging a further six and savaging six armed rescue ships. At the end of a day which had seen the heaviest fighting so far the Luftwaffe had lost 31 aircraft – but succeeded in destroying only 19 RAF fighters.

Compared to the previous day, August 9

Women were a vital component of Britain's defence forces. This reconstruction of a 1940 dressing-table includes examples of an Auxiliary Territorial Service (ATS) peaked cap, First-Aid Nursing Yeomanry (FANY) beret and Women's Land Army (WLA) insignia. The small silver compact bears the pervasive emblem of the ARP service.

was almost quiet. Between mine-laying and sporadic raids against convoys plying their trade along the east coast, the Luftwaffe was preoccupied with finalising its operational plans for Adler Tag. But with the inclement weather improving all the time, the first phase of the oncoming assault was scheduled for the 10th. By nightfall, however, it was obvious that climatically things had not improved sufficiently – and the planned raids against Britain's coastal airfields and radar chain were again postponed.

It was not until August 12 that the attack could begin in earnest. Although Luftwaffe intelligence had failed to identify the true purpose of the prominent radar masts that stood like sentinels along England's coastal perimeter, radio intercepts had indicated that they were indeed employed as part of the ground-to-air control system. With this in mind Luftwaffe operations staff wisely added the radar stations to the list of priority targets which, along with coastal airfields, were to be attacked in the first phase.

By damaging the radar chain the Luftwaffe hoped to "blind" Britain's defences and

ABOVE RIGHT An Me-110 C5 of 4/Aufklarungsgruppe 14 was forced down by RAF fighters above Goodwood House farm in Sussex on July 21, 1940.

RIGHT This photograph clearly illustrates the powerful nose armament of the 110, revealed by the removal of the nose cowling.

BELOW Another view of the crashed 110 stranded near Goodwood House farm.

probably paralyse the control system. If the exposed and poorly defended coastal airfields were eliminated then Fighter Command would be unable to react quickly enough to an approaching air-raid and German bombers would be free to roam inland. This, at least, was the theory. Unlike the British, German strategists were unaware of the difficulties of toppling the tall latticework masts which, despite their appearance, were surprisingly resistant to the effects of high explosives. They were completely ignorant of the partial overlap in the Chain Home (CH) network, which reduced the extent of any breach caused by an individual station going off the air.

Unperturbed by these technical constraints the Luftwaffe prepared to strike at the CH radar stations at Dunkirk, Dover, Rye, Pevensey and Ventnor. In an attempt to confuse the defences Goering ordered a series of feint attacks against embattled Dover, and while Dowding's pilots and their controllers were preoccupied with defending the ancient harbour other Luftwaffe crews hoped to slip past undetected towards the morning's real targets – the radar stations. At nine o'clock the first of the CH stations singled out for attack found themselves tracking unidentified raids which appeared to converge immediately overhead. Within minutes, in simultaneous attacks, Dover, Rye and Pevensey radar stations found themselves in the midst of the battle.

At Dover, although the apparently fragile 350-foot masts reverberated in the shock waves of explosion after explosion and several cross-members were damaged by bomb fragments, the aerial masts remained defiantly erect and functional when the smoke cleared. Plotting was not even disrupted at Dunkirk CH station, even though the heavy concrete transmitting block shifted on its foundations after a 1,000-lb bomb detonated close by. Rye CH station was severely damaged by German bombing but it too survived, thanks largely to a back-up power supply that ensured the radar coverage resumed by lunchtime. At Pevensey the station's power main was severed, though fortunately only temporarily, and it too remained on the air.

The Luftwaffe achieved its most significant result of the day later in the morning when it attacked Ventnor CH station on the Isle of Wight. As a large bomber force slipped through the balloon barrage at Portsmouth 15 Junkers 88s peeled away to assault the easily identifiable radar installation; and as the fast twin-engined bombers lined up for the attack they selected the collection of huts at the base of each mast as their target. But the very size of each mast proved a valuable defence against attack. Though they made excellent aiming points the masts were so tall that they prevented the dive-bombing Ju-88s from releasing their bombs at the optimum height. To avoid colliding with a rugged spire each bomber had to pull up from its dive before the vital operations rooms – which the masts virtually straddled – could be accurately targeted. So although fires were started and the compound at Ventnor was cratered the receiver and transmitter huts were not irreparably damaged. Nevertheless the Luftwaffe's heavy attack did succeed in crippling Ventnor to the extent that it was off the air for 11 vital days until a mobile station at nearby Bembridge was patched in to the network on August 23.

Alongside attacks on the radar stations Goering's Luftflotten were directed at coastal airfields – and yet more convoys. RAF facilities at Lympne, Manston and Hawkinge were also attacked. Lympne was singled out twice in the day and 383 bombs were delivered, rendering the airfield unserviceable. Hawkinge was temporarily put out of action by craters on the airfield and two badly damaged hangars. At Manston, a heavily escorted raid by Dorniers from KG2 succeeded in catching No. 65 Squadron's Spitfires on the ground as they scrambled to intercept their attackers. One of the Spitfires, flown by Pilot Officer Hart, was just about to take off when the blast from a near-miss stopped its engine dead and slightly damaged the machine's airframe. Although most of 65 Squadron's Spitfires managed to take off intact and join the aircraft of No. 54 Squadron, which were already aloft, they could not prevent Manston from receiving the first of a series of devastating attacks that would virtually result in the airfield's elimination from the RAF's order of battle.

August 12 did not go entirely in favour of the attackers. The leader of the group of Ju-88s that attacked Ventnor, Geschwader Kommodore Oberst Fisser, died when his aircraft crashed into Godshill Park on the Isle of Wight. His two crew members survived and were captured. Fisser's plane, an aircraft of Stab KG51, was shot down by a vengeful Hurricane of No. 145 Squadron which rushed

MAJOR H. ADLER

WILHELM LIMPERT-VERLAG · BERLIN SW

Major Adler's popular paperback pulled no punches with its graphic illustration of bombs raining down on a beleaguered Britain.

surviving Luftwaffe bombers were severely damaged and barely made it home. Some wave-hopped back to the French coast, streaming oil and coolant, and others landed heavily, bearing dead and dying crewmen in testimony to the increasing ferocity of the air war over England.

Early on the morning of August 13 Goering's headquarters flashed the codeword "Adler Tag" to Luftwaffe bases in France and the Low Countries. The attack of the eagles was on. To his intense frustration, the Reichsmarschall was forced to postpone the morning's attack and had to stand-down his aircrews as they were poised to take off for England. Poor visibility in Europe and low cloud over England were to blame, making assembly and navigation impossible.

By the time the order to postpone the assault until the afternoon had been relayed to unit after unit, part of the attacking force was already in the air and preparing to follow its pre-arranged schedule. Ironically 74 Dorniers of KG2 led by none other than Kanalkampführer Fink had taken off at 5.30 am, minutes before the stand-down was issued. As they formed up and scanned the heavens for the balance of the bomber-force, Fink's aircrews watched a twin-engined Bf-110 throw itself across the sky in a spontaneous aerobatics display. In fact the fighter was part of the escort assigned to KG2 and its pilot, having received the order to return to base pending further instructions, was desperately trying to attract Fink's attention in an effort to persuade the diligent colonel to call off the attack.

But the 110's stunts were in vain. Although Fink was surprised at how empty the sky appeared, he continued to lead the Dornier formation on towards England. Through having different crystals in their radios, the Bf-110 fighter-leader could not get in radio contact with the bomber force and, having exhausted all means of communicating to Fink, reluctantly left his charges and ordered his fellow fighter-pilots to land. Thus, Fink and his Dorniers of KG2 pressed on relentlessly towards England. Alone and unprotected, they were still confident that they were about to strike the Luftwaffe's first blow on Adlertag.

As KG2 approached England mountainous cloud rose to greet them. When at last a break appeared in the thick white layer all eyes were fixed on the site of neat rows of aeroplanes parked on an airfield below. At 7 am Fink's

to the rescue from RAF Westhampnett. In fact the Luftwaffe lost a total of ten Ju-88s in the attack against Portsmouth and the Isle of Wight. Two of them limped home badly damaged after a mauling by RAF fighters, force landing at Le Havre, and another made it back to its base in France with two crewmen wounded and its airframe peppered by .303-inch bullets.

At the end of a fierce day's fighting, which was only intended as a preliminary to the main event, Fighter Command had vectored 732 sorties and lost 22 precious warplanes. The Germans lost a total of 31 machines, but many

Now the guns turn their attention to the infantry. The enemy ...join in the

The invader will meet more than he bargains for . . .

13

formation commenced its bombing run and sticks of bombs tumbled towards the sitting target. When they struck, however, the bombs exploded not on an important No. 11 Group airfield (as claimed later in the day by Luftwaffe intelligence) but on the relatively unimportant Coastal Command light-bomber station at Eastchurch in Hampshire.

No. 111 Squadron was patrolling over Folkestone when it was vectored to intercept the Luftwaffe raid on Eastchurch, and as the unprotected bombers completed their work they were suddenly set upon by the squadron's Hurricanes. Within minutes five Dorniers were shot down and Fink's force, dispersed and fleeing for their lives, raced for home. The remainder were intercepted by Hurricanes from No. 151 Squadron and Spitfires from No. 74 Squadron, the latter led by the South African "Sailor" Malan, one of the RAF's greatest aces.

Later in the morning two more Luftwaffe attacks were mounted. One, involving Ju-88s heading for targets in Hampshire, including the Royal Aircraft Establishment at Farnborough, was harried by three Fighter Command squadrons and because of this, and thick cloud, missed its targets altogether. The other formation, approaching the coast at Portland, was picked up by radar as it climbed above Cherbourg. The two RAF squadrons which were sent to intercept were surprised to find not bombers but about 20 Bf-110s which had arrived without the Dorniers they were detailed to escort. Six were instantly destroyed and the remainder, finding they had no apparent job to do, wisely turned and fled back to the safety of the French coast.

Adler Tag did not get properly underway until the afternoon of August 13, when the improving weather encouraged Goering to launch bomber after bomber into the skies over France. Soon waves of Ju-88s and 87s and their escorting Bf-109s and 110s were moving towards their targets in southern England. Radar first detected large formations of enemy aircraft coming from the direction of the Channel Islands.

The formation split into two before it reached the English coast. To the west Southampton was bombed and the docks set on fire. A group of Ju-87 Stukas attempted to penetrate inland and bomb Middle Wallop airfield in Hampshire, but in further evidence of their unsuitability for modern combat they were once again bloodied by the fighters of the

RAF. With the sun and altitude on their side Spitfires of 609 Squadron scattered the Stukas across three counties. Nine Ju-87s were shot from the sky and their twisted wreckage added to the increasing amount of scrap that now littered the fields and hedgerows of England.

To the east, the other section of the attacking formation concentrated on Detling airfield and Rochester in Kent, with Detling receiving the full force of a successful Luftwaffe attack; the station's commanding officer was killed and many buildings were destroyed. An increase in cloud cover prevented Rochester from being identified, however, and its would-be attackers jettisoned their bombs over Canterbury, Lympne and Ramsgate before setting course for France.

August 13 had severely tried Fighter Command's defence system. The Luftwaffe had piled on the pressure by mounting a variety of raids simultaneously, preventing Dowding from guessing a target before it was too late. Nevertheless his pilots had performed admirably and accounted for 45 German aircraft. The myth of the Stuka had been finally exploded, and as tales of its vulnerability to attack were exchanged in squadron messes right across Fighter Command, pilots were more anxious to have a crack at the unwieldy dive-bomber when it next appeared in British skies.

As always Luftwaffe intelligence overestimated the success of all the day's raids. Targets were thought to have been destroyed and minor airfields damaged in the day's fighting were claimed as being important sector stations. Goering was told that 88 RAF aircraft had been destroyed. With such inaccurate reports it can be understood why the Reichsmarschall could perhaps be forgiven for demonstrating a pronounced overconfidence. Convinced that his plan to knock

This page from a 1940 children's book clearly illustrates the spirit of defiance which permeated all sections of British society.

The Hurricane was a considerably larger aircraft than the Spitfire. Its graceful outline reveals the large wing area which contributed to its great manoeuvrability.

out the RAF was running according to his naïvely ambitious timetable, Goering went to bed sure that his fleets would do even better during the coming days.

The expected resumption of effort did not materialise on August 14 and the Luftwaffe resigned itself to dispatching only a third of the previous day's sorties. The RAF's defences were, however, still under strain, not so much because of the extent and weight of the attack but more from the baffling diversity shown in Luftwaffe target selection. Although targets were often strategically unimportant, they all had to be defended.

Dowding was unable to detect any logical pattern in the Luftwaffe's operations and his controllers were kept on their toes plugging the gaps in the island fortress, trying in vain to predict where the next raid would occur. The victory ratio was still favouring the RAF, which it had to if Fighter Command was to survive; 19 German aircraft were destroyed that day as against only eight British planes.

On August 15 the ridge of high pressure that had been slowly creeping in from the Azores finally settled over the British Isles. The day dawned warm and sunny – perfect weather for the Luftwaffe to deliver its decisive hammer blow.

The previous day Goering's staff had circulated a set of final operational orders. The Luftwaffe plan of attack was going to be an all-out effort with, for the first time, all three Luftflotten employed across a wide front to inflict maximum damage and disruption against the Royal Air Force facilities.

Targets as far apart as the West Country and the North of England were selected. It would be the task of Luftflotte 5, operating from Scandinavia, to penetrate what the Luftwaffe assumed would be light defences along the north-east coast. Goering's staff had assured him that Dowding would have only a skeleton force of fighters left in the north, the remainder having been drained off to shore up Fighter Command squadrons in the south. Once the three Luftflotten reached the British coast their brief was to punch a series of holes through the radar chain and then head directly for Fighter Command's airfields. If they were not destroyed on the ground, Dowding's Spitfires and Hurricanes would be torn to pieces as they climbed to intercept the heavily escorted bomber formations.

While the skies over Europe lightened in the early hours of August 15, Luftwaffe aircrews studied the latest intelligence updates and poured over reconnaissance photographs of the targets they had been allotted. After reconnaissance aircraft had checked that all was in order, the first Luftwaffe bombers were sent on their way to England.

The familiar drone of an incoming raid was first heard in the gentle countryside of Kent. Armies of Londoners engaged in the yearly ritual of hop-picking donned their steel helmets and stared skywards as the quiet summer morning was pierced by the pulsing throb of bomber after bomber. About 100 German aircraft, consisting of a large force of Stukas and their escorts, struck the forward airfields of Hawkinge and Lympne; Hawkinge was only lightly damaged but Lympne received several direct hits on operations buildings, including the station sick-quarters. Nearby, the Rye and Dover Chain Home Low stations were blacked out after sustaining a pinpoint attack. Two RAF squadrons were vectored to intercept the early raid over Kent but were unable to prevent the attackers from achieving a notable success.

At midday on the 15th one of the most memorable, and for the defenders, stirring events of the entire conflict took place. Flying from bases in occupied Norway and Denmark 65 Heinkel-111s of KG26 and 34 Bf-110 "Destroyers" of ZG76, both part of Stumpff's Luftflotte 5, were hoping to reach England's north-east undetected and unopposed. With orders to pulverise RAF stations in the north of England – ones that Luftwaffe intelligence

Pilots of No. 111 Squadron patiently await the next scramble order outside their dispersal caravan.

THE HAMMER AND THE ANVIL

claimed were undefended – German aircrews were confident of a successful mission and a safe return.

Even though the radar chain along England's north-east coast was newer and less practised than its southerly equivalent, the broad wilderness of the North Sea enabled it to achieve good uncluttered reception. There was no substitute for experience, however, and as operators in receiver huts along the barren coastline peered into the cathode-ray tube screens they consistently underestimated the size of the raid.

Just after noon a formation of more than 20 bandits was detected approaching the Firth of Forth, and this estimate was revised to over 30 as the formation split into three and was plotted heading for Tynemouth. Regardless of the actual size of the raid No. 13 Group's controllers had sufficient warning to scramble a formidable number of Spitfires and Hurricanes (and even a squadron of Blenheims) to arrange a reception committee to meet the enemy raiders before they could inflict any damage.

It was the Spitfires of 72 Squadron that converged onto the target first. To their surprise they discovered not 30 enemy aircraft as predicted but a massive formation of nearly 100, neatly paraded in rows before them. Luftwaffe pilots were equally shocked as they made out the distinctive shape of Spitfires blocking their path in the distance. However their surprise was tinged with anxiety as No. 72 Squadron split into two, one section

attacking the faltering bombers and the other taking care of the fighter escort.

Heinkel gunners threw themselves in all directions in a desperate bid to bring their weapons to bear, but 72 Squadron's flank attack exposed the bombers' vulnerable fuselage to withering fire and prevented nose and dorsal machine-guns from being used effectively. One by one the Heinkel bombers broke formation; some wheeled round and headed home while others dived low, either dropping their cumbersome bomb-load or bravely racing on towards England.

Meanwhile the Bf-110s formed their familiar defensive circles, flying nose to tail in the vain hope that this would dissuade the aggressive Spitfires from closing for an attack run. The unlucky 110 pilots had been forced to leave their rear-gunners behind in Scandinavia due to the weight penalty of such a long-range mission, and as a consequence the expedient of employing mutually defensive formations was of little practical use.

Without waiting to see what happened to their bomber colleagues, most 110 pilots jettisoned their long-range fuel tanks and ran for home. Seven of their number were not so lucky and were shot down. Many badly damaged machines managed to limp home at low level, their pilots scrutinising fuel and pressure gauges and scanning the skies to see if any Spitfires had decided to pursue them.

Those Heinkels that survived the initial encounter with 72 Squadron's Spitfires resolutely pressed on towards the English

In July 1940, in order to accelerate the supply of trained pilots to operational squadrons, Dowding reluctantly reduced the length of Operational Training Unit courses from six to three weeks, and to remind crews of the importance of concentration the Air Ministry commissioned the cartoonist "Fougasse" to produce a series of posters designed to help pilots avoid dangerous situations. The series was titled "Once is too often". The examples shown here warn of the danger of braking too hard and of the need to use the maximum area of the airfield while accelerating for take-off.

coast, but for these hapless crews worse was yet to come. As they reached the shoreline in two ragged formations the Heinkels were bounced by four more RAF squadrons. This attack was the last straw for the unfortunate airmen. Many bombers had already sustained battle damage and some carried injured crewmen. Their confidence shaken and facing the likelihood of a further mauling at the hands of RAF aircraft they had been told no longer existed, most bomber-pilots banked their aircraft and wisely turned for home. As they chased after the Bf-110 fighters that were supposed to escort them to and from the target the Heinkels increased their performance by dumping their bomb-loads in the sea. The bombers' objectives – the airfields at Usworth, Linton-on-Ouse and Dishforth – survived the "attack" unscathed.

While the Heinkels and Messerschmitts

were being scattered by Fighter Command in the north, one hundred miles farther south another Luftwaffe raid met with rather more success. Some 50 Junkers 88 bombers, unescorted due to their speed and agility, slipped through the line of RAF fighters strung out like a net to trap them and proceeded towards their targets in small groups difficult to intercept. Even though they penetrated air-space patrolled by Leigh-Mallory's 12 Group (at this stage still eager to increase their profile in the battle), the powerful Junkers bombers roamed far and wide, seriously damaging a Bomber Command station at Driffield and writing off ten Whitley bombers. They also scattered bombs at Bridlington, hitting an army ammunition dump in the process. Only a tenth of the Ju-88s were shot down by the defences, the rest returning safely to their base at Aalborg in northern Denmark.

Luftflotte 5's onslaught in the north had been unexpected, but on the whole Fighter Command had been able to contain its effects and in many instances thwart it altogether. In the south of England, Goering's primary target, it was a different matter. At noon Manston was subjected to yet another raid. This time hedge-hopping Bf-109s racked the station with machine-gun and cannon-fire, destroying two Spitfires and adding a further 16 casualties to the growing RAF list.

Later that afternoon the Stukas reappeared and struck RAF Martlesham Heath and its environs near Ipswich. The Ju-87s were supported by Bf-110s and together the aircraft caused enough mayhem to disrupt the airfield's operational capabilities for over 24 hours. At the same time a huge force of Luftwaffe aircraft, consisting of nearly 250 machines in two waves, brushed aside four RAF fighter squadrons then on standing patrol and crossed the south coast at Deal and Folkestone. Aircraft factories in Rochester were bombed and the production line containing Bomber Command's newest "heavy", the four-engined Short Stirling, was brought to an abrupt halt. But though this was a significant victory for the Luftwaffe, it did not alter the balance as far as the contest with Fighter Command was concerned.

As the afternoon wore on the Luftwaffe continued to apply pressure relentlessly against Fighter Command. A feint attack in the south-west was designed to distract the defenders from the real thrust, which once more would fall against the battered south-east quarter of England. In fierce fighting over Hampshire Fighter Command destroyed 25 raiders but lost 16 aircraft of its own. As their colleagues staged an elaborate and costly diversion in the west, 70 German aircraft climbed to fighting altitude above Calais and set course for Kent and Surrey.

Fortunately Keith Park received early warning of the raid from the trusty radar chain and was able to field two squadrons above the coast to intercept. His tactics were sound and although his fighters were low on fuel they were present when the raid eventually materialised. Disrupted by the attention of RAF fighters, the raiders split up and were deflected from their primary objectives of Biggin Hill and Kenley. They did locate West Malling, however, and scored several direct hits from high altitude. Some bombers got as far as Croydon and unloaded their bombs on the London suburb spread out below them.

In the first recorded air-raid on Greater London since war had been declared nearly a year before, more Luftwaffe aircraft, this time at low level, struck Croydon. Bf-110s and Bf-109s flashed across the neat rows of semi-detached houses that lined street after street; diving to 2,000 feet, they sped towards Croydon aerodrome and the as-yet officially unoperational No. 111 Squadron. Eighty casualties were recorded and several important aircraft component factories were damaged in the raid. In fact 111 Squadron's Hurricanes were on patrol above their station and, after seeing what had happened, dived from their altitude of 10,000 feet and joined No. 32 Squadron from Biggin Hill in pursuit of the now-unladen raiders. Four Bf-110s were destroyed before they reached the coast.

The Luftwaffe continued its operations after sunset. That night over 70 bombers hit Birmingham, Southampton, Bristol, Swansea and half a dozen smaller targets across England. At the end of a weary day Fighter Command flew 974 sorties and destroyed 75 German aircraft, although at the time Fighter Command claimed more than twice that total. For its part the Luftwaffe shot down 34 RAF machines, but they also destroyed and damaged bomber and trainer aircraft on the ground along with a wide range of manufacturing facilities; 17 RAF pilots were killed, a sad loss Dowding could ill afford, and a further 16 were wounded.

Goering held a post-mortem on the events

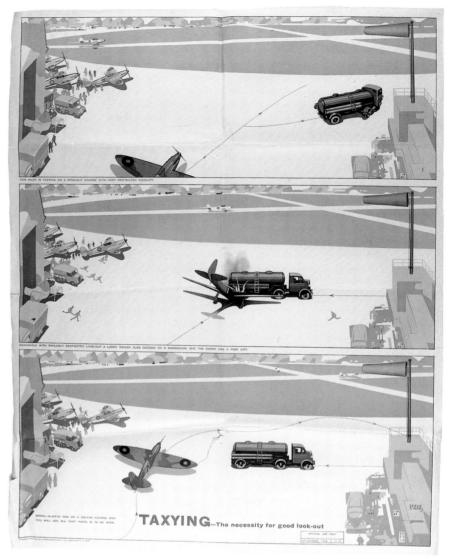

TAXYING—The necessity for good look-out

of August 15 while his Luftwaffe was still in action. Speaking at Karinhall, the Reichsmarschall pointed out the increasingly high loss rate among his coveted Stuka units, and forthwith Stukas would be escorted by Bf-109s to prevent the attrition that was thinning the dive-bomber squadrons. As if this was not enough for the 109 pilots (who already had to contend with a limited flight duration over England due to fuel consumption), Goering further restricted their offensive capabilities by ordering them to escort the twin-engined Bf-110s as well. Ironically the Luftwaffe thus found itself ordering fighters to protect fighters, and unwittingly aided Dowding by tightening the leash on the 109s.

The reception which greeted Luftflotte 5's foray over the North Sea had come as an unwelcome surprise and it was decided to limit the air-fleets' operations in daylight.

The nose-high attitude of all fighters with tail wheels meant that forward vision was reduced. In the case of the Spitfire, with its extremely long nose and broad wings, it was almost impossible for pilots to see where they were going. Unless they weaved the aircraft while taxiing, or followed the instructions of an airman stationed at the aircraft's wing-tip who was able to guide them, pilots could find themselves colliding with airfield vehicles or buildings. This superbly illustrated Air Diagram skilfully highlights the importance of keeping a good look-out during taxiing.

The intense aerial fighting littered the countryside of southern England with so many shattered aircraft that from the air the burning wreckages of both German and British machines resembled so many funeral pyres marking the end of a brief fight to the death. This smouldering Heinkel 111 came to rest in Kent after one such brief engagement.

Instead aircraft were transferred from Scandinavia to France, where they helped to fill gaps caused by the mounting losses over England.

Goering also turned his attention to the attacks on radar stations which, up to now, had been a facet of most Luftwaffe attacks. His pronouncement was yet another bonus for Fighter Command: "It is doubtful whether there is any point in continuing the attacks on radar sites in view of the fact that not one of those attacked has so far been put out of action." Ventnor had in fact been knocked out and was presently the scene of some frenetic repair work; Luftwaffe intelligence had yet again failed the Reichsmarschall.

In London Winston Churchill, watching the dramatic events of the day unfold in the underground operations room at Stanmore, was extremely impressed with Fighter Command's performance. On his return to Westminster he asked his private secretary, John Colville, to telephone Neville Chamberlain, the Lord President, with the news of the RAF's success. Chamberlain was overjoyed – and grateful that Churchill had been so thoughtful to think of him at such a hectic time. Colville passed on Chamberlain's thanks to the Prime Minister; Churchill, in ebullient mood, turned to him and said, "This is one of the greatest days in history."

For two days after August 15 the Luftwaffe

reduced the scale of its operations over Britain. However, depending on the perspective, the situation could still appear very hot indeed. Late in the morning of the 16th the Luftwaffe mounted sporadic raids against targets across England and once again struck at Manston and West Malling, putting the latter out of action for four days. At midday the Chain Home network passed information indicating that three simultaneous large-scale raids were approaching England; 50 raiders headed for the Thames Estuary, 150 pressed on towards Dover and a third, flying from Cherbourg, proceeded to the Southampton area. Squadrons from all three southern Fighter Groups were ordered to intercept the enemy formations, but the enemy's sheer weight of numbers (the total was some 350 aircraft) prevented them from deflecting the many raids.

While the Luftwaffe caused chaos and misery all over the country, damage was especially severe in the Portsmouth and Southampton area. At RAF Tangmere in Sussex a large formation of Stukas took advantage of the confusion caused by their colleagues who were bombing Ventnor, Gosport and Lee-on-Solent. Some were intercepted by RAF fighters but most dived out of the bright midday sun and managed to drop their bombs within the perimeter of

THE HAMMER AND THE ANVIL

Tangmere. Five hangars were hit by the bombs that plummeted from the under-belly racks fixed to each Stuka.

Two of the station's camouflaged Belfast hangars were completely destroyed and three more badly damaged. The station workshops, fire-hydrant pump-house, stores, sick quarters and officers' mess were also wrecked. Bombs fell on an air-raid shelter and severed all the station's power, communications, water and sanitation networks. Six Blenheim bombers, seven Hurricanes and one Magister trainer were destroyed on the ground along with more than 40 motor vehicles. The human cost was tragically high – ten RAF personnel and three civilians were killed and 20 injured. Tangmere's station operations record stated: "The depressing situation was dealt with in an orderly manner and it was considered that the traditions of the RAF were upheld by all ranks."

A huge column of acrid black smoke hung over Tangmere, advertising its agony for miles around. One spectator to the destruction was Nobby Kinnard, a woodsman and rabbiter in his late twenties who was home from army service in Dover for what he hoped would be a relatively quiet leave. For weeks his battalion had endured a barrage of fire from the Luftwaffe and, more sinisterly, long-range guns positioned across the Channel in occupied France.

"We certainly knew the Battle of Britain was real," says Nobby, "because we were stationed in Dover and were continuously shelled by big German guns. There wasn't any glass left in the windows of buildings around St Margaret's Bay because of the shell-fire." From the fields around his home at Patching on the South Downs east of Tangmere, Nobby Kinnard enjoyed a grandstand view of the unfolding spectacle above the beleagured airfield. It was not only the calm of his well-earned leave which was shattered, however, for within minutes RAF and Luftwaffe aircraft crashed from the sky like so many dead game-birds.

Soon the coppices and hedgerows around Patching resounded to the ear-splitting noise of tearing metal and splintering wood. One aircraft, British he thinks, came thundering through the undergrowth north of Myrtle Grove Farm, only a few hundred yards from where he stood. Racing to the scene, he was amazed to see the shattered plane nose-deep in a hillock of juniper bushes and surrounded by

dozens of dead rabbits. The crashed aircraft had unwittingly ploughed into an ancient warren, achieving more in a day than Nobby could accomplish in a fortnight's work!

In fact planes from both sides were dropping like stones all over Sussex. One Heinkel 111 of KG55, attacked by RAF fighters over Brighton, had its fuselage perforated by hundreds of .303-inch rounds, and the bomber force-landed high on the Downs at High Salvington, north of Worthing. By the time a local army unit had arrived on the scene two of the crewmen had died of bullet wounds.

ABOVE It was not only Fighter Command airfields that were subjected to attacks. Here a bomb has blasted a huge crater at Driffield, a Bomber Command station on the east coast and home to several Whitley squadrons.

BELOW Driffield again, this time showing a Whitley sheltering in a damaged hangar. Driffield was re-equipped with Halifax bombers in 1941.

A NATION ALONE

Bemused motorists travelling along the B2145 towards Selsey had to swerve past the starboard wing of a Stuka from StG2 which was spread-eagled, minus its undercarriage, on top of a grass verge on the left-hand side of the carriageway. Both crewmen were captured, badly injured but grateful to be alive. The Stuka was in fact one of four which fell to RAF fighters during the raid on Tangmere.

More horrifying was the death of Oberleutnant Ernst Hollekamp. His Bf-110 was intercepted by RAF fighters above Eastbourne and suffered several accurate bursts of machine-gun fire. All Bf-110s were structurally unsound in the tail-area and, weakened still further by raking machine-gun fire, the tail of his 110 separated from the rest of the airframe. As it broke up in mid-air the twin-engined fighter scattered wreckage across three-quarters of a mile of Sussex countryside. The largest part of the fighter smashed into a privet hedge in Aldro School in Eastbourne.

Hollekamp's rear-gunner had baled out from the stricken aircraft before it disintegrated but the young Oberleutnant was not so lucky, falling helpless from the wreckage as it ripped apart above Eastbourne. His body was later discovered perched on the ridge-tiles of a house in Gaudlick Road, Eastbourne; it had cut a swathe through the apex of the roof, dislodging tiles and masonry in the process. A fireman of the Eastbourne brigade climbed the roof to dislodge Hollekamp. On reaching the

pilot he stretched out and grabbed at his flying-suit but grasped instead the dead man's parachute D-ring, instantly deploying the silken canopy which now threatened to drag Hollekamp off the roof and into the street. After a struggle both the pilot and the parachute were retrieved.

In total, eight British airfields were attacked on August 16, but thanks to the Luftwaffe's unreliable intelligence estimates only three of them belonged to Fighter Command, and repair work at most of Dowding's stations continued without serious interruption. In tallying up the results of over 1,700 sorties, Luftwaffe analysts again produced wildly inaccurate statistics and claimed that barely 300 serviceable RAF fighters remained. The actual figure was 700, and although Fighter Command's total establishment was 209 pilots below strength its weary airmen were still very much in the fight. The battles on the 16th cost the Luftwaffe 49 aircraft, while the RAF had expended a further 22 precious fighters and eight irreplaceable pilots.

The 17th was a relatively quiet day, both sides taking stock of their respective situations. The Luftwaffe restricted its activities to random raids which ranged as far afield as Merseyside, and the RAF survived intact throughout the day, managing in turn to dispatch three German bombers.

During this phase of the Battle of Britain Dowding had not only to contend with the enormous problem of judging the Luftwaffe's every move but also put up with the uncertainty of his own position as Figher Command's C-in-C. Throughout the battle a steady flow of letters was exchanged between Dowding and his bosses at the Air Ministry concerning the terms of his employment.

July 14 had been set originally as the date for his retirement, but the steadily worsening situation in Europe led the Air Ministry to drop this demand on the 5th and propose an extension until the end of October. Dowding had hoped to stay in his job for a further two years, retiring when he was 60. The discourtesy shown by the Air Ministry and the low priority they appeared to give to his employment naturally irritated him. In a letter to the Chief of Air Staff, Cyril Newell, he wrote: "I am anxious to stay because I feel there is no-one else who will fight as I do when proposals are made which would reduce the defence forces of the country below the extreme danger point." His veiled references

THE HAMMER AND THE ANVIL

to his run-in with Churchill concerning the dispatch of fighters to France had not gone unnoticed in high places, and his request for a definite retirement date after the present emergency had passed was not forthcoming.

On July 14 Dowding wrote to the Air Ministry outlining Churchill's recently expressed view that he "should remain on the Active List for the time being, without any date for my retirement being fixed". Hoping the Prime Minister's welcome, if vague, commitment would satisfy the Air Ministry and allow him to concentrate on fighting the Luftwaffe, Dowding set the matter aside. On August 12, a day of significant enemy activity, he received a letter from Newell which, though agreeing to cancel the time limit, offered no firm long-term commitment.

Six times Dowding had been informed of his imminent retirement, only to be reprieved at the very last moment and at a time when he had to concentrate all his energies on the task of directing his 52 squadrons, some of them untried, in battle. The irresponsibility shown by the bureaucrats in the Air Ministry at a time when Britain faced such genuine peril defies the imagination. Only Dowding's enormous strength of character and his dedication to the young pilots under his command prevented the strain he must have felt from clouding his judgment and preventing him from fulfilling his crucial duties. Not surprisingly, when he later looked back at his time as the commander of Britain's front-line defences, Dowding reflected: "I never quite knew exactly where I stood."

Each evening, as Fighter Command's activities declined with the setting of the sun, Dowding spent long hours studying the numerous reports of the day's events at airfields throughout the British Isles. He made notes containing considered judgments regarding individual requests or particular problems that his executive officers had encountered and suggested improvements to the command's organisational procedures. Often he would be driven to one of the many battered fighter-stations that were involved in the battle to see for himself dogged groundcrews toiling under artificial light to patch up, repair and rearm the bruised planes for another day's combat.

Everywhere he went Dowding prepared copious notes that would form the basis of a stream of directives issued the following day. Usually he refused the assistance of aides,

"Eu pessoalmente garantirei que nem uma só bomba cairá no Rure"

GÖRING, Agosto de 1939.

Em 12 meses a R.F.A. levou a cabo mais de 530 BOMBARDEAMENTOS NO RURE e mais de 1000 ataques no resto de Alemanha.

preferring to leave them at Stanmore to arrange things for the following morning's work. Each morning he descended the stairs down to the drab operations room at Stanmore, dubbed "the Hole" by his staff, and scrutinised the plots which hour by hour were added to the huge table spread out before him. Frequently Dowding would descend to the plotting table's perimeter to gain a better view of a particular detail of the fighting. The WAAFs who pushed and pulled at croupiers' rakes and assembled the jigsaw of aerial activity were generally too busy to notice "Stuffy" peering over their shoulders; but when they did turn round and catch a glance

Although Portugal was officially neutral during the Second World War she was also Britain's oldest ally, and British propagandists undermined German prestige there at every opportunity. This postcard pokes fun at Goering's claim that "I will personally guarantee that not a single bomb will be dropped on the Ruhr," pointing out that in the year since August 1939 the RAF had carried out over 530 bombing attacks on the area.

141

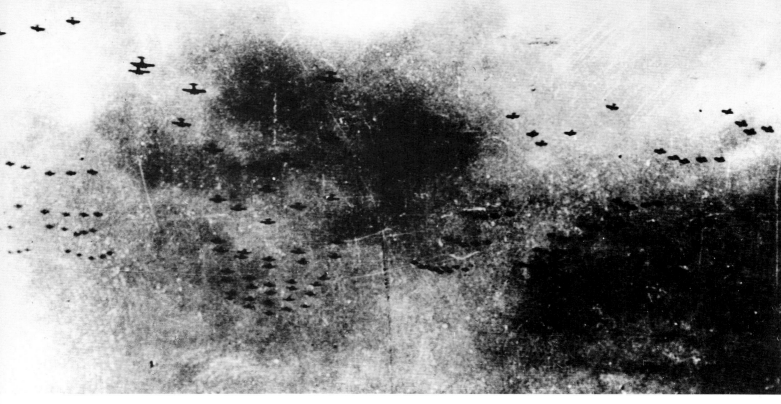

Varying the heights at which their bombers attacked RAF airfields helped Luftwaffe planners confuse Britain's defences. As high-level raids were plotted and intercepted other formations, flying lower, were often able to slip under the radar shield and assault targets from tree-top height. This photograph shows a high-level Luftwaffe formation passing above Biggin Hill aerodrome in Kent. It illustrates clearly the precision with which Luftwaffe crews were able to maintain formation when, by this stage in their journey, they would be subjected to both anti-aircraft fire and the attentions of marauding Spitfires and Hurricanes.

from their commander-in-chief their efforts were usually rewarded with a warm smile and a quiet but sincere "Well done."

Fighter Command's Bentley Priory displayed none of the noise and confusion usually associated with a military headquarters. Even when enemy activity reached its peak those who worked there were encouraged to discharge their responsibilities in a dignified and calm manner. Dowding's fatherly bearing and his simple style tended to encourage an atmosphere (particularly within the hushed confines of his office), which his personal assistant during the battle, Robert Wright, later his biographer, likened to "a somewhat staid and old-fashioned family business office in a provincial town".

As he sat down at his small undistinguished desk on the morning of August 18 and dipped his worn out but favoured fountain-pen into the ink-pot before him, Dowding must have wondered whether the previous day's respite signalled a dramatic change in the Luftwaffe's activity. Below ground, not far away, his staff were beginning to receive information indicating the return of Goering's mighty air fleets— and thus promising Fighter Command a resumption of the relentless bludgeoning it had so recently endured.

The Luftwaffe began its activities on August 18 in the usual fashion – with high-altitude reconnaissance sorties over England and out into the Atlantic to determine the weather situation. Most reconnaissance aircraft were too high and fast to be caught by the variety of fighters which were scrambled to intercept them, though today one Spitfire of 54 Squadron did have some success, clawing its way to 31,000 ft quickly enough to shoot down a Messerschmitt 110 above Manston.

By noon the Chain Home network detected a build up of activity above St Omer and Abbeville in France, with over 80 enemy aircraft steadily moving towards Britain. In sector operations rooms all over No. 11 Group, controllers issued instructions to their squadrons standing at varying states of readiness throughout southern England. One by one squadrons were scrambled with orders to patrol the skies above their airfields or move forward to the front line above the cliffs and beaches of the south coast.

Having learned to their cost the rudiments of the detection capability of radar (though still largely unaware of Fighter Command's control procedures), the Luftwaffe employed a new technique to give their bombers a better chance of hitting the target. From now on two consecutive high-level escorted bomber formations would approach the target, followed by a sudden low-level raid by a third. Clearly the first two formations would be detected by radar and could expect to be met by fighter opposition when they approached the British Isles. However the third, hedge-hopping raid would confuse the operators manning the radar stations and with luck planes might reach their targets unmolested.

THE HAMMER AND THE ANVIL

Even though the high-level raiders were likely to meet some stiff opposition sufficient bombers would succeed in fighting their way to the target and some bombs were thus guaranteed to reach their mark. In this way the fires that were started would mark the target for the low-level aircraft that followed, enabling them to concentrate more on flying than on navigation. This then was the theory by which the Luftwaffe hoped to hit the sector stations which, it was becoming increasingly obvious, were of crucial importance to the RAF's defences.

The first target selected for attack using the new procedure was Biggin Hill, but poor co-ordination between the high- and low-level German formations resulted in a fiasco as the hedge-hoppers arrived over the airfield to find it undamaged and very much ready to repel an air-raid. As nine Dorniers raced low across the airfield perimeter they were suddenly confronted by a wall of anti-aircraft and small-arms fire. After narrowly escaping the lethal spray of shells and bullets that arced towards them from below, the Dorniers had the misfortune to encounter fire from above as well; two of Biggin Hill's three squadrons had been patrolling high above the airfield in anticipation of an encounter with the high-flying aircraft, and after witnessing the activity below they dived down to attack the nine intruders. Only two Dornier bombers succeeded in running the gauntlet. When the high-level raid did arrive it too was welcomed by withering fire and four more bombers fell.

A short while later the Luftwaffe enjoyed more success when it singled out another of 11 Group's sector stations for punishment – RAF Kenley in Surrey, six miles to the west of Biggin Hill. Here the Luftwaffe managed to co-ordinate both its high- and low-level attacks with commendable precision. Radar had given sufficient warning of the predictable high-level raid to enable the station's duty controller, Squadron-Leader Norman, to position Kenley's two resident squadrons, Nos 64 and 615, high above the airfield. The low-level force, consisting of nine specially armoured Dorniers of KG76, would have arrived undetected had it not been for the vigilance of the Observer Corps. Speeding low and fast above the Channel the nine Dorniers, led by Staffelkapitaen Hauptmann Roth, actually trailed wakes across the surface of the sea. As they climbed to cross the coast the observers at Post K3 on Beachy Head

identified them and enabled a warning to be passed to all RAF airfields that stood in the bombers' path. Although Roth did not realise it, his bid to slip underneath Britain's radar curtain had failed. As a precaution against a possible low-level incursion No. 111 Squadron from nearby Croydon was detailed to patrol above Kenley at 3,000 feet.

Below, within the airfield's perimeter, the station's ground defenders checked their motley assortment of weapons. The 31st Light Anti-Aircraft Battery manned the most up-to-date armament – four 40 mm Bofors guns. Firing 120 two-pound high-explosive shells a minute the Bofors was lethal against low flying aircraft, but it was new in service and too few were available; to protect Kenley adequately at least eight Bofors were needed.

The 148th Light Anti-Aircraft Battery was responsible for the care and attention of two obsolete three-inch guns of Great War vintage, slow-firing weapons that lobbed 13-pound shells into the air. When used at low altitude the weapon was aimed through open sights but being slow and cumbersome was of little use against high-speed targets. The balance of Kenley's conventional defensive armament consisted of 20 Lewis guns manned by Army and RAF gunners and one Hispano 20 mm cannon of the type then being tested in RAF fighters.

Their job was made all the more difficult by the airfield's hangars and a row of tall trees which obscured the view to the south. But though they could not see the enemy aircraft

This fascinating photograph, taken from one of the low-level Dornier 17s which attacked the sector airfield at Kenley on August 18, 1940, shows a Spitfire of 64 Squadron sitting in its protective E-pen at dispersal, narrowly escaping the effects of Luftwaffe bombs. An alternative version of this image, from the original negative, was circulated by German propagandists and used heavy retouching to exaggerate the precision of the Luftwaffe attack. The raid nevertheless succeeded in destroying four RAF Hurricanes, one Blenheim and three training aircraft – all on the ground.

A NATION ALONE

This children's painting and story-book demonstrates the cruder aspects of over-zealous national pride, depicting a flaming German fighter falling to earth at the hands of an invincible and somewhat fanciful RAF interceptor. As the air battles raged overhead bookshops and newsagents were flooded with cheaply produced literature, usually in simplistic style, the RAF's defence of Britain.

The whine of 18 Bramo radial engines, running at full throttle, was an unmistakable announcement of their arrival. As the sound grew louder with the approach of the nine Dorniers, Kenley's gunners tugged at the straps of their steel helmets and crouched lower over their loaded weapons.

Sweeping across the North Downs in V-formations ("vics") of three aircraft, the Dornier crews suddenly caught sight of Kenley laid out before them. It was obvious they had arrived in advance of the high-level raid but the pilots were not unduly worried; so far, they had flown unhindered across southern England and it was clear their high-altitude colleagues had lured the RAF fighters away from their target. Birds scattered from the trees as the Dorniers brushed past the highest branches and levelled out for the bombing run. Each pilot selected his target and made the final adjustments to achieve the most accurate results.

Suddenly the sky in front of the German aircraft erupted into an impenetrable barrier of tracer ammunition and exploding shells. The Dornier which was leading the left-hand section of bombers reared up as a well-aimed shell exploded against the aircraft's bulbous birdcage nose. Immediately it fell away to starboard and, out of control, crashed in the grounds of a large house near the airfield. The pilot leading the right-hand section was struck by bullets from a Lewis gun and slumped, mortally wounded, across his controls. Only the swift action of his observer, who reached over him and grabbed the column, prevented his aircraft from crashing.

In the centre of the formation Hauptmann Roth pressed on with the attack, but he too could not evade the concentration of fire that raced up from the ground. Struggling to avoid the mysterious columns of smoke and flame that soared in front of his plane, he felt the Dornier shudder as its wing was smashed by an anti-aircraft round. In seconds, as fuel poured from a damaged fuel tank, the aircraft's wing burst into flames. Trailing thick smoke Roth's machine quickly lost height. Only the skill of the pilot succeeded in preventing the plane from crashing out of control; instead it alighted, still on fire, in a stubble field six miles from Kenley. As it passed over their unit, a local Home Guard detachment loosed off a few rounds at the stricken bomber.

Fortunately for the four crew members their fire was ineffective and all escaped with injuries. Along with Hauptmann Roth the aircraft contained a second officer, Oberleutnant Lamberty, yet only two days before Goering had strictly forbidden the presence of more than one officer among Luftwaffe bomber crews in an attempt to reduce the steadily mounting losses among his more experienced senior personnel.

At the same time Roth's aircraft was hit the Dornier flying on his starboard beam struck one of the cables that had materialised out of the tall plumes of smoke straddling the airfield. Luckily for the Dornier's pilot, Feldwebel Raab, the cable merely grazed the leading edge of his port wing and he managed to take his shaken crew home to France.

As Kenley suffered in the flames the Hurricanes of No. 111 Squadron arrived over the airfield. As they dived towards the remaining Dorniers, by now unloading their bombs across the area, the Hurricanes flew into the hail of anti-aircraft fire and Flight-Lieutenant Connors, who was leading 111, was hit by ground-fire and crashed. Gunners had mistaken his Hurricane for an escorting Messerschmitt and had thus targeted him accordingly. In fact the low-level raid was unescorted – and the Hurricanes of 111 were the only single-engined fighters in the vicinity.

THE HAMMER AND THE ANVIL

With empty bomb-bays the lightened Dorniers which survived the conflagration above Kenley raced for the coast and safety. Each chose an individual route home, weaving through the tree-tops and dodging electricity pylons and tall chimneys, but No. 111 Squadron clung to them like a pack of terriers determined to drag their quarry to the ground. Three Hurricanes dropped out of the chase after sustaining hits from some particularly accurate machine-gun fire. The heavy 20 mm cannons of the Dorniers could only be directed downwards towards ground targets, and the pursuing Hurricanes were spared the effects of these formidable weapons. Five Dorniers made it back to France but only one landed at KG76's airfield at Cormeilles-en-Vexin, south of Le Havre, the others force-landing as soon as they crossed the coast.

Meanwhile, back above Kenley, both 615 and 64 Squadrons succeeded in intercepting the high-level bomber force, shooting down five bombers and damaging a further four. Four Hurricanes from 615 were shot down as they fought to defend their airfield.

As the smoke cleared and the full extent of the damage at Kenley was revealed it became evident that the Luftwaffe had enjoyed a large measure of success. Over a hundred bombs had struck the airfield, each one a 110-lb weapon with a built-in delayed-action fuse to enable the bombers (which released them at just 45 feet) to escape the ensuing blast.

Nine station personnel were killed and ten wounded in the attack. Three out of the airfield's four hangars were destroyed, only their buttressed walls remained standing. Nine fighters were wrecked on the ground before they could be moved from their exposed blast E-pens. A Blenheim and some trainers were also crippled, along with 30 vehicles, the station headquarters, sick quarters and both the sergeants' and officers' messes. Because the runway was badly cratered Kenley's still-airborne fighters were ordered to land at Croydon, but due to the efforts of Royal Engineers, who toiled among over 20 unexploded bombs to fill the craters which littered the runways, Kenley was operational again within just two hours of the raid. Land-lines to the station were damaged and the airfield's reserve operations room at Caterham was used to direct the station's aircraft while Kenley's damaged operations building was patched up.

That afternoon RAF airfields at Croydon,

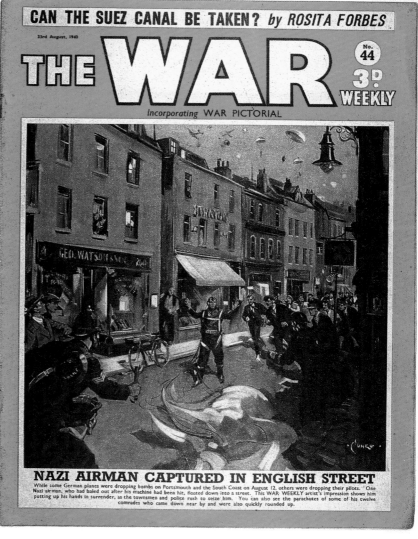

CAN THE SUEZ CANAL BE TAKEN? by ROSITA FORBES

23rd August, 1940

THE WAR WEEKLY

No. 44

3D.

Incorporating WAR PICTORIAL

NAZI AIRMAN CAPTURED IN ENGLISH STREET

While some German planes were dropping bombs on Portsmouth and the South Coast on August 12, others were dropping their pilots. One Nazi airman, who had baled out after his machine had been hit, floated down into a street. This WAR WEEKLY artist's impression shows him putting up his hands in surrender, as the townsmen and police rush to seize him. You can also see the parachutes of some of his twelve comrades who came down near by and were also quickly rounded up.

West Malling, Gosport and Thorney Island received treatment similar to that meted out against Biggin Hill and Kenley. The Fleet Air Arm station at Ford near Arundel in Sussex was also attacked, the Luftwaffe succeeding in igniting fuel storage tanks which belched dense black smoke across the water-meadows surrounding the airfield. Poling radar station between Arundel and Littlehampton was also hit during the same raid; the damage caused to the station was so severe that a mobile unit had to be brought in to plug the resultant gap in the Chain Home network.

In virtually their last engagement during the Battle of Britain the Stukas again received a mauling – losing 12 machines, all from the same unit – as they bombed targets in Sussex and Hampshire. Even a Blenheim managed to shoot down two Stukas, testifying to the Luftwaffe dive-bomber's unsuitability for air-to-air combat.

Although Britain had been at war with Germany for almost a year before the Battle of Britain the struggle had been fought at arms length on the continent. With vapour trails patterning the skies above southern England the British people had their first opportunity to come face to face with the enemy as, with alarming regularity, German airmen descended on English soil by parachute – or, if they chose to crash-land their stricken aircraft, were plucked from the wreckage and frog-marched through suburban streets to captivity. This cover of *The War Weekly* is heavy with sentimentality in its portrayal of a surrendering Luftwaffe pilot.

A NATION ALONE

Late in the afternoon the Luftwaffe returned to the skies above England. Manston was attacked yet again, as was Croydon. Spectators peering out from cover at Dover gasped at the spectacle of a barrage balloon contorting in its death throes as it fell flaming earthwards after a decidedly one-sided encounter with a Bf-109. Raids resumed later in the evening when the Luftwaffe roamed largely unopposed through the night skies above England and Wales, dropping bombs and mines in the Thames Estuary and the Bristol Channel and scattering bombs across East Anglia.

The day's fighting had been long and bloody but it was still the Luftwaffe who suffered the heaviest losses, 71 of their aircraft falling to combined ground and air fire over England. The RAF, for its part, lost 27 fighters with ten of their pilots killed. At the time the RAF assumed that 144 enemy aircraft had been destroyed. Aware that his tired pilots might just be turning the tide of the battle, Dowding remarked to General Pile (the Commander-in-Chief of AA Command), "England is being defended – saved by four hundred young men."

The Luftwaffe's low-level "sneak attacks" were a worrying development since they managed to evade the radar chain. Dowding and Keith Park need not have worried, however; concerned by high losses, the Luftwaffe briefed its crews to fly higher to avoid the effects of ground-fire.

The following day, August 19, Goering lambasted his poor fighter-pilots for what he claimed was a lack of aggressive spirit resulting in heavy losses among his favoured bombers. Equally depressed about the duration of the campaign – it was scheduled for only four days of intense activity as a prelude to gaining air superiority over southern England – Goering gave his units a free hand to select whatever targets they pleased and urged them to press on their attacks with increased vigour.

He again stressed the importance of hitting RAF stations and Britain's aircraft industry, but also extended the Luftwaffe's sphere of operations to targets in the far north of England and in Scotland. Cloudy weather during the day prevented the chastened crews from mounting many operations, though when they did venture out across the choppy waters of the Channel six German aircraft failed to return.

Poor weather again reduced activity on August 20, the day that Churchill chose to deliver (to the Commons) his most famous speech of the Battle of Britain period. Praising the heroism of Fighter Command's pilots the Prime Minister paid his memorable tribute

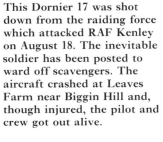

This Dornier 17 was shot down from the raiding force which attacked RAF Kenley on August 18. The inevitable soldier has been posted to ward off scavengers. The aircraft crashed at Leaves Farm near Biggin Hill and, though injured, the pilot and crew got out alive.

THE HAMMER AND THE ANVIL

with the words: "Never in the field of human conflict was so much owed by so many to so few," and he continued: "We are toiling up the hill. We have not yet reached the crest-line of it, we cannot survey the landscape or even imagine what its condition will be when that longed-for morning comes . . . I hope – indeed I pray – that we shall not be found unworthy of our victory if after toil and tribulation it is granted to us."

The toil and tribulation continued throughout the warm days and nights that followed that summer. To the frustration of Luftwaffe units sent on missions over Britain a thin shield of RAF fighters was always raised in defiance. Skirmishes would break out above the seas surrounding the British Isles and combats often continued as the opposing sides wrestled across the skies and moved inland over the landscape of southern England. Fields and meadows in Kent, Sussex, Surrey and Hampshire became graveyards for stricken aircraft of both sides. Huge dumps sprang up where wrecked machines were piled prior to salvage. Rumours abounded among the public concerning both secret Luftwaffe weapons and the poor standard of equipment within German aircraft.

RAF pilots had frequently reported that, when attacking Luftwaffe bombers from the rear, German crews appeared to throw out small boxes that trailed wires in an attempt to foul the propellors of Spitfires and Hurricanes. Examination of wrecked Luftwaffe bombers revealed the source of the mystery to be a small weapon, known as the SKAV grenade-launcher, mounted in the aircraft's tail. On firing, the launcher ejected a series of 106 mm grenades, powered by bursts of compressed air, which were aimed at the bomber's assailant. Once the grenade was clear of the bomber a parachute was deployed from inside the small one-pound missile, the intention being to slow it down before it detonated one or two seconds later, hopefully in the path of the pursuing fighter.

Stories appeared in the newspapers about German fighters which, on examination by the Home Guard or Police, appeared devoid of modern flying instruments. In fact anything of interest was stripped from an aircraft's cockpit – taken by RAF investigators or stolen by locals – long before the carcass was handed over to the volunteer authorities for disposal.

Spent cartridges that fell from each aerial combat gave rise to a belief that the Luftwaffe

The final moments of a Luftwaffe Me-110 are graphically recorded on the gun-camera footage from a British fighter. Gun-cameras exposed film automatically when the pilot fired his wing armament. Their scrutiny by intelligence officers frequently revealed that marksmanship was the exception rather than the rule and that RAF pilots often engaged the enemy at too great a range for an effective weight of fire to be brought to bear.

was indiscriminately machine-gunning civilian targets. Although there are confirmed instances of German aircrews casually firing at defenceless targets, by and large the clattering hail that struck roofs and pavements was the by-product of gunfire and did not indicate a callous straffing attack by a dastardly enemy.

On both sides the death toll due to immersion into the sea after a pilot had exited

A NATION ALONE

The distinctive bubble shape of the moulded canopy of the Spitfire, clearly indicated in this photograph of a Mark 1 modification on the original design, was introduced to give sufficient clearance above the heads of taller pilots. Visibility through the windscreen was hampered by the necessary positioning of the gun-sight and the thickness of the armoured glass section directly in front of the pilot's face.

his burning aircraft was causing increasing concern. Even in summer the water temperature in the English Channel barely reaches 14°C, cold enough to cause death by exposure after only four hours. As a precaution some Luftwaffe crews strapped commercially produced airbeds to their flying clothing in an attempt to stay out of the chilling water. If clear of the water their thick, kapok-filled life-jackets provided extra protection from the cold.

On August 22 Air-Marshal Harris instigated a conference at the Air Ministry to investigate ways of protecting British pilots from the perilous seas. The result was a plan to combine Coastal Command's rescue service with boats from the Naval Auxiliary Patrol and place what few RAF launches that existed under local naval authority. RAF Lysanders were used for air search and helped to pinpoint

downed aircrews in time for help to arrive. With trained manpower a priority, every effort was taken to ensure that if possible a shot-down fighter-pilot was saved . . . and able to fight another day.

Well trained, disciplined and numerically superior, the Luftwaffe appeared almost invincible throughout the summer of 1940. But there was one barrier which proved impenetrable to Goering's air-fleets – the unpredictable and often turbulent weather that, with depressing regularity, engulfed the British Isles. Due to cloudy weather between August 19 and 23, Dowding's exhausted and diminished complement of fighter-pilots enjoyed a welcomed respite from their aerial slogging matches.

But they did not rest long, for on August 24 the skies over Britain once more resounded to the roar of countless German aircraft. The

THE HAMMER AND THE ANVIL

Luftwaffe was back. It too had benefitted from the recent lull in air fighting.

In Luftwaffe airfields all across occupied territory German aircrews, some fresh-faced and wide-eyed, others haggard and disillusioned, had scrutinised the latest reconnaissance photographs. German cameramen had snapped impressive images of Luftwaffe operations, during and after individual attacks – such as the prints showing puffs of smoke rising from dispersal E-pens moments after a Dornier had released its bombs during a low level raid over RAF Kenley. Other images showed plumes of oily black smoke spiralling hundreds of feet into the sky above the broad, flat landscape surrounding Ford aerodrome in Sussex. Biggin Hill, Manston and Hawkinge were pictured battered and bruised – only the twisted skeletons of bomb-damaged hangars identified the pock-marked acres as airfields.

To Luftwaffe crewmen the well-thumbed photographs appeared to reinforce their Reichsmarschall's assertion that the RAF was on its last legs. The edifice of Fighter Command was clearly toppling, and one more push would send it crashing. Briefed to finish the job of destroying Fighter Command and securing air superiority for the invasion (scheduled to receive the Führer's go-ahead on August 27) massed formations of bomber and fighter aircraft swarmed above their continental airfields and headed out across the English Channel in dense columns. They were determined to bring the bloody struggle to a conclusion and pass the baton to a German Army awaiting the outcome of the campaign, and now whiling away the warm summer days in camps all along the Channel coast.

For Fighter Command, too, the phase of the Battle of Britain that began on August 24 was the most critical period. Production of fighter aircraft was well ahead of schedule but the supply of pilots could not be accelerated; 94 pilots had been posted killed or missing in between August 8 and the 18th. Training programmes were cut to the quick but pilots, unlike aeroplanes, could not be manufactured on demand. Keith Park's airfields were shattered and his aircrews were worn out, at the limit of their reserves of energy. Rotation of squadrons enabled tired pilots to enjoy a brief rest but replacements were often young and generally inexperienced. There was no substitute for trial by fire as far as combat training was concerned.

These were young boys fresh from schools, universities or apprenticeships and possessing only a basic understanding of the principles of air fighting. They were no match for the veterans in Goering's FliegerKorps who stalked the skies searching for Spitfires and Hurricanes piloted by jittery novices.

With nothing left but courage and determination to throw into the battle, the RAF stared defeat in the face. As airfield after airfield was struck, the Luftwaffe's tactics at last appeared to be working. For 14 days, commencing on August 24, the Luftwaffe poured across the Channel and hit the RAF's coastal and sector stations.

Park was forced to mount an increasing number of standing patrols as the Germans used more sophisticated feint-attack techniques. Standing patrols were required because it was not until the last minute that an enemy formation, building up in front of Dover for example, revealed its true target and proceeded on to its destination. With his squadrons by now exhausted and battle-damaged, Park was forced to further test the mettle of his pilots (and use up precious fuel and flying hours) by employing his aircraft in a defensive role that radar was supposed to have precluded. Regardless of the presence of an almost unbroken line of defending fighters, sheer weight of numbers enabled the Luftwaffe to reach its objectives time and time again; and almost always these objectives were the RAF airfields scattered throughout the south-east of England.

This close-up of a Messerschmitt 109 cockpit illustrates the Revi reflector sight, the Luftwaffe's equivalent of the RAF's Mk II reflector sight.

This hapless Luftwaffe pilot became the prize of the local Home Guard detachment on August 30, 1940. On a few occasions enemy airmen were not so fortunate and, unprotected by police or military, were set upon by enraged civilians.

August 24 was not only the date when the Luftwaffe renewed its campaign against Britain's defences; it was also the day when the persistence of Goering's aircrews first really paid off – when the first RAF fighter station was forced to throw in the towel. Manston in Kent had long been the focus for Luftwaffe attention and, singled out as a target more frequently than almost any RAF station, the aerodrome was progressively reduced to rubble as wave after wave of enemy bombers pounded its runways, buildings and personnel into submission.

After four particularly heavy raids on the 24th (during one 264 Squadron's Defiants were caught on the ground as they refuelled prior to a defensive patrol above the airfield), Manston ceased to be a viable operational airfield. With its buildings smashed, all communications between the station and 11 Group HQ severed and the endurance of its personnel stretched to breaking-point, Manston was unable to fulfil its role in Dowding's

defence network. Keith Park was faced with no alternative but to evacuate the station. Henceforth the airfield would be used only as an emergency landing ground for RAF fighters which were damaged or out of fuel.

On the same afternoon other important sector stations received a series of body-blows which also threatened their elimination. As a demonstration of its wide-ranging capability the Luftwaffe visited cities like Portsmouth and Southampton and smaller harbour towns like Dover and Ramsgate, causing enormous damage and distress.

When daylight faded the RAF counted the cost. Fighter Command had lost 22 fighters, but had destroyed 38 Luftwaffe aircraft. While the odds appear significantly to favour the defences, the majority of Luftwaffe losses were of the more vulnerable bombers; all Fighter Command losses were, obviously, fighter aircraft. In fighter-to-fighter contests the Luftwaffe was winning: the RAF was consistently losing more machines than the

THE HAMMER AND THE ANVIL

Luftwaffe and its airfields were rapidly becoming unusable ruins.

As the strain on Fighter Command began to tell so its victory margin began to decrease. In the week ending September 6, for example, statistics reveal the RAF lost 161 fighters as against a total of 189 Luftwaffe aircraft of all types. During the fortnight between August 26 and September 6 – the critical phase of the Battle of Britain – the RAF lost 103 pilots killed and a further 128 wounded. Each week Fighter Command's combat strength was being diminished by ten per cent. Clearly such losses could not be borne indefinitely; although aircraft were still in plentiful supply, it would only be a matter of time before there were not enough trained pilots to fly them.

Fate then took a hand in the proceedings and, though it was not immediately obvious at the time, a sequence of events began which would alter the course of the battle and avert a disaster for Britain.

In the evening of August 24 the Luftwaffe once more took advantage of the cover of darkness and the RAF's inability to provide a night defence. Over 170 German bombers ranged almost at will over South-East England in search of a variety of "military" targets. The impenetrable blackness and commendable ARP precautions on the ground made target identification a difficult task, but even so the oil-storage tanks at Thameshaven should have presented a reasonably easy target, given their distinctive regimented layout and the proximity of the characteristic folds and inlets of the Thames Estuary. Yet for ten Heinkel bombers no amount of distinguishing features would appear to have helped. Hopelessly lost, their bomb-aimers peered through the night desperate to pinpoint their target. When at last the decision to release bombs was taken the aircraft were not above the industrial suburbs of London but directly over the East End.

For the first time since Gotha bombers visited the city during the Great War, streets in London's East End and within the square mile of the City echoed to the crash of exploding bombs. Fires were started and the still relatively unfamiliar sound of jangling fire-engines racing to the scene of the damage was added to the cacophony of aircraft engines, the crump of explosions and the shattering of glass as the temperature rose within stricken buildings.

Churchill ordered a reprisal raid for this latest example of German aggression. On the evening of August 25 Wellington, Hampden and Whitley bombers lumbered into the night skies bound for Berlin. Briefed to hit selected military targets they too were unable precisely to identify their objectives and consequently civilian areas were bombed. Each night Bomber Command continued its retaliatory operations and on the 28th something Hitler had promised could never occur happened: Berliners were killed during an enemy air-raid.

Hitler was furious, but he still reserved the decision to bomb London for himself and as yet refused to sanction such an escalation of the air war. However Goering did order his air-fleets to attack Merseyside and between August 28 and the 21st the busy port and towns around it were subjected to a nightly blitz. Though of little material consequence their action indicated a significant shift in Luftwaffe priorities.

Round-the-clock the Luftwaffe piled on the pressure. The attacks subjected tired workers to sleepless nights and kept the firefighters of the Regular and Auxiliary Fire Service on their toes. But these raids were still little more than an extension of the daylight nuisance raids which towns in the South-East of England had been subjected to for over six weeks. It was the daylight attacks on Fighter Command that caused the most concern and

The remains of a Messerschmitt Bf-109 E-3 shot down in Kent and scattered on farmland. The poles in the middle distance, a common feature of 1940 landscapes, were introduced in an effort to prevent German airborne troops using such open spaces as potential landing grounds for gliders.

"It all depends on me" was the motto of this cigarette card set. Comprising a total of 25 cards, the collection features a fascinating cross-section of contemporary 1940 society and concentrates on civilians rather than military personnel.

threatened to lay Britain open to invasion if they continued for much longer.

On August 26 Biggin Hill, Kenley and Debden were yet again bombed. On the 28th it was the turn of Eastchurch and Rochford, and on the 29th most airfields across the South-East received visits from the Luftwaffe. But the worst was still to come.

On August 30 a strong formation of German aircraft evaded an equally impressive force of RAF fighters and headed for Biggin Hill. Luck favoured the attacking side and the bombers managed to avoid a squadron detached from 12 Group which was briefed to provide protection for the aerodrome. Several attacks were successfully pressed home and soon Biggin Hill was reeling under the impact of scores of massive 1,000-lb bombs. Broken gas and water mains poured their contents uselessly over the airfield, telephone lines were down and the station's armoury, workshops, stores, hangars, barracks and living quarters were reduced to rubble. Worst of all, when the smoke cleared, 39 personnel were dead and 26 were injured – many of the dead found in the bottom of a shelter trench that had received a direct hit. The same afternoon the radar stations at Dover, Pevensey, Rye, Forness, Fairlight, Whitstable and Beachy Head were blacked out when the cable supplying their power was severed by bomb damage.

The next day Luftwaffe aircraft again darkened the skies above Biggin Hill. While station staff toiled to repair the damage

wrought by the previous day's attack, out of sight high above them German bomb-aimers followed their recently released sticks of bombs as they tumbled to the airfield. More serious damage resulted, with temporary telephone lines that had only been operational for a few hours cut and hangars once again shattered by explosions. The prize of the day for the bomb-aimers was a direct hit on the station's operations block. As the ops room was plunged into darkness and WAAFs, airmen and RAF officers crawled through the smoke and dust to try to make sense of the confusion, RAF stations and Observer Corps posts surrounding the airfield informed Keith Parks' headquarters that all communication with Biggin Hill had ceased.

As personnel at Biggin Hill were dusting themselves off, convinced that the Luftwaffe had singled them out, pilots of 54 Squadron at Hornchurch were equally certain that they, above all others, were reaping the whirlwind of German aggression. As the squadron's Spitfires bounced across the aerodrome's grass runway bombs exploded all around them. Great sods of earth rained down on the Spitfires as their pilots desperately attempted to weave a path through the smoke and columns of earth that erupted before them.

The high nose of a Spitfire made forward vision impossible and taxiing and taking off was no easy matter, even in peacetime. Trying to guide a fuelled-up fighter through a barrage of flame and air-blasts was a positively terrifying experience. Three aircraft were unable to avoid the explosions: one was thrown into a field, another was lifted up and deposited across the airfield on its belly and the third, caught by the full force of a blast, somersaulted and crashed upside down. Amazingly all three pilots stepped from their wreckage unhurt and were back in the air later in the day! At the same time the Chain Home network was again attacked but this time with little conviction and it quickly recovered. And because of the appalling losses suffered by the turret-fighters an order was issued on the 31st restricting the deployment of Defiants to night operations.

Biggin Hill was raided for the third successive day on September 1. One squadron's exhausted ground-crews were so shattered by recent experiences that they took cover in a nearby wood rather than use the exposed and demonstrably vulnerable shelter trenches provided. No amount of coercion by

THE HAMMER AND THE ANVIL

a pistol-waving officer would persuade them to break cover and return to their posts.

The airfield's runways already looked like they had been subjected to the busy curiosity of giant moles they were so littered with filled-in bomb craters. But this did not dissuade German bombers from peppering them with even more. Catastrophy struck when the station's sector operations room was finally smashed by several well-aimed missiles. One bomb penetrated the defence teleprinter network room where two WAAFs had courageously remained at their posts despite the chaos and destruction surrounding them. Taking cover at the last moment, when the room suddenly seemed to swell and contract under the effects of the explosion, the brave women emerged from the wreckage shocked but alive. Sergeant Helen Turner and Corporal Elspeth Henderson both received the Military Medal – an award usually reserved for soldiers under fire – in recognition of their heroism.

Emerging from the shelter in the early evening of September 1, station personnel were confronted by fire, smoke and destruction in every direction. Spitfires lay where they had been blown up, their backs broken by blast and bomb fragments as if they had been made of balsa wood and covered in doped tissue. Wings pointed skywards as if making a final vain gesture of defiance. Craters were full of water and gas. The wrecked operations block was swarming with Post Office engineers picking their way through the smouldering debris to see if repairs were possible to the station's telephone network. Within hours the efforts of these tireless men had resulted in an improvised communications link being installed in a butcher's shop down the road from the aerodrome. Everywhere, people tried to resume their duties and struggled to patch up the airfield.

The scenes of dogged determination to "get on with the job" were repeated at Detling, Hawkinge and Lympne airfields which other

With Bomber Command mounting nightly raids against the German mainland, air-raid precautions in the Third Reich were as stringent as they were in Britain. The fear of gas was as real to the German population as it was to the British and their reactions against such a terrifying prospect were equally comprehensive. The photograph shows a German civilian gas-mask and an apparatus designed for babies – the latter an interesting comparison with the British version pictured on page 177. The armband was worn by "Luftschutz" (ARP) personnel.

Without the enormous efforts of dedicated ground-crews of armourers, riggers and fitters, Fighter Command would never have been able to field so many aircraft throughout the Battle of Britain. Here armourers are hastily rearming a Hurricane.

Luftwaffe bombers had attacked at the same time as their colleagues wreaked havoc on Biggin Hill. The bitterness of the day's fighting was evident in the final tally of victories. For the first time the Luftwaffe was ahead on the scoreboard – losing only 14 aircraft as opposed to 15 RAF fighters. Nine more next-of-kin notices would be dispatched by the Air Ministry.

On September 2 Eastchurch, North Weald, Rochford, Detling, Kenley and, once again, poor Biggin Hill were all heavily attacked, and this time Eastchurch and Detling came off worst. At the former, an ammunition dump exploded and the defence teleprinter network of GHQ was written off. Detling was so badly damaged that it was left unserviceable for many hours.

On September 3 North Weald, Horn-church and Debden appeared on Luftwaffe target rotas and fierce fighting ensued. At the end of the day the "score" stood at 16 aircraft on each side – an extremely alarming statistic since it implied that the trend was towards a Luftwaffe victory. The war of attrition was sapping Fighter Command's strength, reduc-ing morale and beginning to threaten its already limited reserves. On September 4 the aerodromes at Eastchurch, Lympne, Roches-ter and Brooklands were bombed. The attack on Brooklands was significant because the site of the famous prewar racing circuit was the location of Vickers-Armstrong's main Wellington bomber plant; 88 workers

were killed as girders and heavy equipment crashed down amid the workshops. Pro-duction of Barnes Wallis' revolutionary geodetic bomber [light but strong alloy basket-weave construction] was halted for four precious days. The RAF slightly improved its performance, however, destroy-ing 25 German aircraft for the loss of 17 of its own fighters.

The Luftwaffe's daytime activities were supplemented by attacks against a wide variety of targets across the country after nightfall. Each evening enemy bombers roamed the skies above Britain in an effort to maintain pressure on frayed nerves and worn-out bodies. Liverpool was a regular target and experienced a nightly "mini-blitz", but other cities with some degree of military significance like Bristol, Birmingham and Portsmouth were also raided. However, in Germany, plans were afoot to extend the Luftwaffe's sphere of operations to cover an area that contained the greatest concentration of civilian dwellings and commercial property in Britain – metropolitan London.

The capital had never been completely eliminated from the Luftwaffe's list of targets. Indeed a German High Command directive dated August 16 outlined plans for air-raids against London, but these were only to be mounted immediately prior to invasion and were not part of the general policy of attrition aimed at wearing down Britain's defences. The massive air attack which Londoners had

dreaded for a year would take place once the invasion flotilla had slipped its moorings, designed to "cause the population to flee from the city and block the roads". Thus a terror attack had never been ruled out; but it was seen essentially as a necessary military tactic which, the High Command hoped, would clog arterial roads and communications networks with the same degree of success that a similar polich had achieved in France and the Low Countries.

By pressing home their attacks against Berlin – the heart of "Nazidom" – Bomber Command not only surprised and enraged Hitler but also provided the catalyst which provoked him to order massive retaliation against London. The last moral impediment to a justified escalation of the campaign had been removed. The Führer now turned to his air force chiefs and ordered them to punish the impudent British and commence a bombing offensive that was to prove unprecedented in the history of warfare. The rule-book was torn up and gloves removed. Britain had refused to see reason, and the consequences of such obstinacy would be a terrible but direct result of British belligerence.

On September 3 Goering conferred with Feldmarschalls Kesselring and Sperrle and informed them of Hitler's desire to see a change in Luftwaffe strategy to include an all-out assault on London. Kesselring, who had always considered London to be a prime target, enthusiastically endorsed his Führer's

plan. He was convinced, rightly as we know, that the RAF was on its last legs, and supported by Major Josef Schmid, the officer responsible for the Luftwaffe's generally inaccurate intelligence summaries, Kesselring argued that the RAF would have no option but to defend London – and as such could be finished off in one last engagement by the application of a simple strategy.

Sperle was not so sure. The RAF had survived far longer than anyone had thought possible, and perhaps it was much stronger than had ever been anticipated. He urged a continuation of the attacks against RAF

ABOVE A Hurricane is fed high-octane aviation fuel from an RAF bowser ready for the next sortie. Refuelling aircraft during the battle, when enemy aircraft could strike at any minute, was always a risky business.

BELOW Looking tired and numb from constant air battles, pilots await the next sortie in the bleak interior of the dispersal hut.

A NATION ALONE

Rescue Buoys.

"Fitted Buoys" are selected navigational buoys around the coast and the areas are shown by shading on the map. There is a rope slung round the buoy for you to catch hold of and to guide you to a ladder which reaches from well below the water line to an opening in the buoy. ————
On climbing through this opening you will find a wood box slung inside the head of the buoy containing rations, first-aid box, a flag to fasten to the buoy distress signals etcetera ———
A.S.R.S. want to get you off as soon as possible so if you do land up on one of these buoys, follow out the instructions in the box. — — — —

British Rescue Floats.

The British Air Sea Rescue Floats consist of a boat-shaped hull painted a bright red and orange, placed roughly as shown on the map. They are not manned or armed but will hold at least six men. They are equipped with signal apparatus, bunks, cooking stove, clothing and food. The stern of the float is sloped down from the hatch to the water to enable a man to climb aboard with the least difficulty. The slope is fitted with a grid and bars extending below the water line and act as foot and hand hold. the raised sides of the float afford some shelter to those lying or resting on the grid.

Inside the float are full instructions for crews to follow to ensure a speedy rescue. W/T is fitted there are distress signals, flags a lamp and whistle One or more of these methods of signalling should be set going as soon as possible and a keen lookout kept.
There are complete changes of dry clothing, food, drink books and games, also cutlery, plate and drinking mugs

Legend

▨ Area within which suitable buoys are fitted as refuges and floats are moored.

Contents of box on Fitted Buoys.

First Aid Outfit
Iron Rations D
Drinking water
Torch
Distress Signal
Knife.
Whistle.
Flag.

German Floats.

There are a few captured German floats moored off the South coast. They are easily distinguishable from the English floats as you will see from the drawing. Only a small quantity of equipment has been placed on these as they are moored near the shore, and should you reach one little time should elapse before your position is noticed.

Contents of British Float.

Clothing	Rations
Jackets, trousers.	Preserved meat.
Sea Stockings, Shirts.	Preserved vegetables.
Underclothing, Boots.	Biscuits, tea, cocoa, Sugar,
Cap comforters, gloves.	Condensed milk, Bovril.
Sleeping Bags, Bunks.	Brandy or Rum
Towels, Washing gear.	Drinking water, cigarettes matches

Signals	Comforts
Wireless, Flags	Books magazines.
Distress Signals	Games, playing cards.

France.

ABOVE The Supermarine Seagull V (Walrus to the RAF), designed by R. J. Mitchell and based on his pre-Spitfire seaplane experiences, was used by the RAF as a reconnaissance and rescue plane. Affectionately known as the "Shagbat" by its crews, it was a sturdy and workmanlike machine with a robust fuselage and hull made from sheet aluminium.

ABOVE RIGHT An official Air Diagram showing the design and location of both British and German rescue floats. The RAF did not have a proper air-sea rescue service in 1940 but the Luftwaffe supplemented its well-equipped safety islands by Heinkel 59 floatplanes of the "Seenotflugkommando" (air-sea rescue unit). In order to prevent downed German airmen returning to their units, and consequently offensive action over England, Dowding ordered that such Luftwaffe planes should be shot down.

airfields and facilities. Though he over-estimated the remaining strength of Fighter Command, he was correct in supporting a continuation of the current Luftwaffe strategy. Fortunately for the RAF the impulsive Goering heeded Kesselring's advice; perhaps he also thought it prudent to concur with Hitler's wishes.

Goering had grown increasingly dissatisfied with the efforts of his Luftwaffe pilots, at times implying cowardice on the part of his aircrews. Unlike Dowding or Park he was unfamiliar with the techniques of modern flying – he had not piloted an aircraft since the days of Richthofen and was so corpulent that the few aircraft he did travel in had to be adapted to accommodate his bulk – and he simply could not appreciate the problems experienced by his fighter-pilots, who every day faced a determined opposition and had to contend with the ever-present problem of insufficient fuel capacity. This not only limited the time available for combat flying but also added to the unsettling experience of operating over enemy territory and the frustrating constraint of flying close escort to slow and vulnerable bombers and, latterly, twin-engined fighters.

Bomber crews were presented with similar problems. Although their aircraft were capable of flying sorties of longer duration they were easy meat for heavily-armed fighters. If opposition was met on the approach to or returning from a target the comforting sight of a large fighter escort frequently vanished, leaving the bombers exposed and their crews unsettled. With only a light armament and the keen eyes of their machine-gunners to protect them, bomber crews soon came to regard missions across the "Scheiss-Kanal" (shit-canal – Channel) with trepidation.

Goering understood none of this and was certain that maximum effort had not yet been brought to bear. Although the Luftwaffe's current strategy of attacks against an assortment of targets was in fact proving successful, it appeared to him to be a dilution of offensive power and he was unable to see the benefits of such an approach. On the contrary an all-out aerial bombardment of London appealed to him and whetted his appetite for dramatic spectacle. The sight of rank on rank of bombers and fighters heading for a single target excited him and the results, he thought, could be more easily gauged. London would be bombed round-the-clock in an unprecedented display of military might.

The campaign against the capital of the British Empire would begin on September 7. The RAF would try in vain to defend it and would be eradicated. The invasion would then be possible and the conquering armies would march on a ruined city and plant their standards amid the charred debris of Westminster. So thrilled by the prospect was he that Goering had his train, *Asia*, moved right up to the coast on the Pas de Calais to be sure of a better view of the sight of his Luftwaffe at

THE HAMMER AND THE ANVIL

last delivering the final blow against Britain.

Hitler was equally enthusiastic. On the evening of September 4 he made a surprise appearance at a gathering of women nurses and social workers at the Berlin Sportsplatz. Seething with anger about Britain's refusal to see reason and surrender quietly to the demands of Nazi Germany and especially furious that his beloved Berlin, capital of the "Thousand-Year Reich", had been subjected to the insult of RAF air-raids, he was in no mood for platitudes. This time Britain had gone too far. The Führer swore revenge.

"In England they are filled with curiosity and keep asking, 'Why doesn't he come?' Be calm. Be calm. He's coming! He's coming!" As he continued, the massed ranks of awe-struck women were gripped by hysterical adulation. In one movement they rose to their feet and screamed their support. But Hitler was not finished: "When the British Air Force drops two or three or four thousand kilograms of bombs, then we will in one night drop 150, 250, 300 or 400 thousand kilograms. When they declare that they will increase their attacks on our cities, then we will raze their cities to the ground. We will stop the handi-work of these night air pirates, so help us God!"

It was clear that in Hitler's mind a struggle that he had originally seen as little more than a sideshow to his intended continental Euro-pean conquests had developed into a bare-knuckle fight between Germany and Britain. With hatred contorting his already animated body he raged on at the Sportsplatz, "If they attack our cities, we will rub out their cities from the map. The hour will come when one of us two will break – and it will not be Nazi Germany!"

Over the next two days Fighter Command continued to be bludgeoned by repeated attacks and lost a further 43 fighters. To the pilots tasked with defending the people of Britain it seemed as if time itself had stopped and there would be no end to the daily routine of confronting an enemy who always enjoyed vast numerical superiority. Utterly worn out, fighter-pilots dragged themselves out of beds and armchairs and, often in a kind of somnambulistic trance, climbed aboard their battle-stained aircraft in preparation for another day's gruelling combat.

On landing many pilots fell asleep in the cockpit the moment their aircraft's propellors stopped turning. Others stayed strapped inside their machines between sorties and grimly awaited the next scramble. The only

ABOVE First-Aid Nursing Yeomanry (FANY) motor-vehicle badge. Formed in 1907, the First Aid Nursing Yeomanry was the first women's service to be motorised and during the First World War it ran self-contained motor-ambulance units in France and Flanders. By 1940 its personnel were involved in sterling work in support of the war effort. Female SOE operatives assumed the cover of FANYs to conceal their true activities.

LEFT The wheeled vehicle is a trolley accumulator – or "trolley-acc" as it was more usually known by RAF ground-crews – and was used to supply electrical power to start the engines of fighter-aircraft. The flying equipment arranged on it is of the type worn by fighter-pilots in 1940. The parachute harness was cumbersome, heavy and difficult to run in, so pilots generally slung the parachute into the cockpit and fastened the harness once aboard. The parachute pack became a basic and not too comfortable seat. The face-mask pictured was known as a "D-type" and along with an integral microphone it supplied oxygen via a hose [missing here] from a supply in the cockpit. A quick blast of oxygen was found by many pilots to be an instant cure for a hangover.

thing of which RAF personnel were certain, from Dowding down to the grubbiest "erk", was that Fighter Command would soon cease to exist if the pressure was not reduced. Its survival could be measured in days, not weeks. Aerodromes across the South-East were wrecked and operational ability was diminishing daily. The Luftwaffe had discovered Britain's Achilles heel and was bit by bit dismantling Britain's defence system.

The Luftwaffe had stumbled across its formula for victory. Goering's aerial battering-ram was gradually breaking down the island fortress's main gate. Amazingly the Reichsmarschall was unaware that the battle was all but won. At the moment when victory was within his grasp, the ineptitude of the "Iron Man" and most of his senior advisers let it slip away. Hitler's desire for retribution compounded the error and, ultimately, would prove Germany's undoing.

Germany lost the Second World War in September 1940 when she decided to toss aside the bleeding but alive remains of Fighter Command. The suffering of Londoners over the next nine months guaranteed the eventual freedom of Europe and sealed the fate of hundreds of thousands of German civilians who came to realise the full horror of total, unrestricted warfare. As September 7 dawned Fighter Command's salvation was at hand, and it was delivered by the RAF's most unlikely benefactor – Adolf Hitler. The Battle of Britain was about to be decided.

Chapter Six

"I staggered out of the woods to be met by two or three characters wielding pitchforks . . . They couldn't tell what I was because I was burnt black. My uniform was still smouldering. They didn't know what it was in front of them until I opened my mouth and swore at them. Then the farmer's wife came over and tore up her petticoat to wrap my wounds as best she could."

Squadron-Leader Desmond Fopp,
Sergeant-Pilot, No. 17 Squadron, 1940

WARRIORS OF THE AIR

King George VI inspecting the pilots of No. 611 Squadron at Digby, south of Lincoln, in 1939.

The achievements of pilots on both sides have been thoroughly recorded in dozens of books and it is not the intention of this work to repeat what has been covered exhaustively elsewhere. Yet to appreciate fully the situation faced by pilots who clashed in the skies above England in the summer of 1940 there is no substitute for first-hand accounts.

What follows conveys a feeling of the Battle of Britain from pilots who flew for Britain . . . and pilots who flew for Germany. They shared a common goal – a determination to perform their allotted duties to the best of their abilities – and an intense desire to survive. Their stories are echoed a hundred times in biographies and diaries written in English and German, but for each of them the Battle of Britain was an unforgettable and often painful personal experience.

Flight-Lieutenant Brian Kingcome

In 1940 Group Captain Brian Kingcome was a young Flight-Lieutenant with No. 92 Squadron. During the Battle of Britain he was stationed at Biggin Hill in Kent and was thus frequently in the thick of the fighting. Debonair, witty and charming, Kingcombe was the epitome of the Battle of Britain fighter pilot. A natural flyer in the manner of Stanford-Tuck and Bader, he was respected by his contemporaries and was one of "The Few" selected to be drawn by the war artist Cuthbert Orde. He learned his trade over Dunkirk, quickly recognising the importance of constant vigilance. "You soon learned to watch your tail as much as you watched your nose," he explains. "Most people who were shot down were shot down by something they

A NATION ALONE

RIGHT A pencil drawing of Brian Kingcome by the official war artist Cuthbert Orde, who did portraits of many of the "aces" of the RAF during the conflict.

BELOW Close-up of the port side of Flight-Lieutenant Kingcome's Spitfire Mk1A of 92 Squadron at Biggin Hill in May 1941.

"If you attacked from the beam or from astern this was the way their bombers were designed to be attacked, so they could bring the maximum weight of their own artillery on you. But if you attacked them head on it scared the shit out of them! As soon as you started to approach a bomber formation from the front it started to get jittery and began to bounce about. So whenever I was scrambled and we were told where the enemy aircraft were I would always fly north and try to reach their height and then turn round and hope to meet the incoming formation head on. Usually you met them roughly halfway between Maidstone and the coast.

"Approaching them head on you enjoyed a much quicker and softer target. They had nothing in the front to protect them, while in the back they were armour-plated around the cockpit and the engines to some extent. But in the front they were totally vulnerable. The driver had nothing between him and you but a thin sheet of Perspex. Closing at about five or six hundred miles an hour you probably started to open fire at about a thousand yards – much farther than you should. You went on firing until you just ducked over or under the target. Then you went through the entire formation and if there was any chance then you tried to attack them from the flank or the rear. By that time, of course, the 109s were usually coming down on you. The other reason for the head-on approach was that you could get to the bombers before the 109s could get to you – and at least you got one bloody good decisive attack.

"After the first attack on the formation they broke up. We normally fielded only six or seven aircraft and so flew in loose Vics one on top of the other, the twos and threes of each Vic spreading out so that we covered as broad a front as possible. By the time you reached the other end of the formation normally the 109s were down and you would be involved with them. Hopefully another RAF squadron would then come along to help out! After the first pass some German bombers held and some broke – it depended on the pilots. Certainly their morale was dented. They didn't like it at all!"

At high speed and amid the confusion of battle it was often very difficult to judge the effect of combat procedures. Brian Kingcome is convinced that some claims made during the Battle of Britain are doubtful simply because pilots were busy trying to stay alive and were

never saw, concentrating on someone else's section and not their own."

When the fighting moved from France to England Flight-Lieutenant Kingcombe was ready to put into practice all the experience he gained during his encounters with the experienced Luftwaffe pilots over the sand dunes of Dunkirk. Recognising the superiority of the Luftwaffe's finger-four formation in fighter-to-fighter combat, he nevertheless considered the RAF's traditional "Vic" of three aircraft to be more suitable when attacks on bombers were the priority. "In my view, the old Vics was the best formation for Fighter Command during the Battle of Britain, because as far as I was concerned there was only one safe way to attack a bomber formation – and that was head on.

WARRIORS OF THE AIR

usually unable to see whether an enemy aircraft, once hit, was destroyed or not.

"If you went through a bomber formation head on you would probably start smoke – probably start something coming from the engines. Occasionally by the time you were through you would look back and you might find one or two aircraft in the formation going down. Whose they were you never really knew. I personally never saw one blow up in front of me. In order to do that you had to be sitting right on the tail."

Like all seasoned fighter-pilots Brian Kingcome had a healthy respect for Luftwaffe gunners. "Because the tracer was just a fraction of a second behind the actual bullet that was fired, you never quite knew where the bullet was. You could see the tracer coming all around you, even in bright weather. It was terrifying. Starting off rather slowly, it accelerated at enormous speed past you. If it hit there was a loud rattle. Quite often you came down full of bullet-holes."

Although wary of the Bf-109's cannon armament Flight-Lieutenant Kingcome was satisfied with the performance and reliability of the eight Brownings mounted in the elliptical wings of his Spitfire. "Eight machine-guns gave you a very comfortable feeling when you fired them. They made a strange noise, though. They didn't sound like guns – more a sound like someone tearing calico, a distinctive ripping noise. On firing the aircraft would judder and you could easily stall. You had to exercise a lot of discipline because you only had fifteen seconds of ammunition. The tendency was to give much longer bursts than was really justified. The ideal was perhaps to give six or seven two-second bursts."

Fighter Command in 1940 appears to resemble a somewhat exclusive club whose members found it difficult to relate to outsiders and spent a great deal of time swopping anecdotes with each other or simply getting blind drunk before they had to return to their squadrons and adjust to yet another day living on a tightrope. Brian Kingcome's recollections tend to bear out this rather clichéd impression. "Fighter Command was a very small, compact organisation. You soon heard who was leading which squadron or which wing and you probably met him either at a Fighter Command conference or at an 11 Group conference or most likely in the 'Shepherd's' pub in Shepherd's Market in the West End of London."

Drinking was certainly an important feature of an off-duty pilot's life. The White Hart at Brasted was the local for pilots on active service at Biggin Hill, for example, and each evening its bar was filled with blue-grey serge as pilots and those that "flew desks" rubbed shoulders and quaffed pints. "You had time to get down there after you were stood down," recalls Kingcombe. "You were stood down half an hour after last light so you just had time to get down to the boozer before it was shut!

"At Biggin Hill we were dispersed in houses off the airfield to prevent one bomb on the mess knocking off a couple of squadrons. So the modus operandi was that each evening we would nip down to the White Hart until they

Conjuring up the spirit of 1940, two Spitfires scramble across a summer backdrop during filming for the television series *Piece of Cake* in 1988.

closed and from there we would go back to our marvellous country house with its piano and take back some girls and plenty of beer and have an enormous party. I don't remember going to bed for a long time; I knew that if I went to bed I would never get up in the morning, because they roused us at about four. So I used to sleep in a chair – I probably didn't get into it until about two or three in the morning. Then you were woken up at about half past three or four and then taken down to dispersal. When we arrived there we were met by our doctor, Doc Jones, who dished out medicine from a pail. Then we would nip into our aircraft and have a couple of huge blasts of oxygen and in no time we felt as right as rain, even if you had a hell of a hangover. As soon as the bell went, adrenalin took over and you forgot about it."

Brian Kingcome flew almost throughout the entire period of the Battle of Britain. When he was finally shot down his exit from the battlefield was as spectacular as it was startling. Just before noon on Tuesday October 15, 1940 Flight-Lieutenant Kingcombe, flying Spitfire No. X4418, was returning from the scene of enemy activity over Maidstone and was steadily descending towards his squadron's airfield, which was clearly discernable in the midday haze.

"I was flying at between 15 and 20,000 feet. It was a perfect day and I could see Biggin Hill in the distance. I looked around and I could see nothing except a section of three Spitfires somewhere behind me. Then, like an absolute idiot, I thought 'this is a good time to practise a forced landing'. I throttled back and started to glide towards Biggin. Suddenly there was a rattle and a whole lot of bullets struck the aircraft, one of which went into my leg. I let out a startled cry – as one would!

"The three Spitfires drew up alongside, took one look at me and then half-rolled away. Whether they had shot something down, off my tail, or whether one of them had in error fired a quick burst at me – which had happened on more than one occasion previously – I'll never know.

"I was shot through the right calf, although at the time I didn't know I had been shot – I just felt a thump in the back of my leg. It was a bit later when blood starting coming out of the top of my flying-boot – which is pretty conclusive – I realised I must have been hit!

"I jettisoned my canopy and undid my straps and was about to push the stick forward – I couldn't turn the aircraft over as recommended because my lateral controls were damaged. Suddenly I was sucked out from the cockpit as if a giant hand had plucked me from it. But I was alarmed that I was wearing a German Mae West, which I had taken off a chap I had shot down over South Wales a bit earlier. There had been quite a lot of stories of pilots, especially Poles, being rather badly mauled if people on the ground suspected them to be German – and here I was dangling in my German Mae West. I saw some people gathering in a field below me and thought 'bloody hell' – but luckily my Spitfire came down close by and I was alright."

Brian Kingcome's Spitfire crashed at Wybornes Farm, High Halstow in Kent at precisely 11.47 am on October 15. It was officially attributed to a lone Messerschmitt 109 but Kingcombe is far from convinced about this. After surviving the worst part of his ordeal – a rough examination by a doctor at the Royal Naval Hospital at Chatham, which threatened to cause the pilot to bleed to death – Kingcome went on to complete a long and distinguished career in the RAF. He now runs an interior design business.

Major Adolf Galland

Like his good friend and rival, Werner Mölders, Adolf Galland was already a distinguished fighter ace when the Battle of Britain commenced. His neatly combed jet-black hair, distinctive moustache and ever-present cigar singled Galland out in scores of propaganda photographs taken by German cameramen during the period. His flamboyant style (he had an ashtray fitted to the control panel of his aircraft) and his natural hunter's instinct set him apart from most contemporaries. One of the few Luftwaffe pilots of the period to survive the war, he was in combat up until 1945, the year he flew the world's first operational jet-fighter, the Messerschmitt Me 262.

In the summer of 1940 he was stationed in the Pas de Calais, in command of the third Gruppe of Jagdgeschwader 26, which was equipped with Bf-109 fighters. On August 19 both Mölders and Galland were promoted and each given command of an entire Jagdgeschwader in recognition for their outstanding combat and leadership abilities.

Galland is now widely acknowledged as an authority on the Luftwaffe during the Second

OPPOSITE PAGE Luftwaffe pilots, especially Major Adolf Galland, had great admiration for the courage and flying skill of Douglas Bader. This picture was taken shortly after Bader's capture in 1941. Shot down over France, Bader's artificial legs (fitted after an accident in 1932) had remained firmly lodged in his crippled Spitfire's cockpit. Galland, pictured on the left, chivalrously organised for a replacement pair to be delivered from across the Channel, via the RAF, and treated his prisoner with courtesy prior to Bader's eventual imprisonment at Colditz Castle.

WARRIORS OF THE AIR

World War, and his views enable the reader to achieve a better understanding of how the Battle of Britain appeared from the German perspective. In preparing this book I was fortunate enough to have an opportunity to ask General Galland various questions about the campaign, and his answers provide a valuable perspective on Luftwaffe strategy and tactics in 1940.

On the subject of pilot and aircrew morale and satisfaction with equipment General Galland made the following observation: "Since we had entire air superiority over Poland, France and the Low Countries we were happy with the performance of our aircraft. Morale and confidence were very high amongst our fighter-pilots after the 'Blitzsiege' [Blitz-victories]. We definitely knew, or very soon learned, that our opponents, especially the RAF fighter-pilots, were very well trained. They had high morale and their Hurricanes and Spitfires, especially the Spitfires had about the same performance as the Bf-109 with more maneouvrability."

Galland confirms that one of the glaring inadequacies of the Luftwaffe's strategy was its poor intelligence gathering. "We were not at all accurately briefed about Fighter Command and the British air defences as a whole. Our knowledge of the English radar installations and the fighter guidance system was almost zero. The fact that the British High Command knew all our operational orders at the same time as us by means of Ultra was also absolutely unknown to us."

ABOVE Adolf Galland at rest between sorties. The leading Luftwaffe ace to survive the war, Galland was one of the most skilled pilots of the period. By the war's end he had progressed from piston-engined Me-109s to the jet-engined Me-262 and claimed a total of 105 confirmed kills.

A NATION ALONE

In common with most Luftwaffe veterans General Galland feels that the campaign over Britain in 1940 favoured the defenders. "We hated the Channel, especially when running short of fuel, or when our aircraft were damaged in combat. Our tactics of flying in wide open formations at different altitudes proved to be superior against the closed formations adopted by Fighter Command. Surprise attacks were often in our favour.

"The lack of success of our Stukas against England was not a surprise to us at all. We had already discovered this during joint tests and exercises at the time. Escorting Stukas was very difficult indeed. Goering must have known that the Me-110 was easily outclassed by modern single-seat fighters – this was known from tests in peacetime. But he did not want to admit it as a fact. Soon we learned that the so-called 'Elite-Fighters', the Me-110s, were not able to escort the bomber formations at all. Goering insisted on a defensive fighter escort for his bombers since the bomber-pilots requested it strongly. This was his biggest mistake: fighters can best develop their superiority only when they act offensively. The escort fighters of the US Eighth Air Force finally did it the best way.

"We knew that we were close to knocking out the RAF, but we did not know how close we were. Switching over from attacking the British air defences to the air battle against London and other civil targets was a big strategic mistake. RAF fighters could never be totally destroyed because of the limited range of our own fighter aircraft. Their radius of action just reached as far as London, without having more time for air combat. To us the Battle of Britain presented a major campaign for which, we were soon to learn, the Luftwaffe had not been equipped. It was not strong enough to conquer England."

Galland supports the general German view that the Battle of Britain was more an extension of the European campaign than a decisive contest in its own right: "Operation Seelöwe [Sea-lion] was never seriously considered and prepared. Hitler did not want a war against England. Britain was not supposed to be the enemy."

Sergeant-Pilot Desmond Fopp

Desmond Fopp's experiences during the Battle of Britain were shared by scores of young men who flew with Fighter Command in 1940. In common with most veterans of the conflict he is casually pragmatic about his contribution to the defence of Britain and self-effacing about his exploits as a fighter-pilot.

As an NCO during the Battle of Britain he experienced little discrimination and was accepted by his officer colleagues in No. 17 Squadron on more or less equal terms. The high casualty rate among officer pilots meant that NCOs were frequently in command of flights and at times even led squadrons into battle. Most, like Desmond Fopp, were quickly commissioned as their combat experience increased. However, he explains, the lot of sergeant-pilots sometimes left something to be desired, especially as they were often employed as "Tail-end Charlies" or "Weavers" to stooge around behind the squadron formation and act as flying sentries.

"As far as your flying went", he explains, "the basic rule in 1940 was that the officers flew in the lead position and NCOs flew as number twos, threes or fours. I can remember at one stage being the Tail-end Charlie, which was the worst job of the lot – you really got the chop there if you weren't very good. You had to keep up as well which was the awkward bit because you were flying across, as well as ahead, to keep the tail of the squadron covered. The thing to remember was that while the officers were doing all the shooting there was an NCO keeping their tail covered and he didn't get the chance of shooting at the enemy aircraft. If he was doing his job properly he should be looking after his number one."

Desmond Fopp remembers clearly how he felt during his first engagement with the enemy. "I felt quite excited by the fact that at last I'd got a chance to have a crack and get a squirt at the enemy. There was no feeling of hatred – it was just a target, a Heinkel 111.

"We treated them more or less as equals. As far as I was concerned a bomber was a target and I never gave a thought to anybody in it. We were obviously outnumbered, but we didn't feel particularly worried about it because the more there were the more you had a chance of hitting them. However, as far as we were concerned in Hurricanes, the enemy was invariably above us. Messerschmitt 109s who had come over as top cover were already up high above us. The Spitfires were supposed to be up there attending to them but it never worked that way. If the Spits didn't get there in time or were in the wrong place the 109s would be down among us as well.

"Once you'd seen them coming you could out-run them. They were faster but they couldn't do a lot to you if they were behind you as you just turned around and got behind them in turn. But they got away so fast that unless you got a quick burst in, you wouldn't catch them."

Desmond Fopp's log-book is still intact. The entry dated September 3, 1940 reads:

> Sept 3 Hurricane YB-E
> Ops Intercepted 60 EA
> 1 Do-17 Probable
>
> Shot down in flames by three
> Me-110s
> Baled out 17,000 ft
> In hospital 2 months
>
> Sortie 50 mins duration (15 mins descent by parachute)

This straightforward record conceals the details of a drama that resulted in Desmond Fopp suffering the injury feared most by fighter-pilots – burns. The series of events that culminated in a conflagration 17,000 feet above Essex started in the morning as his squadron prepared for the first sortie of the day. He describes it thus: "Hurricane YB-E [the aircraft Sergeant Fopp was given as a replacement for his trusted YB-I] had been until quite recently a replacement aircraft. One of our new pilot officers at the time had taxied it from the hangar across to the dispersal blast bays but as he was coming into the blast bay he didn't stop and he hit the bay. The aircraft went over onto its nose and chipped three inches off all the prop tips. The fitter at the time then trimmed the tips a bit further, using a saw. It made the engine rev a bit too much."

Not surprisingly the damaged Hurricane was a poor performer but Sergeant Fopp was still expected to use it operationally. At approximately 9.30 am Hurricane P3673, with Fopp at the controls, took off from RAF Debden and along with the rest of No. 17 Squadron climbed to intercept a formation of 60 Luftwaffe bombers approaching North Weald aerodrome. After intercepting the formation and claiming a Do-17 as "probable", Fopp and his lack-lustre Hurricane found themselves in a tricky situation.

"I thought I'd bluffed my way out of this spot with three Messerschmitt 110s that were

LEFT Sergeant-Pilot Desmond Fopp, No. 17 Squadron, RAF Fighter Command, Debden, 1940.

BELOW Official letter sent to Mrs Fopp explaining in typically unsentimental terms the fact that her son had suffered injuries while involved in air combat against the Luftwaffe. Notifications of deaths were equally clinical.

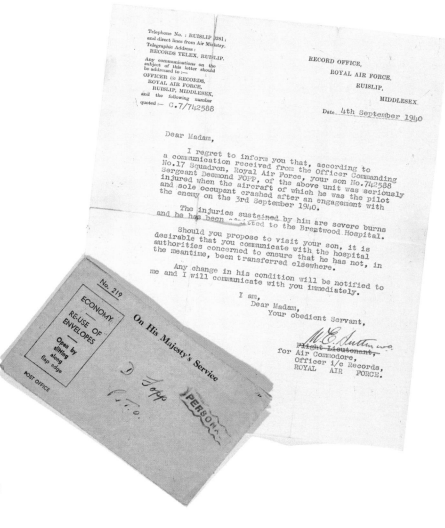

coming straight for me. I hadn't got any ammunition left so I thought the only way to get out of it was to turn on them, which I did, and they broke up. As I dived away, one of them got underneath me and hit my belly as I was going down. The Me-110 couldn't manoeuvre but once in a good position it was lethal as it had a very powerful armament. You could cope with them if you could see them. I thought I'd succeeded but I hadn't seen the third bloke. He hit me in the radiator and I caught fire – very rapidly. All of a sudden I was sitting in a ball of flames and it became very painful very quickly. My gloves and my boots were burnt off. Within seconds my trousers were burnt away to just below my knees.

"My instinctive reaction was to get out. The first thing I did was try to get out with all my straps done up, but of course I realised this and as soon as I had undone the straps and opened the hood I went out like a startled rabbit. The parachute harness was smouldering even when I touched the ground. I came down near Brentwood in Essex, in the wood in fact. I couldn't have done it better actually because I went through the trees and finished up with my toes about three inches off the ground. The trees broke my fall but I did get a few scratches on top of my burns. All I did then was release the harness and I finished up on my hands and knees.

"I staggered out of the woods to be met by two or three characters – they were wielding pitchforks because it was hay-making time. They couldn't tell what I was because I was burnt black. My uniform was still smouldering. They didn't know what it was in front of them until I opened my mouth and swore at them. Then the farmer's wife came over and tore up her petticoat to wrap my wounds as best she could. Then I was whipped off to Brentwood District Hospital, which was very lucky for me because at the time they were experimenting with burn cures.

"One cure in being at the time was a thing called Tannifax, which was tannic acid. It used to work but it had one big fault – it contracted everything. I had Tannifax on my hands but not on my face. As it tended to gather the skin together one of my hands is smaller than the other. People who had it done on their faces used to require rebuilds of their faces because it burnt straight through the bridge of their nose. I was lucky because the doctor at the Brentwood District Hospital wouldn't have anything to do with that treatment on the face. He used olive oil. He took the whole hospital stock of olive oil and used it on me because I was the only one in there for this treatment. I stayed there for two months and was never transferred to a service hospital. I was blind for the first month."

Archibald McIndoe, one of the innovators of plastic surgery and famous for his Guinea Pig Club of burns victims, was as sceptical of the tannic acid and gentian violet treatment then in use as was Desmond Fopp's doctor at Brentwood. Instead, McIndoe developed a specialised saline bath into which his burn victims were immersed. The solution in it was kept at blood temperature and was a soothing relief from the pain and inflammation of burns. Although it has since been claimed that pilots who were burned and who landed in the sea enjoyed a better chance of survival than those who baled out over the land, it is unlikely that this had anything to do with the water's salt content. It was probably more a consequence of the cooling properties of cold water which perhaps reduced the shock as well as the pain of burns.

Sergeant Fopp was commissioned in November 1940 and promoted to the rank of Pilot Officer. During a morale-boosting (or "line-shooting" tour as it was known by pilots) he visited factories up and down Britain shortly after the Battle of Britain had finished and once his wounds had healed. At one establishment a worker was surprised to discover how poorly paid the fighter-pilots were. After reflecting on this for a few seconds the employee offered a justification for the apparent anomaly: "Well," he said, "I suppose we do carry on working throughout the air-raids." Pilot Officer Fopp's reaction is best left to the reader's imagination.

Fopp was fortunate in escaping from the stricken Hurricane's burning cockpit. Many pilots were not so lucky, and one of the most terrifying features of aerial combat was the risk of cremation, trapped in a cockpit rapidly becoming engulfed in flames.

RAF pilots invariably sat behind their vulnerable unarmoured fuel-tanks which, if hit, would stream blazing fuel backwards into the cockpit and all over its hapless occupant. In a few brief seconds the intense heat and ferocity of the flames could peel away layer after layer of skin to expose bones and muscle. Flying helmets and gloves helped to shield the skin but many pilots omitted to wear goggles because they so restricted peripheral vision.

It is interesting to compare the rapid and inelegant exits Sergeant Fopp and Flight-Lieutenant Kingcome made from their stricken aircraft with the officially recommended version that was issued to air-crews. The Air Ministry prepared instructions insisted that: "The sequence of operations is most important, even if you are in a hurry. First, lift your seat to the full 'up' position, slide back your hood and lock it fully open. Undo your harness, take hold of the parachute rip-cord, and then either stand up on the seat and put the stick forward, or roll onto your back . . . If you are on fire don't open the hood until the last moment, as it will draw flames into the cockpit. If your clothes are soaked in petrol, switch off the engine switches and leave the throttle open, otherwise as you get out the sparks from the exhaust may act like the flint in your cigarette lighter. Keep hold of the rip-cord as you leave the aircraft, but if you are very high there is no need to pull it for the time being. Pilots who have pulled the rip-cord immediately after getting out in a high-speed dive have been badly injured. You will fall more slowly out of your aeroplane than in it, so do a delayed drop whenever you can. The '109' will also find you harder to hit with the umbrella shut than open. You only fall 1,000 feet in five seconds, so there is really plenty of time."

One wonders whether Pilot Officer Cardale Capon of No. 257 Squadron had followed the official instructions or employed a more expedient method of evacuation before baling out over Kent on October 12, 1940. His Hurricane was hit by cannon fire at 27,000 feet and was so badly damaged that the 20-year-old pilot had no option other than to abandon it. Jumping at 26,000 feet, Capon displayed amazing grit by not opening his parachute until he had descended to a mere 1,500 feet. As air battles raged around him the plucky pilot performed an involuntary free-fall descent for nearly five miles!

He was lucky not to have been shot at, for the reference to trigger-happy Me-109 pilots contained in the official instructions was based on many recorded incidents of pilots suspended from silken canopies succumbing to a final burst from a departing foe. The straffing of baled-out aircrew was not solely the domain of Luftwaffe pilots; Brian Kingcome confirms that he witnessed RAF pilots machine-gunning defenceless German crews as they floated down above southern England.

First Lieutenant Hans Schmoller-Haldy

One Luftwaffe pilot with very vivid memories of the Battle of Britain is Hans Schmoller-Haldy. During the summer of 1940 he held the rank of first lieutenant and led a squadron of Bf-109 fighters stationed at Campagne Sud, an airfield about ten miles south of Calais. In 53 days of continuous fighting, seven of the nine pilots from his squadron who were present at the beginning of the campaign had been killed. It is little wonder that he refers to the period as "merciless battle".

Hans Schmoller-Haldy (centre, facing right) pictured at Defence Headquarters in Deelan, Holland, in 1944. On the left is Adolf Galland, by now promoted to General, scrutinising yet another report.

A NATION ALONE

In keeping with the two other branches of the German armed services the Luftwaffe employed a dramatic range of regalia to reinforce the national identity and encourage a strong feeling of "esprit de corps". Clockwise, from top left: metal Luftwaffe jacket emblem, two Luftwaffe arms of service badges; air-gunners badge (left) and Luftwaffe ground combat badge (right); next to the cloth Luftwaffe emblem is an elaborate officer's dress dagger and scabbard; below the blue painted alloy Luftwaffe belt buckle is the standard Luftwaffe pilots badge as introduced in 1935 and worn below the left breast-pocket of the uniform tunic; centre right is the badge and lanyard award to Luftwaffe personnel for marksmanship proficiency.

Schmoller-Haldy's account of his many experiences during the Luftwaffe's offensive over England provides an illuminating insight into the daily business of German aircrew during the Battle of Britain. And it is included here to offer a valuable contrast to the more familiar experiences of RAF pilots.

"Today we know exactly how the war went on and finally ended," he says. "In 1940 the view and the aims of the higher political and military German leaders were completely unknown to me. Certainly, I realised the rearmament of the German forces from 1934 onwards, but not what was wrong with it. From 1936 until 1938 I served as a so-called combat-ready pilot as a young flight-lieutenant in a fighter group near Munich. There were at the same time some 30 other young flight officers and the same number of flight NCOs. We young officers lived in a double-roomed flat on the base. We were all unmarried. Our home was very nice with a spacious mess-hall and all the facilities we needed. We had each received the same education in school concerning civil and military matters and shared the same spirit and dedication to our profession.

"Our day-to-day duty was to fly. We were proud of our fighter-planes, which we handled with great skill. Our service was hard and we had our first flying accidents. You may believe it or not but politics was never a subject of our discussions. And Goering, he was also rarely a

subject. He was a former First World War pilot together with Richthofen and he was a builder of the new German Air Force in which we served.

"And Hitler? He was the German leader. We knew that there were some reservations against him personally and against his policies in general. But these reservations were not a subject of our discussions either. We knew that many foreign statesmen negotiated with him either by visiting him in Berlin or through their embassies in the German capital. These diplomatic activities, which mostly took place in a friendly manner, unfortunately produced the dangerously wrong impression, in the eyes of many foreign statesmen, that Hitler was a sincere person and not the unscrupulous criminal which he was in fact, right from the beginning of his chancellorship. We were all deceived."

Schmoller-Haldy recalls his role with characteristically Teutonic precision. "With the exception of a few days of bad weather during the six weeks I flew with my squadron over England we normally flew two missions a day, sometimes three. These missions lasted between 70 and 90 minutes.

"I arrived on August 1, 1940 at Campagne Sud with my squadron and some 150 airmen, 11 Bf-109E aircraft and nine pilots; two Bf-109s were flown by pilots who returned to Schipol in Amsterdam. Our entire fighter group was located here – three squadrons and the group staff of four pilots (group commander, adjutant and two NCO pilots). There was a total of approximately 35 Bf-109s.

"I had left hospital in Holland at the end of July after my accident with a Bristol Blenheim on June 26. [During an encounter with the Blenheim near Rotterdam Schmoller-Haldy's 109 was hit by fire from the bomber's rear-gunner. Shot in the left foot and bleeding profusely, he managed to bring his stricken fighter home. The 109 nosed over on landing and Schmoller-Haldy was rushed to hospital at Tilburg.] My left leg was still bandaged and not very moveable. I always hoped that the Bristol Blenheim, which was apparently severely hit in its port wing, returned safely to England.

"A Bristol Blenheim which was attacked in enemy territory by a flight of four 109s should have been easy prey, but it defended with courage and did not give in. The rear-gunner sent me down with some 20 bullets in my aircraft's body and heavy bleeding from a painful wound in my left leg. I have thought very often during and after the war about this particular incident and hoped that the crew of the Blenheim survived the war.

"Looking back the entire battle seemed to be like one long single day: getting up in the morning pretty early from my room in a farmhouse in the village, with no light, no water, no wardrobe and just a bed and a chair; driving with the pilots in a truck, mostly silently, to our little hut on our airfield; flying missions; trying to do one's duty and lead the squadron with courage and skill; trying to preserve the lives of our pilots and survive oneself; leaving the airfield after darkness; driving home in the same truck – hopefully with the same number of pilots as in the morning; enquiring about the successes or losses of the other two squadrons and their personnel; and, finally, planning and looking ahead to the next morning and the same business all over again.

"Yet I do remember some specific events. When, after a dog-fight 20,000 feet above London, a Spitfire chased me right down to the deck. When Lieutenant Kinzinger, my deputy and friend, shot at and hit a Hurricane right on the top of a loop and the English pilot baled out. When a flight of four Spitfires just 1,000 feet below me shot four Do-17s down in flames over Canterbury and I could do nothing to help.

"When our fighter group was ordered to escort some 20 Ju-88s, which had just arrived from Norway and were completely in-experienced over England. Due to miserable weather we were separated from them and had to leave them alone and return to our airfield feeling very badly about it. Later in the evening we heard from headquarters that the majority, including the group commander, had been shot down over England.

"When my wingman, an NCO pilot, got hit during an escort mission to Biggin Hill. He was wounded and bleeding and asked me over the radio to lead him home to our base. He flew at a distance of 20 to 30 metres from me, undetected and unnoticed by many Spitfires and Hurricanes who did not realise that the two Bf-109s could not defend themselves on their way home. When we reached the French coast I talked to poor Sergeant Ripple and told him that we were going to make it and that we were already close to our airfield. I realised that he was getting weaker and weaker. Finally, shortly before our airfield, his engine stopped and he killed himself attempting a crash landing only one hundred metres from the airfield. All our efforts and hopes had been for nothing.

"These are things which you never forget in your life. How difficult it is for all of us to recall what our psychological condition was during the battle – our feelings, our moods, our fears, our hopes. What were my feelings the evening I discovered one of our pilots had

Luftwaffe flying clothing was practical and of extremely high quality. Displayed on the wing of the RAF Museum's Me-109 can be seen a leather fighter-pilot's jacket, a cloth flying-helmet, silk-lined with leather-covered earphones and integral throat microphones. There were two other styles of helmet: one was all-leather with a woollen fleece lining, the other was made from a cotton-mesh material for use in hot weather and in tropical climates. The goggles have one-piece lenses and rubber frames and the oxygen-mask is the standard three-strap demand type. The kapok-filled life-jacket did not need inflating like the RAF type and would still provide buoyancy if damaged, but it was awkward and prone to snagging against aircraft interiors.

been shot down over the Channel, had baled out and was most probably alive, knowing that he would most likely be driven by the currents towards the direction of the Netherlands and so would not survive?

"What did I feel when I heard that two or three chaps in other squadrons had been killed over England? We all knew each other very well and were friends. It did not matter what rank we held. Each evening we asked the same questions: who got lost in our group, in our wing, on other wings?

"There was an excellent communication system between the eight or nine wings which were located within a radius of ten to fifteen miles. The squadron leaders had their staff cars and the means to visit their friends in other nearby villages, to find out who was lost, to exchange battle experiences and to talk to each other.

"Arriving in the morning at the airfield, we could already hear the good, confident sound of some 20 Mercedes-Benz 601 engines which the ground-crew were warming up. A short while later the group commander, Major Von Bonin – my former squadron leader in Spain and after that a friend who was killed in Russia – called the squadron leaders to his little headquarters. Time for the first briefing. Three escort missions deep into England were on our flight plan. It was mentioned that strong British fighter activity could be expected.

"What did I feel when the loudspeaker called: 'Pilots to board the aircraft, get the engine started; take-off time in exactly five minutes.'? Corporal Mattner, the chief of my aircraft's maintenance team since the beginning of the war, helped me to put on the parachute and the life-jacket and helped to get me into the cockpit. He fastened my seat-belts, passed the oxygen-mask and the helmet with earphones to me, smiled at me with his friendly face then closed the cockpit canopy and started the aircraft's engine.

"From now on I was alone and everything happened very quickly. The first 109s took off. I rolled slowly to the take-off point, lined up until it was my turn and got the aircraft into the air. Then weapons were armed, oxygen turned on, the aircraft trimmed [flying control surfaces adjusted for straight and level flight] and the engine stabilised. The entire fighter group of about 20 aircraft had by now assembled and quickly climbed behind the staff-flight already in the air to the front.

"The missions were so precisely prepared with respect to time, meeting point with the bomber group and bomber type (Do-17, He-111, Ju-88) that there was never any difficulty meeting the bombers at the pre-planned points. This was normally over Cap Gris Nez at a height of 12,000 feet.

"Remember that all the German fighter wings, at this time, were located within a radius around Calais of approximately 20 to 25 miles. Remember also that in July, August and September roughly between 700 and 800 Bf-109's were flying – at least in the major missions against British fighter bases like Biggin Hill, Croydon and Hornchurch. Also some 100 to 150 Bf-110's took part, which were located about 50 to 100 miles to the rear of Calais.

"Nobody who has not seen it can imagine the crowd of Bf-109s which took off simultaneously and then tried to assemble. I myself remember clearly seeing two air collisions of two 109s each, minutes after my squadron had taken off. Frequently 109s that had got separated from their own squadrons in this unbelievable mess of aircraft were suddenly hanging around your squadron. Slowly as we climbed higher and higher the chaos was disentangled. Soon the bombers came into sight. Our group commander, Major Von Bonin, flew over the bomber's 'point' aircraft, shook his wings and 'said' to him; 'Here we are.' On some days there were hundreds of 109s and hundreds of bombers proceeding towards England – an unimaginable and dreadful spectacle.

"This was the moment when your tension diminished a little bit. But not for long, for when the first faraway cries of 'Spitfire' were heard in the earphones you knew the battle had started. After we crossed the British coast Spitfires and Hurricanes attacked the slowly moving and almost continuous bomber stream. The nearer we came to the British fighter bases around London the more violent the British fighter attacks became. We all saw the first burning bombers and fighters, we all heard the screams of wounded 109 pilots and we all saw the descending parachutes of both friend and foe.

"After we had landed back at our airfield the ground-crews surrounded the aircraft, camouflaged them and serviced them to make them ready for the next mission. Pilots got together, their faces strained, drinking coffee, smoking cigarettes, slowly calming down. The

greatest relief: there was no loss. But everybody knew the next mission would start in two or three hours – the same game, the same procedures from beginning to end of the mission. And so on. Day in, day out.

"How could these men endure such a life? If someone would have asked me or one of my friends: 'Why are you doing this terrible business day in, day out?' I would not have had an answer in those days; and I have no answer today. We just did it. Perhaps we thought it was our duty, just as thousands and millions of soldiers have done in the past thousand years.

"I believe that after it became clear to everybody on our side that the battle over Britain was lost, for many of us a bell began to ring and a warning surfaced deep in our conscience. It was not the feeling that a turning-point had arrived but it was a realisation that something exceptional had happened. The losses of our fighter-pilots went into the hundreds. All had gained great battle experience in the Netherlands and France and could not be replaced. These disastrous losses were concealed back at home in Germany.

"On September 24, 1940 I landed late in the evening at the big air-base at Wilhelmshaven after flying direct from Campagne Sud. On that very morning we had flown our last mission over England, with only three pilots of my original squadron left—myself, Lieutenant Kinzinger and Sergeant Knipscher. A free-chase mission was ordered at 10 o'clock in the morning, and a young pilot was ordered to join us in order to form a flight of four. We were caught by four Spitfires over Ramsgate at 10,000 feet. Knipscher was hit – I saw him going down in smoke and flames. The young pilot was hit by more than twenty bullets and could not make it home. It was our last mission in the battle. That evening Kinzinger and myself flew back to Germany.

"At Wilhelmshaven I reported to the station commander, a friendly elderly colonel. We were the only survivors of the squadron. The commander asked me to get all my pilots into the briefing room as he wanted to welcome them. I answered: 'Sir, there are only two pilots left of the former squadron, and they are in your front office. The rest of the squadron are either killed, drowned in the Channel or in England in a prison camp.' I will never forget the pale face of the colonel as he heard my words.'

Kinzinger, who was a wonderful man and one of my best friends in those days, was killed on the first day in Russia while flying fifty metres on my right side. His death was the

A British soldier guards a downed Me-109 against over-curious locals and children hunting souvenirs. Soon investigators from the RAF's technical branch would comb the wreck for any unusual modifications or new pieces of equipment that might yield useful information.

final loss of my original squadron. The Russian campaign is a different subject, where cruelty prevailed on both sides.

"Most wing commanders, group commanders and squadron leaders who fought in the battle over Britain were known to me personally. I am sure that I speak for the majority of them when I say there was no hatred or bitterness in our feelings towards the British pilots."

Pilot Officer Pat Hancock

Though the Battle of Britain was not perhaps always the chivalrous affair that popular myth would have us believe, it is clear that much mutual respect existed between Luftwaffe and RAF pilots. Pilot Officer Pat Hancock, for example, considered the Luftwaffe crews to be "tenacious fighters – their bombers certainly didn't turn and run at the drop of a hat." And he believes the RAF should have taken a leaf out of the Luftwaffe book of tactics earlier.

"Looking back we were very slow, really. We should have adopted the German tactics much more quickly than we did as we always had poor 'arse-end Charlies' being knocked off. Every time he weaved he got further away from the formation. The actual flying, apart from fighting the enemy, took quite a lot out of you in terms of nervous energy. You had to keep in the same piece of sky because you didn't want to be lost – and because you faced the wrath of your leader, be it your flight commander or section leader.

"It was a stressful situation. Your aeroplane required a certain amount of physical handling, since there were no power controls in those days and it was all done by strength. The wear and tear on your arms was quite noticeable. The faster you went the more you had to pull. It was a physical as well as mental exercise."

For Pat Hancock and scores of other young pilots the skies above Britain in 1940 were the nurseries where individual skills took root and blossomed, turning 19- and 20-year-olds into battle-hardened veterans before they came of age. Hancock's Battle of Britain was un-exceptional for he did not excel at his craft until later when, as a squadron-leader in the Western Desert, he developed a penchant for daring low-level attacks that earned him the Distinguished Flying Cross.

Thus his experiences in the summer of 1940 are perhaps more typical of the average fighter-pilot's lot than the familiar exploits of the handful of aces popularised in the press, in books and in film. This is his story.

"The second that bloody phone rang [in the dispersal hut], even if it was only to tell the airman of the watch it was time he went and had a cup of tea because another airman was coming on duty, it had an effect. I don't care a damn what people say – it didn't get any better for your heart because it was 'we're off, or are we?' and 'are we all off?' It was a jangle for the nerves. You always hoped to come back but only some of us were lucky.

"We stuck to our own planes so long as we had them and they hadn't been shot down. Although it wasn't our personal property as often as we could we flew 'our own' aeroplanes – except of course the aces, who got shot out of their aircraft or used so many planes they didn't have much time to get to know one before they shot somebody down and were so shot up as a result they had to get another. If you were shot down in the morning and getting airborne in the afternoon, you obviously didn't have the same aeroplane. I suppose it's a measure of my incompetence that I kept mine for so long!

"When you were flying around you could see bombs dropping and things burning. We knew we appeared to be holding our own to some degree although the number of pilots was reducing at a frightening rate. When you drop from 22 to 13, which we were until we were pulled back to rest at Wittering in 12 Group, it's pretty obvious that you're losing out in terms of pilots.

"You could quite often see another squadron of your own people and in fact you would meet up with other Spitfires and Hurricanes. And at times you could see great masses of Germans. At other times there would be smaller groups, maybe 20, but it varied. You always tended to see more Germans than your own because we were coming individually as it were, not having the wing set-up that 12 Group adopted later on.

"From the air you could see wrecks on the ground or aircraft burning. I saw bits of German aircraft when the odd chap would bring back a bit of aileron from an aircraft he shot down or a swastika from the fin of a plane. But you seldom saw any Luftwaffe aircraft intact, close up.

"I came back with holes in me seven or eight times, but occasionally I put holes in Germans too. I had smoke coming out of a

WARRIORS OF THE AIR

Heinkel but I never had the satisfaction of seeing one blow up in front of my very eyes in confirmation. The most I ever got was a possible. I was just a terrible shot at that stage, spraying the countryside – in fact most people thought I was flying for the Luftwaffe!

"By and large we opened fire too far away. The real killers – the aces – practically went up the backside of the enemy plane. Very often in the process, when you blow up an aeroplane right in front of you, it will damage your own machine. Quite a number of people destroyed German aircraft but damaged themselves at the same time.

"When we were released to go off-station a group of us would go to our favourite haunt – the 'Bag-o-Nails' in London. We would drink extensively, more than we should have done, to relieve the stress that was always there. Between scrambles you could well be having a brief on the last effort – whether it had been OK or a cock-up, depending. The leader would say, 'This is where we went wrong – why the hell didn't you do so-and-so? This is what we'll do next time.' There were silhouettes of enemy aircraft to look at all the time and the intelligence officer would come and have a natter about something or other. Otherwise you would play cards or read. It was a mix really.

"If new people joined us we knew we had to depend on them because they were going to be flying with us at some stage. So we imparted whatever knowledge we could to encourage them as much as possible. We certainly didn't look down on them – far from it. Whether they were sergeant-pilots or pilot officers mattered not a whisk. Even though they were often the same rank, new pilots looked up to the old hands who had been through France.

"We couldn't form real friendships at that stage though. A particular friend of mine was in a squadron prewar and went to France with them in 1939. During the phoney war they all became close friends because they were not hacked about too much. During the Battle,

Pilot Officer Pat Hancock sitting on the leading edge of a Hurricane in 1940. Note that the gun-ports are taped up but just visible; this was done to prevent moisture from entering the muzzles of the machine-guns.

however, the turnover was such that you couldn't make close friends because he'd be gone or been posted, or was dead, or wounded. You would suddenly ask, 'Where's old so-and-so?' There was so much movement – postings, courses, transfers – not just casualties. If it was a promotion you'd know because there would be a party, but otherwise colleagues could disappear abruptly.

"Life was very different. Quite frankly I was desperately keen to acquire a girlfriend and to get married. I was frequently expecting to get knocked off – not that I went round in a sort of hang-dog mood, of course. You sought female company as an antidote to excessive male company. WAAFs were thin on the ground by and large and you could really only meet girls in pubs. Moving around a great deal didn't help, either."

In common with many of his contemporaries, Pilot Officer Hancock was shot at by an eagle-eyed Luftwaffe fighter-pilot. He was more fortunate than most recipients of such attention, however, landing shaken but unhurt. "The aircraft that shot me came straight out of the sun. I hadn't the slightest idea of his presence. One round struck my aircraft but fortunately it didn't explode, just severed both the lower longerons [lengthways running fuselage supports] of the Hurricane. It was quite alarming, for I could feel the wobble in the air-frame that set in after the impact. I could almost feel the fuselage bending because instead of having four supports it had only the two top ones. I wanted to abandon and was going to get out but there was no fire and so I thought, 'Well no, I'm not going to jump because that's even more frightening.'

"So I nursed it gingerly back, but it was a bit saggy and I could feel that the aircraft was badly hit. I got to the point of almost undoing my straps and standing up to get out – I had opened the lid anyway in case. Fortunately I got home and didn't collapse in a heap on the airfield!"

Chapter Seven

"Within 50 feet of a large bomb its wind-blast will tear a
man to pieces and will shatter a solid brick wall. Further away,
the blast will deafen people by bursting their ear-drums,
and may kill them by paralysing their lungs."

*"A Practical Guide for the Householder
and Air-Raid Warden", 1940 (price 6d)*

LONDON'S BURNING

Weary firemen hang a Union
Jack from a lamp-post after
a night blitz on Plymouth in
March 1940. In common with
many wartime pictures the
background has been
retouched to prevent any
chance of the enemy
discovering the true extent
and accuracy of their
bombing.

The eternal summer of 1940 was a time of
extremes. While seven weeks of almost
continuous fighting was taking its toll among
those engaged in the front-line defence of
Britain, behind the lines, in the areas
untouched by the turmoil of conflict, life was
in many respects relatively normal.

Apart from giveaways like taped-up windows, the occasional fire-bucket and the total
absence of road signs, most of the nation was
unscarred by the ravages of military conflict.
The ignominy of Dunkirk had receded and
was replaced by a growing conviction that
blitzkrieg could be countered after all. As the
novelty of air combat wore off the population

soon became increasingly contemptuous of
Germany's battle prowess.

Radio and newspapers were the main
sources for information but knowalls fleshed
out the rather dry bones of official statements
with salacious accounts about the results of
dog-fights and the effects of enemy bombing.
Over breakfast householders reviewed Fighter
Command's performance during the previous
day's combat; the press reported the RAF
victories as though they were cricket scores
and were consistently inaccurate, generally
overestimating British "kills" by three times.

At times the fighting came too close for
comfort. The sight of Luftwaffe aircrews

disentangling themselves from their parachutes on the village green or the discovery of the gory remains of a less fortunate aviator could prove alarming in the extreme and brought home the reality of the conflict to those on the receiving end. In parts of Britain, of course, the war was very real indeed. In Kent especially, people lived cheek by jowl with danger as their homes stood directly beneath the most hotly contested skies in Europe.

Dover had been embroiled in every stage of the Battle of Britain since the early coastal phase. Bombs, bullets, aircraft and even shells from France had fallen on the town since early July. Throughout 1940 Mary Shulver lived with her husband and three young children in Eythorne, a village inland from Dover. Eythorne stands high above the harbour town and during the battle was an ideal vantage point from which to view the almost daily activity above Dover. Often stray aircraft passed uncomfortably close overhead or duelling pairs broke off from the main battle and tumbled towards the village, frequently threatening to collide with buildings. Hardly a day passed without some kind of drama which drew Mary, along with her fellow villagers, into the streets to rush towards the latest

crash site or gasp at a dog-fight above the treetops.

"One day a plane came low and flew straight through the streets. I thought, 'Any minute it's going to come and hit a house, it's got to.' The aircraft went right across the village but didn't hurt anything. It landed in the park and blew up. We went over to have a look. The pilot was shot out and the engine landed more than a mile away. The plane crashed right opposite our doctor's and I called for an ambulance. I'll always remember it. We had recently got a new ambulance. The driver said, 'I'm having no dirty German in my ambulance – put him in the lorry!' The pilot, who was laying face down and spread-eagled near the wreckage, was then covered in a tarpaulin and dumped in a lorry to be taken away.

"Shortly afterwards I saw a Spitfire, piloted by a Pole we later found out, shot at by a German fighter that appeared overhead. The Spitfire pilot knew he'd been hit so he pulled straight up, directly underneath the German aircraft, and crashed into him. Both pilots were killed.

"I was down in the shelter most of the time. You could tell the sound of the aircraft, you got used to the different noises and you knew

Home ARP outfits were available in abundance, but they included dressings and medicines which would have been useful only for treating very minor injuries. Of particular interest is the steel "ARP Helmet" manufactured by Head Protectors Ltd. of Grimsby in 1938, produced in response to the hysteria caused by the Munich crisis.

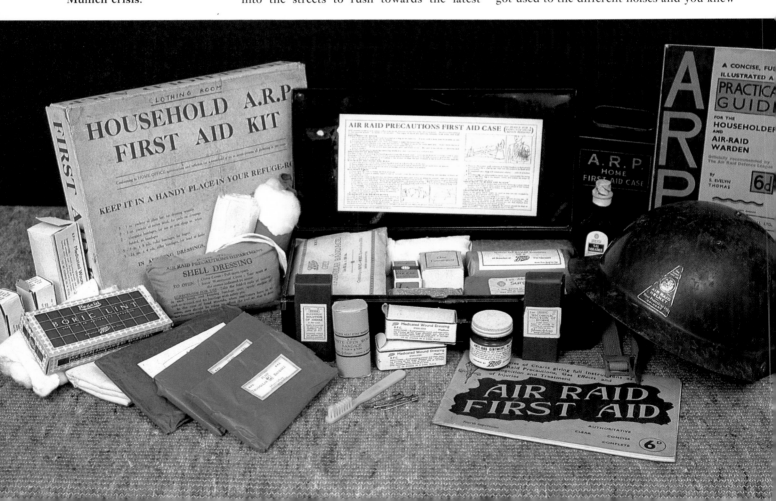

just which aircraft it was. Every now and then you would pop your head out and have a look. When I think of it now I just can't believe I watched what I did. What an awesome spectacle passed right over our heads.

"The Germans used to drop what were called 'flaming onions' on the convoys in the Channel. We could watch them and see the coast of France from the top of our hill. Once a shell came so close it whizzed passed us. We were standing near a lot of fir trees and it cut the tops right off the trees right in front of us. If we hadn't stopped to talk to a man we knew we would have been in trouble. The shell landed directly ahead of us and buried itself in an earth-bank.

"We were told to remove everything from dressers and window-sills at the beginning of the war. When the shells passed nearby the windows rattled and any plates or ornaments would fall to the floor. The place was never quiet. The noise of a shell, a whine like someone was taking their last breath, is the most frightening noise I've ever heard. But of course if you heard it you were safe.

"There were loads of cartridges falling all about but we never touched them. While I was sewing one day a bomb landed so close my sewing-machine jumped straight into the air. My husband, Jim, was in the shed and the bomb lifted the shed up and dropped it about a foot from its original position.

"One afternoon I heard someone shouting outside, so I went into the street to take a look. We realised that a plane, one of ours, had been shot down and one of our pilots had baled out. Then we saw that his parachute was on fire. It was a horrible sensation. We were all transfixed and holding our breath. Everyone was shouting, 'Come on! Come on!' as his parachute burned. Before he reached the ground it flared up and the last bit broke away. He fell heavily to earth and was killed.

"During the lunch-hour at Dover, every day, the German aeroplanes used to nip over and machine-gun civilians in the streets. The bombers followed in a great vee-shape, like a big cloud. We stood rooted to the ground. After one raid, I remember standing at the bedroom window watching a Dornier, the flying pencil – I recognised its shape from pictures we had studied – pass at low level close to our house. It was so low and near I could clearly see the pilot staring back at me.

"Dog-fights were common-place. After one, a Messerschmitt passed overhead trying

to get home. It was losing height all the time and its pilot crash-landed in a nearby field. The villagers grabbed hammers, pitchforks and axes and rushed to confront the raider. The pilot emerged and seemed so young, like a boy. He put his hands up and smiled. He was unhurt. Protected by the police he was led to a lorry, where six Home Guards thrust their rifles at him and escorted him on his journey to a prison camp. Each day during the summer the sky was darkened by hundreds of aircraft twisting and turning and dog-fights, which we clearly witnessed, and I will never forget."

Yet Mary was an exception. Considering the enormously serious nature of the struggle a surprisingly small proportion of the population was really aware of the peril it faced. Government propaganda and the press over-simplified the crisis, comparing it to a straightforward contest between good and evil; right would prevail as long as everyone stayed calm and did their bit.

At No. 11 Group, Fighter Command, Keith Park was under no such illusion. He fully realised just how dangerously close Britain was to losing the battle. The forecast for September 7 promised a day of fine weather and with it yet more pulverising Luftwaffe attacks against RAF airfields.

Due to their inability to draw air through the type of filters incorporated in adult gas-masks, special anti-gas helmets were designed specifically for babies. Once securely strapped in air was pumped inside the gas-proof compartment via a rubber bellows mechanism operated by the infant's parents. The sturdy steel frame gave an element of extra protection against flying debris. Nurses were expected to ensure that mothers were fully briefed about the fitting and operation of such units.

A NATION ALONE

Across the Channel, Goering and his entourage moved to a specially prepared observation-post high on the cliffs at Cap Gris Nez. Powerful binoculars were provided to allow the spectators a clear view of the coast of England. With the Reichsmarschall's encouragement the coterie of Luftwaffe top brass settled down to enjoy a jovial picnic in anticipation of the afternoon's theatrically staged assault on London.

Park, unaware of this change in plan, was busy making his dispositions in preparation for further attacks against his embattled airfields. His mood was quite different from Goering's. Fighter Command's poor performance over the past few days was giving him cause for concern.

One of his biggest problems was the lack of co-ordination between Leigh-Mallory's 12 Group and his own command. Leigh-Mallory bitterly resented being in a position which he considered was on the periphery of the fighting and was champing at the bit for an opportunity to involve his group more fully in the air-battles which took place each day in the South-East of England, outside his immediate area of responsibility. Dowding and Park were aware of Leigh-Mallory's dissatisfaction, but both insisted that he should employ his forces to provide a defensive perimeter which shielded the Midlands and Park's most northerly airfields.

By late August the Luftwaffe's tactic of hitting sector stations across 11 Group was beginning to pay off, and increasingly Park sought the support of 12 Group squadrons to provide air-cover for his airfields north of London. Despite repeated requests for assistance 12 Group was notably absent on three important occasions: on August 24 North Weald was left unprotected and was heavily bombed, on the 26th it was the turn of Debden and on the 30th Biggin Hill. Each time 12 Group had either proved too slow or unwilling to help.

By the end of the month the relationship between Park and Leigh-Mallory had reached rock-bottom, deteriorating to the extent that 11 Group no longer appealed directly to 12 Group when assistance was needed but instead made its requests direct to the controller at Fighter Command Headquarters in the hope that he might bring Leigh-Mallory into line.

The situation was exacerbated by the behaviour of Squadron-Leader Douglas Bader, then in command of No. 242 Squadron based at Coltishall and flying out of Duxford, south of Cambridge and within No. 12 Group. Bader's achievements are legendary. His refusal to submit to the debilitating effects of a grievous flying accident in which he lost both legs and his stubborn determination to resume flying with the RAF are inspirational. He was unquestionably a great fighter-leader, full of offensive spirit. Younger pilots looked to him for guidance and forgot their fears as he led them into battle.

But for all his virtues Bader was no strategician. Impulsive and hot-headed, he had little time for Fighter Command's system of strict ground-to-air co-operation and was unimpressed with the policy of dispersing what little resources the command possessed. He was convinced that force should be met by force and that the Luftwaffe could best be defeated if attacked en masse and not by individual squadron formations – the method currently employed.

Leigh-Mallory was sympathetic to Bader's arguments and encouraged his wayward subordinate to try out new offensive techniques. His support for Bader's "Big Wing" theories was not out of character. In September 1939 he had been admonished by Dowding for issuing a directive to 12 Group operations staff suggesting a scheme for grouping up to five squadrons at a time on

The Hawker Hurricane, backbone of Fighter Command in 1940. Its sturdy construction and ability to withstand a great deal of battle damage made it a popular mount with most fighter-pilots.

individual airfields. The aim was to provide a single, large offensive force but the result would have been chaos as refuelling and rearming over 50 fighters would have proved impossible. Dowding reminded Leigh-Mallory that strategic control was the province of the commander-in-chief and that rules governing the organisation of squadrons were clearly defined and should be adhered to. Bader's arrival on the scene was fortuitous for Leigh-Mallory, and the air vice-marshal enthusiastically embraced the squadron-leader as a kindred spirit.

Bader can perhaps be forgiven for not appreciating Dowding's strategy; he had joined 12 Group only in February 1940 and was not involved in the years of exhaustive analysis that had spawned the new techniques. Fighter Command did not even exist when Bader experienced his horrifying crash in 1931 and was forced to leave the RAF. Britain's air defences had changed out of all recognition with the advent of radar and radio communications, introduced while he was in civilian employment. Bader was a fighter-pilot of the old school, full of élan and vigour; he simply could not tolerate a system which meant that he could join the battle only when requested by some distant controller.

On August 30 Bader had an opportunity to prove his theories. At about the same time that Biggin Hill was devastated by a Luftwaffe attack which slipped past a 12 Group patrol, he was busy disregarding his controller's orders to patrol above the 11 Group airfield at North Weald and instead led his squadron south-west of the aerodrome to what he considered a better attack position.

Spotting a large formation of enemy bombers in the distance Bader signalled to his fellow pilots to follow him into the fray. Ten Hurricanes dived among nearly 100 enemy aircraft but, with the advantage of surprise, suffered no losses and succeeded in routing the Luftwaffe formation. Twelve enemy aircraft were destroyed and more damaged, while all ten Hurricanes landed without a scratch. Bader excitedly rang Leigh-Mallory and explained that with more fighters even greater success would be possible. Leigh-Mallory thought the idea sounded splendid and proceeded to arrange for more squadrons to be assigned to support Bader's wing.

Such disregard for the cardinal principles of the fighter defence network and the irritating increase in freelancing by squadron leaders

worried Park. His concern was heightened by the news from Fighter Command HQ that, due to increased shipping activity in German occupied ports, invasion was considered imminent. Before he left Uxbridge for a meeting with Dowding at Bentley Priory he issued a stiff instruction to his controllers highlighting certain deficiencies in the ground-to-air control system. He pointed out that some controllers were ordering squadrons, detailed to engage enemy bombers, to patrol too high. With experience, radar operators were obtaining greater accuracy when judging the altitude of Luftwaffe bombers. Based on information from Chain Home network, group controllers ordered squadrons to patrol at a specific altitude.

However, in an effort to ensure that no trouble was encountered from a surprise attack from above, sector controllers added two or three thousand feet to the given height and by the same logic squadron leaders did likewise. The result of all this leap-frogging was that enemy bombers frequently slipped under the defences and were only attacked on their return trip—after they had done the damage.

Douglas Bader frequently ignored the orders of controllers as far as patrol altitudes were concerned; in his biography *Reach for the Sky* no secret is made of his belief that the man on the spot was best equipped to decide which

The Spitfire was an altogether more finely balanced aircraft than the Hurricane. It demanded skilled handling but, in the hands of an experienced pilot, was a lethal and efficient killing machine.

A NATION ALONE

tactics to use. Clearly Bader was not alone in his irreverence but Park, unlike Leigh-Mallory, would not entertain a situation where junior officers dictated policy. No. 11 Group at least would tighten up its act, and controllers were to make sure that group instructions were followed to the letter.

The morning of September 7 seemed to bear out Park's worst fears. Hawkinge was again singled out for attention by the Luftwaffe, and though the raid was not especially significant it did point towards further attacks against sector airfields in the afternoon. Mindful of the need to protect his vital aerodromes, Park drew his squadrons back from the coast and positioned them deep inland to give them a better chance of intercepting individual raids and to plug the gaps that 12 Group seemed unable to fill.

Shortly before 4 pm Goering and his cohorts witnessed the stunning spectacle of

A Home Guard lookout scans the skies for enemy activity above the British Overseas Airways Corporation's offices in Victoria, London.

over 900 aircraft assembled wing-tip to wing-tip in the skies above them. As the swarm of fighters and bombers headed towards England an endless pattern of shadows danced across the upturned faces of the spectators. Goering could hardly contain himself, the sight was so irresistible.

In England radar operators all along the south coast viewed the dramatic pageant through the dim green light of their cathode-ray screens – and no doubt shared the Reichs-marschall's astonishment. Scores of separate plots of 20-plus poured into Fighter Command Headquarters as one by one Luftwaffe units grouped together high above Calais. It was assumed that once the formation had crossed the coast it would split up with individual groups heading for specific targets in the usual way; by the time the operations staff at Bentley Priory realised that the massive assembly of over 300 bombers and 600 Bf-109s and Bf-110s was not following a set pattern but was instead streaming in concert towards London, it was too late to arrange a suitable reception committee of fighters.

The one man who might have correctly guessed the Luftwaffe's intentions – Keith Park – was uncommonly absent from 11 Group's operations room. He was still in conference with Dowding, at a crisis meeting to discuss ways of reinforcing Fighter Command's dwindling supply of experienced pilots in the face of continued Luftwaffe pressure against front-line squadrons. And as Park sped back to Uxbridge the first wave of German bombers reached their target – the East End of London.

With virtually no fighter opposition to upset their work, Luftwaffe bomb-aimers found their mark. London's docks, its oil refineries, gasworks, wharves and warehouses were all subjected to a terrific bombardment. Though the principal targets were the port facilities and gas and oil installations, the East End and the inner suburb civilian areas suffered greatly. Not since Zeppelins paused overhead to release their deadly cargo had the streets been assaulted with such ferocity. As far west as Tower Bridge and south towards Croydon huge fires erupted, their angry flames fanned by the warm summer breeze. By the time the final wave of bombers had passed the boroughs of Poplar, Woolwich, Millwall, Limehouse, Tottenham, West Ham, Barking and Croydon were ablaze with fires of all sizes.

A Heinkel 111 passes over the Isle of Dogs and the serpentine twists of the River Thames. The river was a godsend to the crews of the Luftwaffe bombers, providing a naked guideline to the heart of the enemy capital.

Silvertown in the heart of London's docklands was almost instantly engulfed in flames and dense smoke.

Park did not stay at Uxbridge for long. After hastily reviewing the activities of his controllers he headed for Northolt and his personal Hurricane. Once he was airborne he made straight for the conflagration of East London, and as he flew above the pulsating inferno the scale of the Luftwaffe's attack became clear. Soon he realised that the switch in Luftwaffe tactics was for him a form of divine providence; if the civilian population could take it, his airfields could be repaired without interruption and his command could quickly rebuild itself.

As the raiders headed for the security of their bases in France, Fighter Command did what little it could to regain its composure and stabbed at the bomber stream in a series of unco-ordinated but gallant actions.

At Duxford, however, Bader had trouble assembling his Big Wing in time. Only his own squadron, 242, was airborne quickly enough to intercept the enemy. The remaining components of his formation, Nos 19 and 310 Squadrons, could not catch up. By his own admission the attempt at a combined attack had failed. Leigh-Mallory was not too disappointed; 242's stirring claim of 11 aircraft destroyed impressed him and he urged Bader to continue practising his Big Wing operation.

One RAF unit which did achieve notable success on the afternoon of September 7 was No. 303, one of the Polish squadrons within Fighter Command. In co-operation with a Spitfire squadron, which kept the Luftwaffe fighter escort occupied, and another Hurricane squadron which distracted the attention of the crews of 40 or so returning Dorniers, the Poles staged a classic fighter attack. Diving out of the sun they took the bombers by surprise and, swooping down in an almost straight line, slammed into their hated foe, firing at them until they were dangerously close. Ten Dorniers fell from the formation as the Hurricanes of 303 Squadron flashed away into the distance.

The daylight fighting had cost Fighter

A NATION ALONE

Command 28 aircraft and the Luftwaffe some 41 bombers. The aerial activity was far from over but with darkness it became increasingly one-sided. Guided by the light of fires that still burnt brightly throughout East London the Luftwaffe returned at eight o'clock the same evening. Fighter Command was virtually powerless to intervene. Spitfires were totally unsuitable for night operations and Hurricanes little better. What success there was owed more to a chance encounter – and a lucky burst the moment a pilot glimpsed an unfamiliar object through the murky blackness – than it did to sophisticated technique. The AI radar fitted to Blenheim night-fighters was an extremely early example of a piece of apparatus that would not prove useful until the following year when, in its Mk4 guise, it was fitted to Bristol Beaufighters. In 1940 airborne radar was both unreliable and cumbersome.

With nothing to bar their way a shuttle of nearly 250 bombers flew across from France and stoked the existing fires. The night sky above London glowed a dull red and in the Pool of London the very water of the Thames appeared to burn. Everywhere the air was filled with the choking odour of charred timber and glowing embers danced in the night like a million fireflies. The cobbled streets of the dock area resounded to the ting-a-ling of fire-engines and the hiss, pop and crack of burning wood. The London blitz had begun.

The night raid on London caught the ARP and Civil Defence authorities off-balance. They had been expecting a single devastating attack during the hours of daylight and had made their preparations accordingly. In anticipation of enormous casualties plans had been drawn up for mass burials in pits drenched with quicklime. Decontamination squads clad in black rubber overalls were ready to hose down gas-infected streets and houses should the Luftwaffe rain down poison from the sky.

In the event the air-raids of September 7 reached a crescendo after dark. Gas was never used and although casualties were high they were nowhere near as bad as predicted. The principal weapon used by the Luftwaffe was the fire-bomb, with two basic kinds employed. The first was the oil-bomb. This was a heavy dustbin-shaped missile consisting of a thin casing packed full of oil and various other inflammable materials. On impact the casing

of the bomb burst open, igniting the volatile contents and spewing them forth for many yards in all directions.

The second bomb was more deadly and far more numerous. At about 18 inches long and weighing little more than two pounds the Luftwaffe's prime incendiary – the infamous "Firebomb Fritz" – could be carried in its thousands on board a single aeroplane. It was a formidably efficient weapon. Though light in weight, the stabilised thermite incendiary fell with such force that it could easily penetrate a tiled roof. Once firmly lodged within an attic the incendiary burned furiously, its magnesium alloy container fusing on impact.

"Firebomb Fritz" was far more than an irritating menace; it was a cheap and deadly effective weapon. The hot summer of 1940 had left wooden buildings tinder-dry and created the ideal conditions for fire-raising. All over East London incendiaries in their hundreds smashed through roofs and lodged among stacks of cut timber and densely packed rows of paint and chemicals. This was a blitz of fire, not gas or explosives.

Confronting the fire-storm were 6,000 regular firemen of the London Fire Brigade and some 25,000 volunteers who comprised the Auxiliary Fire Service. The auxiliaries came from all walks of life. They had initially been cold-shouldered by contemptuous regulars resentful about the influx of volunteers whom, they thought, had a depressing effect on wages and working hours. But gradually the office-workers, engineers and artists who donned the dark blue garb of firemen earned the respect of their regular collagues. Anyone who mastered the art of manhandling a 14-foot long hook-ladder atop a 60-foot tower could not be all bad.

The London Fire Brigade and the AFS had spent the first 12 months of war preparing for their integrated debut, and they had not been idle. The gleaming scarlet of fire-engines and pumps had vanished under a coat of drab grey paint in an effort to camouflage them against the dark city streets. Hundreds of London taxis had been similarly coated and were pressed into service as tractors for the vast battery of mobile pumps that supplemented the heavier, traditional appliances. Rigorous training familiarised novices with the intricacies of the powerful heavy pumps (they had a capacity of 900 gallons of water a minute), mobile fire-escape ladders and turntable water-towers. The image of a lone fireman

Hand-cranked sirens were dotted throughout the towns and cities of Britain. Once the handle was turned what Churchill described as "a banshee wail" was emitted.

LONDON'S BURNING

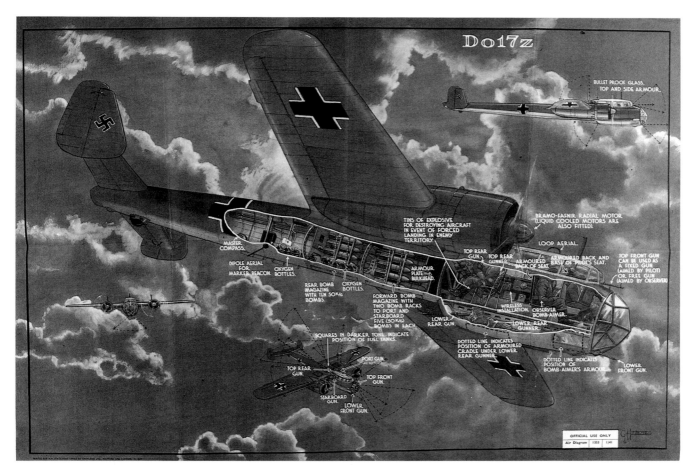

perched on the 100-foot extension or the latter device, aiming the swivelling hose-nozzles into the heart of a raging inferno, characterises the blitz period.

AFS firemen were taught what to expect when encountering a bombed and flaming building. Bursting bottles in a spirit warehouse could be mistaken for automatic gunfire; poorly fixed decorative facades might collapse but did not necessarily mean that perfectly sound walls underneath were about to fall down. On the other hand an oil-soaked floor could appear safe, but once the fuel reached its flashpoint the area was certain to be engulfed in flames and threatened to trap unsuspecting firefighters.

One former Auxiliary Fireman recalled the traumatic experiences of the training school: the enormous difficulty of avoiding kinks and twists in its serpentine lengths while running out a hose; the nerve-racking experience of the escape drill, which meant stepping from a narrow window-sill on to a 50-foot tall ladder which swayed precariously immediately hand and foot was placed on it; the staggering heat generated by even a small fire; the sting of

water, heated to boiling-point, as it jetted from the "branch"; the danger to the fireman holding the branch if he was cut off and surrounded by an overwhelming blaze.

The evening of September 7 was, literally, the AFS's baptism of fire. And they discharged their responsibilities admirably. Steel-helmeted, they lowered their heads in an effort to shield themselves from the heat of the fires they fought, wet through and covered in a slimy film of soot and oil, indistinguishable from their professional colleagues and a credit to London's fire service.

As far as Britain's Chiefs-of-Staff were concerned September 7's massive assault on London was a final indication that the impending German invasion was about to commence. The service chiefs had little faith in the value of secret intelligence due to the inability of the various intelligence networks to co-ordinate their activities and organise a suitable mechanism whereby gathered information could be processed and distributed to interested parties while it was still relevant. "Enigma" intercepts did, however, provide some useful material.

The Dornier 17Z carried a formidable defensive armament of up to eight 7.9 mm machine-guns and at times even a nose-mounted 20 mm cannon – plus a supply of stick hand-grenades which could be thrown into the path of attacking RAF fighters. The Do-17Z's two Bramo 323P radial engines gave it a maximum speed of 265 mph at 16,400 feet when fully loaded.

183

A NATION ALONE

It was a source of great pride to Londoners, as this example of sheet-music showed, that the King and Queen had not fled the city to a less exposed residence. When Buckingham Palace fell victim to Luftwaffe bombs, Queen Elizabeth exclaimed that "now we can look the East End in the face".

On July 29 Enigma had revealed a Luftwaffe order forbidding the bombing of certain English ports to prevent damage from hindering the disembarkation of elements of the invasion force. A similar order had been intercepted immediately before the invasion of France. A further decrypt confirmed that a new German naval wireless network had been established to cover the Channel zone, ensuring efficient communications during Operation Sea-lion. But Enigma was able to provide little more than background information about German intentions during the summer of 1940. Certainly it was not as useful to Dowding as it became for field commanders later in the war.

The unreliability of Enigma intelligence at this stage of the war, and the enemy's annoying habit of relying on secure land-lines when issuing operational orders, forced the Joint Intelligence Sub-Committee (JIC) to look elsewhere for clues concerning German intentions. Photographic reconnaissance was considered the most effective and reliable method available for gathering intelligence and, consequently, Photographic Reconnaissance (PR) flights increased in regularity as the Battle of Britain developed.

Flying from bases at Wick in Scotland and St Eval in Cornwall, long-range Spitfires of the Photographic Reconnaissance Unit (PRU) made repeated visits to the coast of occupied Europe to note any anomalies in enemy shipping traffic. From September 1, PRU became aware of a dramatic increase in the amount of ships moving westward from Ostend along the enemy coast.

At Ostend itself the total number of invasion barges had increased from 18 to 270 in the week up to September 7. Scores of motor-boats and steamers, earmarked as tugs for the invasion barges, were spotted en route from the North Sea to French Channel ports; between the 1st and the 4th 100 large ships appeared at Flushing and similar build-ups were detected at the newly repaired ports of Calais and Dunkirk.

PRU cameras also captured evidence that German long-range guns were in position and available to provide barrage fire in support of the landings. On the 5th yet more barges were seen at Ostend – and intelligence sources revealed that all German army leave was to be cancelled from September 8. On the 6th Signals Intelligence confirmed that the Luftwaffe had completed the redeployment of units from Norway to the French coast and told of the reappearance of Stuka dive-bomber units situated close to the coast in preparation for the imminent assault. The JIC's summary of events on September 6 warned that seaborne raids could be expected, but pointed out that Germany would be unlikely to launch a full-scale invasion until total air superiority over southern England was achieved.

Enemy activity on September 7 removed any doubt on the part of the intelligence chiefs. In the morning PRU Spitfires reported a worrying development on the continent – invasion barges were seen being moved to their

Britain's brave firemen steadfastly refused to be beaten by the blitz. Night after night they toiled in unimaginable conditions to control the conflagrations caused by Luftwaffe explosives. This fireman is kitted out in the uniform worn by auxiliary firemen during the winter of 1940/41. Next to him is an example of the mobile pump trailers that helped firemen to tackle blazes at close quarters. The basket-work filter enabled the feed hose to be placed in any suitable supply – even the River Thames – and firemen frequently pulled fish from the lattice-work of wicker after the hoses had been withdrawn.

LONDON'S BURNING

embarkation points. As this put the unwieldy and vulnerable German flotilla within range of RAF attack it was clear that the rendezvous was a short-term arrangement and heralded immediate departure once loading had been completed. Added to this the relative position of the moon and tides along the Channel coast between the 8th and 10th would provide the ideal conditions needed for landing troops and vehicles. Diplomatic sources tended to confirm British anxieties about the likelihood of invasion.

A disturbing increase in the clandestine activities of German spies was a final indication that the machinery of invasion was about to be set in motion. Germany's military intelligence organisation, the Abwehr, had succeeded in delivering spies to Britain all summer. Fortunately for the defenders, Nazi secret agents were, mostly, lamentable failures. In mid-August an unarmed Heinkel bomber, painted black and bearing no insignia or identifying markings, slipped under the Chain Home radar screen and dispatched its cargo; two Danes sympathetic to Germany's cause were dropped into the night sky over Salisbury. The plan was not a success and one of the pair damaged his leg on landing.

Reluctantly the Abwehr controllers enlisted the help of Germany's senior agent in Britain, the Welshman Arthur George Owens, in an attempt to salvage something from the operation and perhaps recoup some of the considerable cost of training their two new recruits. Within days, however, the injured man, Björnson, was captured. His total ineptitude and unsuitability for espionage work did have its benefits, however, as it appears his captors took pity and had him interned rather than executed (as was usually the case with captured spies). His partner Schmidt managed to keep one step ahead of British Intelligence and, during the Battle of Britain, visited coastal defences around Brighton, photographed airfields and visited London to see how the capital fared in the face of German bombing. Schmidt reported to his Abwehr controllers consistently over the next five years and was lucky enough to survive the war undetected.

Most other German spies were less fortunate. Some landed in the Republic of Ireland, a country assumed by the Abwehr to be united in hatred for Britain. But it seems the Irish were equally disinclined towards the Nazis and one spy, an Austrian called Ernst

Weber-Drohl, was handed over to the police shortly after he landed by submarine. Alone and destitute, he was encouraged to join British Intelligence rather than remain imprisoned in Ireland for the duration. Another German who descended on the Emerald Isle had the misfortune to become known to the police in Ulster, who subsequently offered a large reward for his arrest.

German agents had been told that IRA members were allies in the struggle against Britain but they had not been informed of the IRA's policy of trading spies for cash. Located by the IRA the agent, Hermann Goertz, still wearing his jackboots and in possession of his First World War medals, was exchanged for the reward and handed over to the police. After biting on a concealed cyanide capsule Goertz was found dead in his cell.

The total lack of preparation given to German agents astonished their British counterparts. Nazi spies were betrayed either by a lack of knowledge about the language and customs of Britain (one intruder tried to buy a pint of beer in a pub at breakfast time), or because, lonely and unsure of their duties, they were unable to remain concealed and operationally active.

One story, from the annals of the Northamptonshire Home Guard, characterised German attempts at espionage during the Battle of Britain period. At five o'clock in the evening of September 2 G. C. Beechener, a member of the 11th (Hardingstone District) Battalion, was alerted to the presence of a strange-looking man seen lying under a bush in a ditch in a nearby field. Approaching the site with caution, and with bayonet fixed, the courageous Mr Beechener beckoned to the stranger, insisting he emerge from his hiding-place. The young man, dressed in sports coat and flannels, obliged and stood up, proferring a business card towards the Home Guardsman.

Equipment used by members of the Auxiliary Fire Service. Of particular note is the black Bakelite helmet which was lighter and consequently more comfortable than the more common steel "Brodie" pattern helmet. The axe was of the same type as that issued to bomber crews; it had an insulated handle and was used to sever exposed power-cables and smash out window-frames to permit entry to buildings.

"Firebomb Fritz" – the standard German incendiary – was a horrifyingly efficient fire-starter. To help counter its enormously destructive effects householders cleared their lofts and removed combustibles from stair-cupboards and cellars. Fire extinguishers ranged from buckets of damp earth to devices like the 'Firex' grenade: once hurled at the base of a fire the glass shattered and released a chemical which consumed the oyxgen in the area thus, hopefully, extinguishing the blaze.

A NATION ALONE

During the winter of 1940 Britain had no adequate night-fighter defences. Spitfires proved too tricky to taxi, take off and land in blacked-out conditions. Hurricanes fared little better and radar-equipped Blenheim night-fighters were plagued by teething troubles. The Defiant appeared to offer a stop-gap solution as its separate gun-turret allowed the pilot to concentrate on the tricky job of flying by instruments while the air-gunner scanned the skies for Luftwaffe bombers.

The official history continues: "There was a suspicious error, however, in the card, for the address was in Continental style – street name first and then the number – and in addition the date was wrong. Further, Mr Beechener noted the huge knot in his tie which would have 'given him away anywhere' . . . It was then found that the stranger carried an automatic pistol and when this was extracted he smiled and said, 'I give up.' 'You wouldn't have got me,' he added, 'if I hadn't got a crack on the head from this as I landed,' – and he pointed to his suitcase which, being opened, proved to be a portable radio transmitter.

"Subsequent search revealed that the man had landed by a fine-quality silk parachute and was well equipped with a groundsheet, small clock, compass, maps, torch, tablet of soap, chocolate and flasks of whisky and rum . . . He had a wallet containing approximately £300 in English notes. At an interrogation by Captain Penn, Section Leader E. E. Smart and the local policeman, who had been summoned, the latter tried unsuccessfully to break and unload the pistol. 'Can I help you?' asked the German and, being permitted to do so, while

care was taken to see that he did not 'try any funny stuff', calmy pressed a catch and scattered the cartridges on the table.

"He told his captors that he had come from Hamburg and had been dropped at about 3 am. He believed that he was somewhere between Stratford-on-Avon and Banbury. Since the man was in civilian clothes, he was finally handed over to the County Police."

Events like this, though farcical, reinforced the belief that something was afoot. The Chiefs of Staff and GHQ Home Forces certainly thought so: at eight o'clock on the evening of September 7, as fires raged throughout East London, the codeword "Cromwell" was issued – invasion imminent!

It is hardly surprising that the C-in-C Home Forces, General Alan Brooke, felt the significant increase in enemy activity heralded the invasion proper and warranted the transmission of "Cromwell". From his headquarters at St Paul's School, Hammersmith, he could see for himself the extent of German aggression in the luminous red glow above the East End. Teleprinters chattered ceaselessly and aides barked out

LONDON'S BURNING

instructions, and in the playground outside dispatch riders skidded to a halt bearing news of the devastation of the docklands and adjacent areas. All intelligence summaries were equally pessimistic. Everything pointed to invasion. This, finally, was it.

"Cromwell", however, signified Alert No. 1 and was designed to ensure that the Army's Eastern and Southern commands took to their posts and intensified their vigilance. The codeword meant that invasion was "imminent and probable within twelve hours" – not that enemy landing operations had already begun. It appears that the true significance of the alert was lost on the best part of IV Corps, VII Corps and HQ London District, whose troops were already at eight hours' notice. Many did not know what "Cromwell" meant while others, perhaps aware of the confusion that followed in the wake of the German invasion of the Low Countries, did not want to be wrong-footed and decided for themselves that the invasion was already taking place.

Being a Saturday night, many junior officers and NCOs were on guard duty. Receipt of "Cromwell" caused many of them to overreact and start the alarm bells ringing. Other commands like the Home Guard were on the distribution list of "Cromwell" for information only. Without considering the message's real meaning the volunteers stood to en masse – nearly half a million eager combatants ready to do their worst if the dreaded Hun dared set foot on English soil. For good measure many Home Guard units decided to ring the church bells which had been still and silent for months and were only to be sounded when invasion had actually started.

All over the south of England armed men took up their fighting positions, the Regular Army in its casemates, trenches and strengthened Victorian fortresses, the Home Guard in lonely and isolated vantage points along the coast or high up on the downlands of Kent and Sussex, the Auxiliary Units in camouflaged lairs or secret excavations cut out of the chalk and clay mantle of the Home Counties. Women of the Land Army galloped on horseback across the dark countryside ready to report the first signs of paratroopers descending out of the blackness. Fire-watchers endured a lonely vigil on factory rooftops and Air-Raid Wardens peered into the inky skies, anxious that when the time came they would remember the lessons they had been taught.

The RAF could not, of course, have been at any more advanced state of readiness than it had been throughout the seemingly interminable summer. However, as "Cromwell" was repeated a thousand times across England on that memorable night of September 7, some pilots had a unique and perilous duty to perform. Taking off from blacked-out airfields along the coast Skua target-tugs and other similarly unsuitable aircraft prepared to initiate one of Britain's more desperate defensive measures.

Two months previously 200 "Defile Flame Traps" had been installed along the coast. The Petroleum Warfare Department, with the encouragement of Professor Lindemann, Churchill's scientific adviser, was confident that the flame barrage would prove effective in stopping German infantrymen in their tracks. As darkness fell the RAF's second line of rag-tag formations were ready on the word of command to dive-bomb and thereby ignite those flame traps – and "fire" the sea from Cornwall to Kent. If successful, it would have been a very unpleasant reception.

Likewise steps were taken to ensure that

Air-Raid Wardens – famous for their catchphrase "Put that light out!" – did an unenviable and important job in ensuring an efficient black-out was maintained.

LDV and Home Guard insignia was, of necessity, drab in appearance, but there was no shortage of books available to help the eager volunteer improve his technique. The small brass badge to the right of the picture bears the legend "UTP", which stands for Upper Thames Patrol and was worn by Home Guards who plied the waters of the river in search of possible invaders.

Britain's gas capability, if it was needed, would be ready for immediate use. Intelligence had confirmed that during amphibious operations German troops stacked their cylindrical gas-mask containers in communal lockers onboard their landing-craft. For some minutes after coming ashore they would be totally unprotected from the ravages of gas attack; their vulnerability at this phase of Sea-lion was a disadvantage that, regardless of ethics, Britain's commanders were determined to exploit.

As if part of a modern re-enactment of a medieval siege a ring of steel bristled over the ramparts of England. Tin-helmeted soldiers fixed their gaze towards the silent Channel waters, scanning the horizon in the direction of France for the first glimpse of invasion barges. As if to reinforce their peril the ruddy glow above London brightened the skies to their rear; there could be no turning back, each man standing firm. With so many soldiers keyed up to fever pitch, trigger-fingers nervously twitching against the mechanisms of a vast assortment of weapons both new and old, it is not surprising that accidents happened. It was in the sectors patrolled by the Home Guard that, predictably, chaos reigned most.

With the church bells providing dramatic accompaniment to their activities the enthusiastic volunteers proceeded to do their worst. Bridges were blown, roads blocked, tank-traps installed. Huge 600-gallon petrol-tanks were primed, ready to flood road junctions with a flaming concoction of petrol and oil. Everywhere travellers, official and unofficial, were challenged and urged at bayonet-point to produce identity cards. Encouraged to harness all its aggressive energy, the Home Guard was wound-up like a giant mainspring at full tension; but with no real enemy in sight, tragedies inevitably occurred. However, in view of the number of wild shots loosed off at random that night, the cost of three fatal casualties – Guard officers blown up when their car struck a newly mined road – was surprisingly light.

As late evening approached, equally erratic and fruitless shooting was taking place in London, but by weapons of a much larger calibre than those used by the Home Guard. The blitz of September 7 found the AA gun defences of London falling far short of their anticipated capacity to deter offensive bombing. Anti-Aircraft Command's renowned Commander-in-Chief, General Frederick Pile, was well aware of the shortcomings of his organisation. Writing some years after the Battle of Britain, he admitted that AA Command was at that time "technically entirely unfitted for dealing with any but the bomber of twenty years earlier". In fact so inadequate were the guns that, shortly before the September blitz, Pile had issued a directive ordering searchlight batteries to extinguish their lights during raids as the bright shafts of arc-lights were providing ideal target markers for German bombers, and the guns that ringed the searchlight sites were consistently unable to score hits against their aerial quarry.

The intensive bombing during the first night of the London blitz exposed all sorts of weaknesses in the home defences, and even the Prime Minister was not spared the anxiety of coming to terms with personal vulnerability in the face of the hail of airborne ordnance. For weeks the War Cabinet had been ready to take refuge in a purpose-built facility below the New Public Offices in Whitehall. An underground labyrinth capable of housing the British political and military high command had been constructed within the basement in 1938, at the height of the Munich crisis. By the summer of 1940 an elaborate command centre had been established and the basement had been transformed into an armed citadel in the heart of Westminster.

Although the Cabinet War Rooms, as they are now known, had benefitted from developments that rendered them gas- and blast-proof and included the construction of machine-gun embrasures to counter the effects of enfilade fire along the narrow underground galleries, the complex was a makeshift affair and not entirely capable of protecting its inhabitants from the devastating effects of modern war. With the advent of the blitz the War Cabinet took to meeting within the supposedly safe

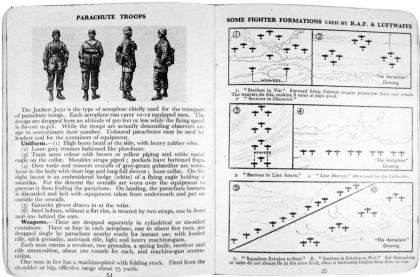

confines of Room 69, but the building's shortcomings were immediately apparent with bombs falling nearby, and all minds focussed on the question of the building's true ability to withstand blitzkrieg.

On enquiry, Churchill was concerned to discover that his underground nerve-centre was not proof against a direct hit from a 500-lb bomb, and clearly further bombing like that of the 7th could have dramatic effects on the Cabinet War Rooms if steps were not taken to improve the situation. Rather than evacuate to "Paddock", an alternative command centre at Dollis Hill in north-west London, Churchill ordered the construction of a defensive layer of concrete known as the "slab", which would provide an impenetrable lid to the vulnerable Cabinet War Rooms.

Although Churchill rarely used his bedroom in the underground complex, the conference and command facility below the New Public Offices was in constant use throughout the war and provided a vital control centre which allowed the government to stay within the capital and thus keep morale high. Churchill considered himself a troglodyte working within his subterranean lair but, like Hitler, he was determined to manage the war from the spiritual and cultural heart of his domain and refused all attempts to move to safer pastures. Unlike the German High Command's bunker in Berlin the Whitehall stronghold was never breached, and 115 meetings of the War Cabinet took place in safety only a few feet below the scarred and ruined streets of London.

As September 8 dawned smoke hung over London's docklands above the charred re-

All members of the Observer Corps were issued with a handbook that included useful information concerning meteorology, range-finding and, of course, aircraft identification. The pages featured here include information detailing the appearance of German paratroops and illustrates some examples of RAF and Luftwaffe aircraft formations.

A NATION ALONE

RIGHT Stretcher parties (SPs) ferried victims of the bombing to ambulances and rest centres to await transport to hospital.

BELOW Despite the disruption caused by enemy bombing, much of life in London went on almost as normal. The reference to "Musso's Lake" on the placard is a comment about Britain's ability to continue military operations in the Mediterranean Sea despite the proximity of hostile Italian forces.

mains of the wharfs and warehouses. The Thames was thick with soot and debris and the streets were slimy with filthy water as a result of the dousing from AFS hoses. Among East London's slums, survivors picked their way among the ruins of homes and desperately tried to salvage any personal belongings that had not been consumed in the fire. Men of the Heavy Rescue Service helped free those unfortunates trapped within the wreckage of collapsed buildings. Later the Army joined in too in a desperate attempt to liberate those still unable to climb to safety from the rubble. Dangerous buildings were brought down by demolition squads and gangs of workmen set about trying to make sense from the crazy tangle of twisted railway tracks, uprooted water-mains and cracked and weeping sewers and gas-pipes.

In all 430 civilians died as a result of that first night's bombing. A further 1,600 were seriously injured and thousands more were left homeless. Rest centres established in church halls within the blitzed areas dispensed

welcomed cups of tea for the survivors, and members of the Women's Voluntary Service (WVS) provided blankets and comfort for the scores of homeless who sought refuge.

Accompanied by Harold Scott, the Chief Administration Officer of the London Civil Defence Region, Churchill spent the morning touring the bomb-sites to see the devastation for himself. Recalling a favourite phrase from the Great War, the Prime Minister asked the crowds of weary East Enders, "Are we down-hearted?" The crowds shouted back "No!" – and Churchill continued on his way with admiration greeting his every exaggerated gesture of defiance.

Other heroes of the hour were the valiant members of the Army's Bomb Disposal and Beach Mine Clearance Units. A new adminis-trative structure, the Bomb Disposal Direc-torate, had only been formed days earlier on August 29. The aim was to co-ordinate all bomb disposal activities and establish a central data-base about bomb types, fuses, defusing techniques and safety precautions. The

Directorate had barely found its feet when the full capability of the disposal squads was put to the test in London on September 8.

Unexploded Bombs – UXBs as they were known – littered the south of England, and disarming them was a perilously difficult and slow job. Prior to the start of the blitz proper over 2,500 UXBs were awaiting the attention of bomb disposal specialists. The havoc caused by UXBs – the closing of roads, schools, factories and houses where they lay – often had a more disruptive effect on everyday life and war production than those that actually went off.

Due to their ballistic qualities bombs often managed to bury themselves well below the surface. Retrieving them meant not only hours of back-breaking digging but also resulted in work that often had to be completed knee-deep in cold, muddy water while all the time the walls of the excavation or the weakened structure of overhead or adjacent buildings threatened to entomb those engaged in such a dangerous task.

Although of simple construction the Anderson shelter was extremely robust and could withstand the effect of bomb-blasts caused by anything other than a direct hit.

Luftwaffe fighter-pilots considered it good sport to take pot-shots at lumbering barrage balloons. Bomber crews, however, wisely avoided the web of steel cables that hung like a veil from their under-bellies.

It is impossible to calculate the value of the property saved, not to mention the thousands of civilian lives, by the gallantry of the bomb disposal units. Houses, factories, even unique architectural legacies such as St Paul's Cathedral were all rescued from destruction by the quiet dedication of a few score of men who daily wrestled with infernal examples of war's callousness and who for the most part have never achieved the recognition enjoyed by other branches of the armed services in the Second World War.

Reports from his returning bomber-crews convinced Reichsmarschall Goering that the night attack on London had been a complete success. The defences had been light and night-fighters non-existent. London, they said, stood out in the night sky, clearly lit by

the fires that raged in its streets. What was more, the River Thames treacherously identified the capital since even from a great distance it could be located by pilots and bomb-aimers who gratefully followed its course to the city's heart.

Goering was sure he had at last found a formula to break the British, sapping their morale and causing so much terror among the myriad cultures of East London that perhaps even civil unrest would result. Without hesitation he ordered his bomber crews to return to London on the evening of September 8, a Sunday, to continue dismantling the very fabric of a nation.

That evening's air attack differed from the previous night's raid in that targets in West London were added to the Luftwaffe's operational orders. Although Target B as it was designated (Target A was London's docklands) was selected primarily because of the abundance of power stations and railway termini in the area, it was clear that the densely populated civilian areas would inevitably be hit by bombs.

The Heinkels and Dorniers of Luftflotte 3 reached London by 7.30 pm on the evening of September 8, and a total of 207 German bombers once again succeeded in stoking the

Petrol rationing, though unpopular, was essential if Britain's dwindling supplies were to be conserved. Coupons like these were required before motorists could fill up and most cars were disabled and laid up for the duration.

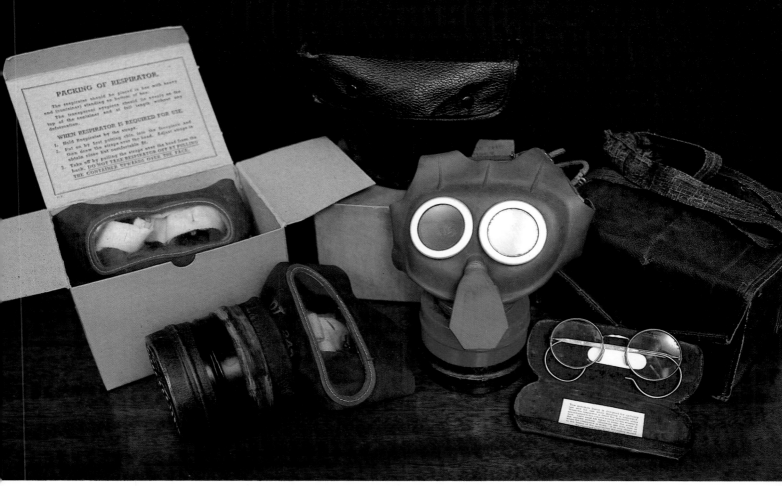

fires in East London and hitting hospitals, railway stations, blocks of flats and even a museum in West London. Londoners sheltering below (many of whom had decided to seek refuge in the deep tunnels of the Underground railway system), had no idea that the Luftwaffe would, in fact, return on almost every clear night throughout the winter and into the spring of 1941 – until Hitler finally gave up trying to bludgeon the British into submission and instead, in May, turned his greedy stare on Soviet Russia.

The raid of the 8th claimed a further 412 lives. As usual the guns were powerless to intervene in support of the civil population. AA Command's commander, General Pile, wrestled with a solution to the problem of how to hit back, but due to the lack of sophisticated radar controlled gun-laying equipment and the unavailability of modern proximity fuses for anti-aircraft shells, he could see no quick or easy answers.

After the heavy air-raid of September 7 the AA defences of London had been steadily reinforced, however, and in two days the number of guns had doubled. Unfortunately it took time to level new gun-sights and lay on the power and telephone cables essential to link a fresh battery into the barrage. The

biggest problem was that the extraordinarily complex Fixed Azimuth system of gun-laying, a vestige of the old Air Defence of Great Britain network, was totally unable to deal with modern bombing techniques. Fixed Azimuth only worked if the enemy maintained a constant height, course and speed whilst approaching and passing over the target. It also depended on antiquated sound location techniques which often meant that information was out of date by the time it was relayed to the gun battery.

So ineffective was the system that although there were 440 large-calibre guns within the 1st Anti Aircraft Division, the unit charged with defending London, the gun barrage brought down only four aircraft by night between the 8th and the 10th. Urged by Churchill to do something, and himself deeply concerned at the apparent failure of the system, Pile called a conference of his subordinates on September 10.

Although the guns had some success during the day it was clear that the Luftwaffe had switched tactics and the main raiding force, now attacking under the cover of darkness, was escaping from London largely unscathed. Pile's solution was simple. On the evening of the 10th the whole AA gun barrage would, on

Civilian gas-masks had been mass produced long before hostilities with Germany began. The masks were issued in cardboard boxes which at first were slung from the shoulder on string; later more elaborate cases were available, as shown here. The children's gas-mask (centre) was known as the "Mickey Mouse" due to its separate goggles and snout-like filter. Specially designed spectacles were available to those who could afford them; these had very thin side-frames which ensured that the gas-mask fitted tightly against the wearer's face.

the approach of the enemy, commence firing simultaneously, regardless of whether the Fixed Azimuth system provided accurate target indication or not. Pile's instructions were clear: the guns would start firing once the enemy was overhead and continue firing until ammunition was exhausted.

The result of his order was a spectacular cannonade of bursting shells which lit up the night sky on September 10 and persisted, conditions permitting, for most nights during the blitz. Although the guns achieved little in terms of direct hits the mass barrage did have the effect of pushing enemy bombers higher and higher, upsetting the aim and preventing what had been some pinpoint attacks.

More important than the military effectiveness of Pile's vertical broadside, however, was the enormous effect the continuous firing of the guns had on morale. Previously the guns had lain silent until a target had been accurately "predicted", a silence that caused much consternation among the civilian population. Curiously people slept far sounder even though the night air was pierced by the crack of nearby guns, the whooshing of falling shells – and perhaps the knowledge that shrapnel was apt to cause more damage to London's houses than Heinkels. Churchill was suitably impressed. At last Britain was giving as well as receiving. In *Their Finest Hour* he stated, "Everyone was cheered by the feeling that we were hitting back."

Hitler was not so cheerful on September 10. Depressed by the Luftwaffe's inability to break the deadlock which prevented Germany from gaining air superiority over southern England, he decided to postpone his decision to initiate Operation Sea-lion until the 14th. As ten days' notice was needed prior to the invasion flotilla sailing, this meant that in theory the earliest date on which a landing could take place was September 24. Time was finally running out.

Chapter Eight

"We knew that we were close to knocking out the RAF, but we did not know how close we were. Switching over from attacking the British air defences to the air battle against London and other civilian targets was a big strategic mistake . . . To us the Battle of Britain presented a major campaign for which, we were soon to learn, the Luftwaffe had not been equipped. It was not strong enough to conquer England."

Major Adolf Galland,
3rd Gruppe, Jagdgeschwader 26, Pas de Calais, 1940

INTO THE LIGHT

By the autumn of 1940 images like this one became increasingly common as the tide of battle turned: RAF personnel proudly display their trophy of a wing panel salvaged from a shot-down German aircraft.

The next day, September 11, Churchill told the nation: "If this invasion is going to be tried at all, it does not seem that it can be long delayed . . . Therefore we must regard the next week or so as a very important period in our history. It ranks with the days when the Spanish Armada was approaching the Channel . . . or when Nelson stood between us and Napoleon's Grand Army at Boulogne."

On September 14 Hitler once again prevaricated and refused to commit himself to Sea-lion. Once again he decided to postpone his decision, this time for a further three days, causing the theoretical start date to recede to September 27. This was the last date when the moon and tide were in a conjunction, making amphibious operations practicable, before October 8. Although there would be other "windows" after that date, the change of season and the unpredictability of Channel waters meant that an invasion attempt would be unlikely.

It was obvious to British military analysts that if Hitler was to take advantage of the few remaining opportunities for invasion, a massive aerial assault aimed at finally securing domination of the skies over England was imminent. Enigma decrypts had pointed to September 13 as the likely date for an all-out attack. When nightfall eliminated that possibility the crypto-analysts of Bletchley Park changed their minds and predicted the attack for the following day.

In fact September 15, a Sunday, was

A NATION ALONE

ABOVE September 15, 1940, now celebrated as "Battle of Britain Day", was to be the final hammer blow delivered by the Luftwaffe – an attack which, German tacticians argued, would lead to the collapse of British morale. But it was not to be. This souvenir calendar was produced shortly after the Battle, when it became clear that the nation had weathered the storm.

scheduled for the Luftwaffe's grand slam against England – a date which to this day is celebrated as Battle of Britain Day. But in reality the Luftwaffe had shot their bolt. The week-long daylight reprieve had allowed Fighter Command to recover from the mauling it had received during high summer. Dowding's pilots were rested, their aircraft repaired or replaced and most airfields had been patched up sufficiently to enable them to regain full operational status. The radar network was intact and its operators well versed in the science of unravelling the mysteries of the flickering cathode-ray tube.

The Luftwaffe threw caution to the wind during the early stages of their attack on September 15. As usual they commenced operations by dispatching several reconnaissance sorties. These were checked by vigilant RAF fighters and an over-curious He-111 was shot down into the Channel. RAF controllers expected to be confronted by an irritating sequence of feint attacks next, as was

usual German practice; but amazingly the Luftwaffe dispensed with such valuable cloaking techniques and, instead, paraded their vast air-fleets up and down while they assembled in ordered ranks above the French coast. All these maneouvrings were carried out in full view of radar operators, controllers and even Mr and Mrs Churchill, who had chosen the 15th to visit No. 11 Group's headquarters at Uxbridge.

Shortly after eleven o'clock in the morning the enormous formations of Luftwaffe aircraft moved towards England. This time the RAF was ready for them.

Immediately, Park scrambled 11 of his 21 squadrons, approximately 130 aircraft, to intercept. No. 11 Group's fighters caught the first raiders head on as they approached Kent and angrily hacked at the bombers as they continued their journey northwards to London. No. 10 Group sent reinforcements, 609 Spitfire Squadron, with orders to patrol west of London and prevent any bombers reaching

Windsor Castle. The royal home was the site of a secret depot established by Beaverbrook for the storage of fighters prior to their delivery to RAF squadrons.

North of London Leigh-Mallory threw Douglas Bader's Big Wing into the fray, and by now it was five squadrons strong. For once there had been sufficient warning for the large formation to gain height and a suitable attack position in time to intercept the intruders while they were still en route to London. Everywhere the sky was filled with RAF fighters. Goering had miscalculated. The RAF was very much alive, and in daylight it was in its element.

In the face of such determined opposition Luftwaffe bomb-aimers were unable to enjoy a steady run to the targets and were forced, instead, to jettison their bombs erratically over a wide area. The fighter top-cover was occupied with saving itself from the intentions of maruading bands of Spitfires and as glowing red lights signalled almost empty fuel-tanks the Messerschmitts were forced to leave the bombers and turn for home.

The Luftwaffe returned once more in the afternoon but again the defences were ready to meet them. Four hundred German aircraft doggedly approached the English coast, a daunting spectacle which onlookers likened to a swarm of giant insects, remorselessly engaged in some ritual mass migration. But if the Luftwaffe armada was large the number of RAF fighters detailed to receive them was equally impressive as 200 Spitfires and Hurricanes filled the skies. Once again the Luftwaffe formations were broken up before they managed to reach the capital. Much

damage was caused but it was random and unco-ordinated – certainly not worth the cost in men and machines paid by Germany.

After a final German attack in the early evening it was clear that the RAF had won a famous victory. At the time radio listeners rejoiced at the news that 185 enemy aircraft had been destroyed and morning papers displayed the day's "bag" in boastful letters across their front pages. Postwar research has shown that this figure was clearly exaggerated, the true total being only 56 machines, but for the British September 15 was the turning point. The RAF's losses for the whole day were just 26 aircraft, with 13 pilots baling out to safety.

The odds were starting to favour the defenders, and from this moment onwards Luftwaffe losses were consistently much higher than those of the RAF. Luftwaffe morale was declining daily and an inefficient repair organisation meant that damaged aircraft remained unserviceable for long periods. German factories were unable to plug the widening gaps in the Luftwaffe's establishment as their production methods had hardly altered since peacetime. As the RAF grew stronger the Luftwaffe grew weaker, its rank and file increasingly disinclined towards further apparently fruitless actions against England.

The next day Churchill broadcast to the nation. "Yesterday eclipses all previous records of the Fighter Command," he said. "Aided by squadrons of their Czech and Polish comrades, using only a small proportion of their total strength, and under cloud conditions of some difficulty, they cut

Spitfires of 610 Squadron (county of Chester) in formation. In September 1940, 610 was stationed at RAF Acklington in the command area of No. 13 Group.

OPPOSITE PAGE A familiar sight during the seemingly endless summer of 1940: vapour trails trace complex patterns across the sky as defenders and attackers jockey for advantage during combat. The aircraft were too high to be clearly distinguished but every now and then the sun would glint off a wing or fuselage and schoolboys would catch the momentary flash of silver and shout "Spitfire!" or "Messerschmitt!"

A NATION ALONE

to rags and tatters three separate waves of murderous assault upon the civil population of their native land, inflicting a certain loss of one hundred and twenty-five bombers and fifty-three fighters upon the enemy to say nothing of the probables and damages, while themselves sustaining a loss of twelve pilots and twenty-five machines. These results exceed all expectations and give just and sober confidence in the approaching struggle."

On September 17 Hitler again postponed Sea-lion, this time indefinitely, and ordered the partial dispersal of the invasion barges and shipping which had been subjected to concentrated RAF bomber attacks since the 5th. However, he still maintained all basic preparations in case of a possible invasion in October. That invasion never came, although it was never officially cancelled and, from October 12, put on ice until the following spring. If the weather was suitable the Luftwaffe continued to mount daylight attacks against targets in Britain after September 15, but rarely with conviction.

Dowding's official dispatch after the Battle of Britain states: "Heavy pressure was kept up until September 25, but by the end of the month it became apparent that the Germans could no longer face the bomber wastage which they had sustained." So confident were the British defenders who had checked German intentions towards invasion that on September 17 the highest state of invasion alert was relaxed.

With the Luftwaffe nightly pounding London with high explosives and incendiaries the RAF was ordered to consider increasing its offensive as well as defensive operations against Germany. Accordingly, on the evening of September 23, 119 Wellingtons, Whitleys and Hampdens of Bomber Command took off into the night sky for Berlin. They caused little damage but were a forceful reminder that Germany was not having it all her own way. As Londoners climbed from their shelters on the morning of the 24th, the news that Berliners had experienced similar discomfort was met with some satisfaction.

The next few days saw the introduction of yet another Luftwaffe tactic – precision bombing runs against key industrial targets, notably the aircraft factories. To achieve

On September 6, 1940 King George VI and Queen Elizabeth visited Fighter Command headquarters at Bentley Priory. Here the royal party are ascending the steps to the terrace accompanied by Sir Hugh Dowding, whose expression clearly reveals the enormous strain he was under as his command reeled from the pounding of successive blows from the Luftwaffe.

INTO THE LIGHT

LEFT Spitfires of 222 Squadron scramble from RAF Hornchurch in Essex on "Battle of Britain Day" – September 15, 1940. Eager for a repeat of September 7, when London was blitzed by a succession of daylight raids which caught the defences off balance, Luftwaffe crews met a more determined resistance from the RAF than ever before and they lost a total of 60 aircraft.

BELOW A Royal Air Force fighter-pilot, fully kitted out for operational duties, climbs into the cockpit of his Hurricane. Note the complexity of the parachute harness and its large, easy-to-grip rip-cord handle. The parachutes were made by the Irvin Company: pilots whose lives were saved by using one were awarded membership to the "Caterpillar Club" and given a distinctive brooch to wear.

meaningful results against such heavily defended sites Luftwaffe planners put even more pressure on their already overworked Bf-109 pilots. Not only had they to contend with the difficulty of a limited radius of operations but now they were also expected to claw their way into the air dragging bombs beneath their fragile superstructures.

Mixed formations of bomb-carrying 109s and medium bombers struck at both the Supermarine factory and the equally important Bristol factory, causing great damage and a high loss of life. The "Freijagd" or "free-hunt" missions flown by Bf-109s, each carrying a single bomb, posed a serious threat into and beyond the new year. Able to come in below the radar curtain or rise high above it and, having released their bombs capable of returning to a full fighter configuration, these fighter-bombers were a dangerous nuisance.

Just as it seemed that the Luftwaffe had returned to pinpoint attacks it once again changed course. On September 27 Goering's air-fleets appeared en masse in the English skies. Such out-dated tactics offered little chance of success and predictably the mixed German formations were torn to shreds. From a total of 380 aircraft, heading in two formations for London and Bristol, 55 fell to RAF fighters.

The next day, as if at last resigned to the fact that Britain would always remain a thorn in the flesh of the Third Reich, Hitler ordered the German economy to direct its efforts towards supporting the invasion of Russia. By the end of September the Luftwaffe was a spent force during daylight over England. Only at night could it hope to penetrate

British airspace and return unscathed.

However, even under the cover of darkness, the Luftwaffe did not get everything its own way. In 1979 Kurt Newald, Luftwaffe bomber-pilot and veteran of Kampfgruppe 126, in conversation with Alick Grant, a British aviation enthusiast and wing commander with the RAF's Volunteer Reserve,

A NATION ALONE

Kurt Newald, a veteran
bomber-pilot of
Kampfgruppe 126, who
was forced to bale out of
his doomed Heinkel 111
over Essex on
October 15, 1940.

recalled his memorable experiences during the early period of the London blitz in October 1940.

Newald's story begins on the afternoon of October 15, at Wittmundhafen airbase in Germany. Not being scheduled to fly a mission in the evening, Newald was relaxing in the station's officer's mess and enjoying a profitable game of poker. Scooping up his winnings, he was interrupted by the approach of an orderly bearing unwelcome news: the "stand-down" was cancelled and Newald and his crew were to replace another crew on the evening's mission. Stuffing his winnings into the pockets of his flying-suit, he proceeded to gather his crew and headed towards their aircraft, a Heinkel 111.

The forecast predicted ground fog for the late evening, so Newald's staffel and another from KG126 were ordered to take off for Schipol near Amsterdam and wait there until the order to head for London was received. While at Schipol, Newald supplemented his bounty of Reichsmarks with Dutch gilders.

At midnight KG126 took off and climbed to 12,000 feet. The sky was clear and a full moon aided visibility enormously. Knickebein was to be used to guide the Luftwaffe crews to their target, but Newald and other pilots were convinced the British monitored the frequencies and gathered their night-fighters over the intersecting beams accordingly. As we know the reality of RAF night defences were a far cry from this German fantasy; but perhaps the

uncertainty that resulted from the possibility of a "beam-riding" reception committee did have a small, if unmeasurable, effect on Britain's war effort.

What follows is best told in Kurt Newald's own words: "I was just about to intercept the Channel 'Knickebein' beam when a burst of tracer-shells traversed the cockpit almost vertically from underneath, smashing into the instrument panel and missing my legs by millimetres. (I realised later on, when I unzipped my boots, that the tracers burnt into the fur of the legs). My immediate reaction was to dive. At the same time I observed the hostile aircraft, lit by moonlight, turning only approximately fifty metres in front of and slightly below our cockpit. I could well identify it as a Defiant.

"My navigator rushed to the front-gun and sent a burst after the disappearing enemy. I meanwhile checked the instruments and tested the condition of the engines, but could not force power out of them anymore. Then, looking to the left engine, I saw flames breaking through the rifts of the cowling. Now I realised that we had no other chance of surviving but to jump as soon as possible and descend by parachute.

Holding the aircraft in a glide I urged my crew members by means of the still functioning intercom-system to get ready for jumping, but received no acknowledgement from the belly-gunner. The wireless operator, realising this, volunteered to go down to him and find out his condition. As he told me later, in order to get about as quickly as possible he unbuckled his sit-on parachute. Just imagine, all that in an already burning aircraft! After seconds which seemed like an eternity to me he reported that our poor comrade showed no sign of life and that he himself was now ready to jump.

"I jumped a few seconds after my navigator and when I felt the jerk of the opening parachute the strain of the last minutes abated a little. During the descent I could watch our spinning aircraft which once approached me dangerously close. I also observed another descending parachute slightly lower and not far away which, a few minutes later, turned out to belong to my wireless operator.

"Then I dipped into the high fog and after a few seconds of uncertainty as to the nature of what was going to be my landing spot my feet hit the ground – fortunately soft, grassy soil. Only about 150 metres away our burning

INTO THE LIGHT

aircraft had plunged into the edge of a wood, setting the trees on fire. From another direction, but still closer, I heard the wireless operator calling for me. We jointly destroyed the secret radio code-tables which he still carried in his pocket.

"Meanwhile we could observe an ever-growing crowd of firemen, steel-helmeted Home Guard soldiers and civilians gathering around the fire. Perhaps they had also caught sight of our discarded white parachutes because a group of Home Guard men spread out, keeping contact by shouts. Since we saw no chance to travel unrecognised in our uniforms through South-East England and to catch a Channel ferry-boat we decided to surrender.

"So we walked straight away to the scene of the fire. It was certainly an experience of victory for the Home Guard men when they got hold of us. Shortly before that happened I threw my pistol into the flames of the burning wreck so as not to contribute to the armament of the British Army. That was the end of one act and the beginning of another, during which I was finally and on 'His Majesty's Service' shipped to Canada and back again one year after the end of the war."

After his capture Kurt Newald was given a receipt for the money he carried in his flying

Major Werner Mölders was the "pin-up boy" of the Luftwaffe in 1940. A great friend and rival of Adolf Galland, he led Jagdgeschwader 53, which was stationed next to Galland's JG 26 on the Pas de Calais.

clothing on the fateful evening of October 15, 1940. The British intelligence officer who interrogated him could perhaps be forgiven for wondering why a lieutenant in the Luftwaffe was in possession of 225 Reichsmarks and a handful of Dutch gilders!

Even though Newald suffered the ironic misfortune of being shot down on the very

Fragment of German Bomb
Dropped at Hambrook Sussex
22 July 1940

Two typical souvenirs collected from the countryside during the Battle of Britain and preserved to this day. The large magazine drum comes from the free-mounted 7.9 mm machine-gun of the Ju-88, situated at the rear of the upper crew compartment. It was apparently discarded and dropped from the aircraft over Sussex while the Luftwaffe air-gunner fumbled to exchange it for a fresh magazine. The other object is a piece of shrapnel from an exploded German bomb. Even a relatively small piece of metal like this could cause terrifying injuries.

evening he enjoyed a substantial win at the poker table, he was lucky to survive the air combat. His navigator, Unteroffizier Konrad Gläser, jumped from the burning Heinkel seconds before Newald himself did, and it is assumed either his parachute was fouled on the shattered airframe or that perhaps the deployed canopy caught fire. Several weeks later Gläser's body was found in a ditch close to the Essex crash site of the burnt-out German bomber.

The last great daylight air combat during the Battle of Britain took place on September 30. The first wave of attacking aircraft was successfully turned back before it reached the coast and later a series of separate dog-fights took place over Kent. At 3.10 pm, a large raid of over 100 enemy aircraft approached the coast, 30 or so breaking through the defensive perimeter of RAF fighters to reach London. An hour later a further 180 enemy aircraft tried to outwit the defences by slipping in towards London from west Surrey. At the same time 40 German bombers selected the Westland factory at Yeovil, but cloud over the valuable target obscured the aim of the Heinkel crews and they jettisoned their bombs over quiet and defenceless Sherborne before turning for home.

Dowding ensured that all Luftwaffe formations were met on the way from their targets as well as en route. As a result the enemy formations were neatly sown into a lethal trap and picked off one by one with

some ease. As the regular nightly shuttle of black bombers approached London after sunset they were unaware that their colleagues operating during the daylight hours had suffered casualties of nearly a fifth.

The same day King George VI decorated Dowding, appointing Fighter Command's skilled leader a Knight Grand Commander of the Bath. Sadly, even though Dowding had soundly defeated the Luftwaffe and frustrated Hitler's ambitions of conquering the British, his troubles were not over, for he seemed to have enemies at home as well as abroad.

The dispute between Keith Park and Trafford Leigh-Mallory continued on into October. The drama was played out against a background of intensive Luftwaffe high-altitude fighter-bomber sweeps which added to the problems of Fighter Command, and especially Dowding. The refinement of the Luftwaffe's fighter-bomber techniques was paying dividends. Unencumbered by the slower two-engined medium bombers, these fighter-bombers were able to race at speed towards their targets. Above 25,000 feet the Bf-109, with its sophisticated two-stage supercharger, enjoyed a far greater performance than the venerable Hurricane and had the edge on the Mk II Spitfires which were then leaving the factories for squadron service.

Flying at such heights the Messerschmitts were also able to escape the keen eyes of the Observer Corps and their radar signature was greatly reduced. Luftwaffe planners cleverly

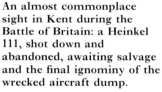

An almost commonplace sight in Kent during the Battle of Britain: a Heinkel 111, shot down and abandoned, awaiting salvage and the final ignominy of the wrecked aircraft dump.

INTO THE LIGHT

A Heinkel 111 drops its bombs over southern England. Though small by bomber standards the He-111 H3 could carry a payload of up to 4,400 lbs vertically in its centre section bomb-bay.

employed a series of inbound raids to further confuse the defences; not all the formations actually carried bombs, so the RAF was forced more or less to maintain standing patrols in order to spot the bomb-carrying flights early enough. New tactics were needed to counter the threat. Leigh-Mallory, as usual, argued that Big Wings were the only sure method of hitting the enemy hard and he made sure that those in positions of power and influence within the air force and even the government got to hear about it.

Subsequent to the Bader Wing action of September 15, Leigh-Mallory endorsed a report about wing patrols carried out within 12 Group and sent it to Fighter Command HQ. Considering the large amount of Luftwaffe fighters that accompanied the Heinkels, Dorniers and Junkers to their British targets, he argued, surely it was prudent to dispatch an equally large RAF reception committee to intercept them?

Dowding's reaction to the report can well be imagined. All summer he and Park had struggled to persuade Leigh-Mallory to see the inherent wisdom in meeting the enemy threat along the widest front possible, and this could only be achieved if the Spitfires and Hurricanes were allotted to individual target formations in small groups. The system obviously worked; not only did it wear down the Luftwaffe but in retrospect it also

prevented Goering's bombers from inflicting irremedial damage to 11 Group's airfields.

Further still, the policy had a dramatic effect on Luftwaffe morale. Everywhere the German airforce operated, it seemed the RAF was waiting to interrupt their missions. Even though the great majority of RAF squadrons were equipped with Hurricanes, German pilots returned time and time again to complain about the ever present "Spitfuers". Spitfire snobbery could not disguise the fact that, in the Luftwaffe's eyes at least, the RAF was consistently able to meet whatever challenge it encountered throughout the entire summer. In reality of course it was the Luftwaffe's constant tactical alterations which at each critical phase of the battle resulted in the RAF being let off the hook.

By the time Leigh-Mallory signed his glowing report on wing patrols the arguments within it were largely out of date; the new German hit-and-run fighter-bomber sweeps negated the usefulness of large scale defensive measures. Increasingly, apart from spectacular successes like the Supermarine and Bristol raids and a later attack on Shorts at Rochester, the edgy fighter-bombers tended to jettison their bombs and run for the Channel as soon as any serious opposition was met. And, as Dowding and Park had always maintained, it was the accurate dropping of bombs that had to be stopped, not lightly-

This He-111 was shot down over Watton early in 1941. The picture clearly shows the rear-mounted machine-gun that British pilots frequently complained about. RAF fighters had also to contend with a variety of missiles such as stick grenades and boxes which trailed wires intended to ensnare their propellers when in pursuit of fleeing enemy bombers.

203

Rescue crews bring a bomb victim out of the rubble caused by a direct hit on a London dwelling. Heavy rescue (HR) crews were responsible for removing large pieces of debris, and they often discovered the most amazing examples of human stamina as people clung to life trapped in cramped air pockets or sheltered from the weight of collapsed masonry by the fortuitous presence of a sturdy wardrobe or dining-table.

armed fighters. An enemy fighter without an RAF fighter to shoot at was in itself an impotent machine.

Nevertheless the Air Ministry, after some machinations, largely based on over-inflated kill ratios, thought it important enough to warrant further attention. Accordingly, both Dowding and Park were called to task about their apparent reluctance to involve 12 Group in the battle to defend London and the South-East. The fact that despite repeated calls for help it was clear that the big wings were unable to climb to 30,000 feet quickly enough, the consensus of opinion within the corridors

of power was that Leigh-Mallory had been held in check by the over-cautious Dowding and Park.

On October 17 a crucial meeting was convened at the Air Ministry in London. Dowding, Park and Leigh-Mallory were all present, and from the Air Ministry came the Deputy Chief of the Air Staff, the former First World War fighter-ace Air Vice-Marshal Sholto Douglas. He came in place of Cyril Newall, the Chief of the Air Staff, who could not attend. Unfortunately for Dowding and Park, Douglas tended to sympathise with Leigh-Mallory's view that offence was the best defence.

With so many distinguished, high-ranking officers there Dowding and Park were concerned to discover that Leigh-Mallory had chosen to bring Squadron-Leader Douglas Bader along to the meeting, to plead 12 Group's case. Bader proceeded to tell the assembled conference that, in his opinion, wing leaders and not ground controllers should control the battle tactics. This was a direct challenge to the Dowding system – and tantamount to direct criticism of Fighter Command's leader.

Despite a concerted effort from Dowding and Park to impress on the meeting the importance of the new sophisticated defensive structure (which relied not just on flying skill and courage but the practical involvement of the latest scientific developments), it soon became clear that the majority favoured the Leigh-Mallory/Bader principle. Indeed there was much talk of "Balbos" of two wings

Throughout the Battle of Britain it was the stoicism of ground-crews which enabled the RAF to continue meeting the apparently inexhaustible challenge from the Luftwaffe. Short of rest and grabbing meals and sleep where they worked, they patched up damaged machines and kept barely serviceable aircraft flying in order to preserve the RAF's small and precious reserve of new machines.

INTO THE LIGHT

FOR FREEDOM!
A PANORAMIC PICTURE STORY BOOK OF OUR
NAVY · ARMY & AIR FORCE

History tends to cast doubt on the motives and morality of most momentous events, constantly throwing up questions and reappraising their significance in the light of new information; but in 1940 most people were pretty sure what they were fighting for – and the likely outcome if they lost the battle. "*For Freedom*" was a panoramic picture book published in 1940 by Raphael Tuck and Sons, the famous postcard and souvenir company.

operating together, so-called because of the massed formation flights by the prewar Italian aviator Italo Balbo.

Later, when the minutes of the meeting were circulated, Park was alarmed that certain key points in defence of his own position had been omitted from the draft. Despite his remonstrations an amendment, clarifying the fact that his squadrons had not operated singly during the battle but in pairs, was not added. Nor was his point showing how smoothly Brand's No. 10 Group had co-operated with his own 11 Group included.

The big wing theory held sway, and as the German daylight raids petered out through October whenever Luftwaffe aircraft appeared over southern England the "Duxford Wing" was scrambled to intercept them. On two notable occasions, however, October 25 and the 29th, Duxford failed to respond quickly enough to Park's requests for assistance within 11 Group's area. In fact in the first instance 11 Group was unable even to locate the wing, so sparse were its transmitted fixes. On both occasions nearly half an hour was needed before the wing climbed high enough to leave the Duxford area south of Cambridge, let alone set course for the rapidly approaching enemy.

This apparent vindication of Park's argu-

ments did no good; wing formations were here to stay. With the battle virtually over, and Germany clearly unable to seriously consider invasion until the spring of 1941, both Dowding and Park's usefulness diminished and on November 25 Dowding was replaced by Douglas. After a succession of rather trivial appointments the man who had masterminded the defence of Britain during the nation's most critical period was shepherded off on a tour of the United States to help wage the propaganda war in encouraging her further involvement in aid of beleagured Britain. Unlike Douglas, Sir Hugh Dowding never enjoyed the privilege of promotion to Marshal of the Royal Air Force. Indeed, so complete was the disregard he was shown that the

If a product was able to carry a message in 1940 it would usually be a patriotic one, and matchbox covers printed with the emblems of the armed forces or civil defence organisations were extremely popular.

By late October 1940 the pride of Hitler's Luftwaffe had been dashed against the stalwart defences of Britain. The twisted carcasses of so many enemy aircraft bore testimony to the scale of Germany's defeat and confirmed the importance of Britain's victory in preventing the most serious invasion attempt of the islands in nearly a thousand years. Unwilling to see the Luftwaffe bled to death, and rapidly losing what little faith he had in the practicability of Operation Sea-lion, Hitler turned his attention to the enemy he loathed most – Russia. Soon the bombers and fighters that flew the short but perilous journey from France to England would be transferred to air-bases in eastern Germany and Poland, briefed to lunge deep into the Soviet heartland. Crews who had survived the dangers of the Channel crossing and air combat over England would once again be subjected to the rigours of operational sorties against a determined enemy . . .

official history of the Battle of Britain that appeared in 1941 does not even mention him.

Park was equally poorly served, and at about the same time that Dowding was asked to clear his desk the New Zealander, worn out and disappointed that his peers refused to accept his operational methods, was posted to Training Command. His replacement was Trafford Leigh-Mallory. With the removal of both Dowding and Park from Fighter Command's front line, the most stirring chapter of Royal Air Force history closed.

As October progressed poor weather and the absence of a strategic incentive reduced the Luftwaffe's daylight activities to little more than nuisance raids. But at night it was still a different matter; the wail of sirens and the ominous phrase "enemy bombers overhead" were routinely heard throughout Britain's principal towns and cities.

Attacks by high-flying German aircraft carried on throughout October but by the end of the month they had dwindled to a trickle. With men and machines earmarked for work on the Eastern Front, the Luftwaffe was reluctant to waste any more of its resources over Britain. In the month of October alone, Germany lost a total of 325 aircraft in the Battle of Britain, with little to show for it.

By common consent the Battle of Britain is considered to have ended on October 31, a day which saw the last concerted Luftwaffe daylight raid against Britain. But the other Battle of Britain continued to be fought, however, as the Royal Navy struggled to maintain the Atlantic supply lines and save the nation from collapse.

On August 20 Churchill had spoken what are the most famous words relating to the air battles of 1940. "Never in the field of human conflict," he said, "was so much owed by so many to so few." While the young pilots who survived may have thought he was referring to their mess bills, he was right. The pilots of the Royal Air Force, the thin blue line of British defence, had denied Germany the opportunity to stage an amphibious landing. Little more

than a thousand young men had frustrated the ambitions of the most skilled, disciplined and, until the battle, unbeaten war machine the 20th century had seen; 415 RAF pilots made the ultimate sacrifice and died in the defence of their country or, in the case of those from the Empire and foreign lands who took part, their temporarily adopted country.

Between July 10 and October 31 the Luftwaffe lost a total of 1,733 aircraft in operations against Britain. Amid the euphoria of the time it was thought the total stood at 2,692 machines. Careful analysis by the RAF soon after the battle and postwar investigations of Luftwaffe records resulted in the reduced figure. In the same period the RAF lost 915 aircraft.

By the end of the year Hitler had his sights fixed firmly on his hated communist foe in the east. However it was not until February 13, 1942 that the German troops detailed for Operation Sea-lion were officially removed from their part in the fanciful scheme. By then, of course, the invasion would have been an almost impossible undertaking.

The night blitz on London ended on May 10, 1941, when the might of the Luftwaffe was swung about and given fresh targets in Russia. Yet throughout the summer Britain continued to keep one eye on the Channel as its armies met the enemy on more distant battlefields, and anti-invasion leaflets continued to be pushed through letter-boxes in an effort to keep the population vigilant. Increasingly, a poll carried out by the Mass-Observation Unit in March 1941 demonstrated that many people still thought Hitler might have another go at attempting an invasion; 42% of those questioned thought it certain or very probable, 30% regarded it as "very improbable".

Significantly the same poll carried out amongst RAF personnel showed that only 20% of servicemen considered invasion a possibility and 48% regarded it as unlikely. Regardless of the reality of an invasion threat, Britain's defences were not relaxed until the huge build up of Allied troops in preparation for D-Day made the German position untenable in 1944.

Today we are used to research or the publication of previously secret documents diminishing previously epic aspects of history into nothing more than squalid political or military affairs with no clear victors and little moral justification. The Battle of Britain is unique in British history in that not only was it a clearly won contest which decided whether Britain would remain free from Nazi tyranny, but also an event that was crucial to the continuance of democracy and freedom in the West. If Britain's defences had failed at a time when she alone was resisting German expansionism, it is doubtful whether there would have been a springboard left for those nations still able to strike back at Hitler. With Britain subdued it is possible that Hitler could have turned on Russia sooner than he did and thereby preclude the calamity of fighting during her deadly winter. Without Britain to offer some form of resistance Imperial Japan would have been able to strike earlier than she did against Western interests in the Pacific.

The Axis plan was to join hands along the Indian border—Japan in the East and Germany and Italy in the West. The United States of America, isolated and, by the standards of the time, unable to mount military operations against continental Europe or Asia, would have had to come to terms with the new division of power or face withering on the vine, cut off from the world economy by the impenetrable bastion of fascism. By staying in the war Britain kept the door to European, and perhaps world, freedom firmly ajar. With the aid of the Allies it would eventually be prised wide open to liberate the occupied nations.

Due to the tenacity and courage of Britain's fighter-pilots and the stoicism of the nation behind them the United Kingdom was spared the blight of Nazism. Apart from the misfortune that befell the Channel Islands, Britons did not suffer the round-ups, death-squads and concentration camps that were a feature of the Nazi regime in occupied Europe. Hitler, ever superstitious, had feared tackling Britain. Against his earlier judgment he tried and failed, but so provoked the indignation of the British that, within a few months, the nation which had stared defeat in the face was striking back and forcing a war against the Reich that had to be fought on more than one front.

The Third Reich threw all its weight against the rocky outcrop of the British Isles— and in so doing opened a wound which it could never staunch. The Battle of Britain was the first victory for modern democracy, the first defeat for totalitarianism; 50 years on, the debt that is owed by those who enjoy the fruits of freedom is undiminished . . . and the valour of The Few untarnished.

Index